THE STATE OF
BLACK AMERICA 1987

Published by **National Urban League, Inc.**
January 1987

National Urban League, Inc.
The Equal Opportunity Building ■ 500 East 62nd Street ■ New York, New York 10021

State of Black America 1987

Editor
Janet Dewart

Copyright © National Urban League, Inc. 1987
Library of Congress Catalog Number 77-647469
ISBN 0-914758-07-1
Price $18.00

The cover art is "The Builders" by Jacob Lawrence, originally created to celebrate the National Urban League's founding over 75 years ago. Used with permission of the artist.

TABLE OF CONTENTS

About the Authors   1

Black America 1986: An Overview   7
     John E. Jacob

The Law and Black Americans: Retreat From Civil Rights   15
     Julius L. Chambers

Taking Charge: An Approach to Making the
     Educational Problems of Blacks
     Comprehensible and Manageable   31
     Sharon P. Robinson

The Future of School Desegregation   37
     Charles V. Willie

Economic Status of Blacks 1986   49
     David Swinton

Blacks, Budgets, and Taxes: 75
     Assessing the Impact of Budget Deficit
     Reduction and Tax Reform on Blacks
     Lenneal J. Henderson

Black Families in a Changing Society   97
     Andrew Billingsley

Social Welfare Reform   113
     Barbara Bryant Solomon

The Black Underclass in Perspective   129
     Douglas Glasgow

Drug Use: Special Implications for Black America   145
     Beny J. Primm

AIDS: A Special Report   159
     Beny J. Primm

Blacks in State and Local Government: 167
     Progress and Constraints
     Georgia A. Persons

Conclusions and Recommendations   193

Chronology of Events 1986   199

Appendix   223
     A Profile of the Black Unemployed
     Billy J. Tidwell

Notes/References   239

Acknowledgements   261

TABLE OF CONTENTS

About The Authors

DR. ANDREW BILLINGSLEY
Professor of Sociology and
Afro-American Studies
University of Maryland

Dr. Andrew Billingsley is a well-respected educator and scholar. He has written extensively on such issues as black education, child welfare, and the black American family. Published in books and magazines and presented in seminars across the country, his works have earned him over 250 scholarly citations. He is the author of *Black Families in White America* and "Family: Contemporary Patterns" in the 1987 edition of the Encyclopedia of Social Work.

Dr. Billingsley received his B.A. in Political Science from Grinnell College; his M.A. in Sociology from the University of Michigan; and his Ph.D. in Social Policy/Social Research from Brandeis University.

Currently, Dr. Billingsley is Professor of Sociology and Afro-American Studies and Affiliate Professor of Family and Community Development at the University of Maryland, College Park campus. He served as President of Morgan State University from 1975 to 1984, providing important leadership in that school's transition from a predominantly black liberal arts college into a multi-racial urban university.

Dr. Billingsley has contributed his educational skills and expertise to Howard University, the University of California, and to social service programs in New York, Massachusetts, Wisconsin, and Illinois. He is a long-time consultant to the National Urban League.

JULIUS LEVONNE CHAMBERS
Director-Counsel, NAACP Legal Defense
and Educational Fund

Julius Chambers, a renowned civil rights lawyer for over 20 years, is known for his work involving the desegregation of the public schools of the Charlotte-Mecklenburg district in North Carolina. His efforts contributed to the landmark Supreme Court decision of 1971, which upheld court-ordered busing as a means of achieving desegregation and educational equality for blacks.

In 1958, Mr. Chambers received his B.A. in history from North Carolina Central University, graduating *summa cum laude*. He was awarded the Woodrow Wilson scholarship to study at the University of Michigan, where he earned his M.A. in history. In 1962 he obtained a law degree and graduated valedictorian from the University of North Carolina. While there, he served as Editor-in-Chief of the Law Review.

Mr. Chambers established North Carolina's first interracial law firm, where he defended segregation suits and fair employment cases. He has taught law classes at the Columbia University Law School, Harvard University Law School, and the University of Pennsylvania School of Law. He has served as president of the NAACP Legal Defense and Educational Fund, Inc., and is currently the newly elected Director-Counsel.

DR. DOUGLAS G. GLASGOW
Vice President, Washington Operations
National Urban League

A noted educator, lecturer, and social scientist, Dr. Douglas Glasgow is an internationally known expert on the poor and the disadvantaged.

Dr. Glasgow received his undergraduate degree from Brooklyn College; a master's degree in Social Work from Columbia University and a doctorate in Social Research from the University of Southern California. He was the professor of Social Policy/Research, and later served as Dean of the School of Social Work at Howard University from 1972–1975. He is currently the Vice President of the National Urban League's Washington Operations Office.

Dr. Glasgow's academic career included the University of Ghana and Makererre University, where he undertook research in systems of African social health. While in Africa, Dr. Glasgow served as policy analyst and research consultant on social development programs to the ministers of social welfare in Ghana, Benin, and Togo.

He is the author of the acclaimed *The Black Underclass: The Oft Debated Issue of the Etiology of Blacks' State of Poverty, Unemployment and Entrapment of Ghetto Youth.*

DR. LENNEAL J. HENDERSON
Professor, School of Business and
Public Administration
Howard University

Dr. Henderson has gained an international reputation as a lecturer and consultant in the areas of economics and public administration. He was a Ford Foundation/National Research Council Post-doctoral Fellow at Johns Hopkins School of Advanced International Studies in Washington, D.C. (1983–84), a Rockefeller Foundation Fellow (1981–83), and is currently a Kellogg National Fellow.

Dr. Henderson received his B.A., M.A., and Ph.D. degrees from the University of California, Berkeley, and is completing the requirements for an M.A. in Science, Technology and Public Policy at George Washington University in Washington, D.C. Currently, he is a Professor in the School of Business and Public Administration at Howard University.

As a noted expert in the areas of Energy Management, Fiscal Management, and Development Administration, Dr. Henderson has lectured and consulted in Canada, England, the U.S.S.R., Africa, Brazil, Egypt, Peru, the Caribbean, and India. He has authored and edited four books, and his writings have appeared in publications including *The Annals, Public Administration Review, The Review of Black Political Economy, Policy Studies Journal, The Urban League Review, The Howard Law Journal,* and *The Journal of Minority Business Finance.* Dr. Henderson has contributed to previous editions of the *State of Black America.*

DR. GEORGIA A. PERSONS
Assistant Professor, Political Science
Howard University

Dr. Georgia Persons has served as a policy analyst in both the public and private sectors, and is noted for her research in the areas of black mayoral leadership and regulatory policy.

Dr. Persons holds a doctorate in Political Science from the Massachusetts Institute of Technology (1978) with concentration in Urban Politics and Public Policy. She received a B.A. degree in Political Science from Southern University, Baton Rouge, Louisiana in 1971, and is currently Assistant Professor of Political Science at Howard University.

Dr. Persons' scholarly writings have appeared in *Phylon, The Policy Studies Review,* and other National Urban League publications. A special collection on "Public Policy and Social Change," edited by Dr. Persons, is forthcoming in the Winter 1987 edition of the *Urban League Review.*

BENY J. PRIMM, M.D.
Co-Founder, Executive Director
Addiction Research and Treatment
Corporation of New York

Dr. Beny Primm is one of the nation's foremost authorities on drug abuse and Acquired Immune Deficiency Syndrome (AIDS) research. Dr. Primm has served as advisor to the President's Advisory Council on Drug Abuse Prevention and the Special White House Briefing Team on Drug Abuse.

Dr. Primm earned a B.S. degree from West Virginia State College in 1950. He then pursued graduate study at the University of Heidelberg in Germany and received his Docteur en Medicine and degree in medicine from the University of Geneva, Switzerland, in 1959. Upon completion of his residency in anesthesiology at Meadowbrook Hospital in Meadowbrook, New York, and directing at departments of anesthesiology at Oyster Bay and Whitestone Hospitals, Dr. Primm began his pioneering work in the field of drug abuse.

Dr. Primm is the Co-Founder and Executive Director of the Addiction Research and Treatment Corporation (A.R.T.C.) in New York and an attending physician at Harlem Hospital. He lectures at colleges, universities, and medical schools on substance abuse and related issues. He has authored several articles on substance abuse and alcoholism for journals and textbooks, many of which have been reprinted in French and Norwegian.

DR. SHARON P. ROBINSON
Director of Instruction and Professional Development
National Education Association

Dr. Sharon Robinson was awarded a doctor's degree from the University of Kentucky in 1979. She received several fellowships and assistantships while completing her education and has worked as a classroom teacher, associate director of an education research consortium, and human relations specialist. She has also served as the Research Assistant of the University of Kentucky's Technical Assistance Project for School Desegregation, Jefferson County Public Schools.

Since 1980, Dr. Robinson has directed the National Education Association's many programs in the area of Instruction and Professional Development. In that position, she has provided staff support for several NEA education reform projects such as the "Excellence In Our Schools" series, The NEA Report, "An Open Letter to America," and The Mastery in Learning Project.

Dr. Robinson has represented the NEA at Congressional hearings and has acted as liaison to numerous organizations and forums, including the American Educational Research Association, The American Association of Colleges for Teacher Educators, and The Association of Teacher Educators. In addition, Dr. Robinson has made media appearances on several major news shows including the "McNeil/Lehrer News Hour," "Good Morning America," and CNN News.

DR. BARBARA SOLOMON
Acting Dean of Graduate Studies
University of Southern California

Dr. Solomon is an acknowledged leader in the field of social services. For more than three decades, she has contributed her skills in psychology and social work to institutions across the country. A widely published author, she has written extensively on the needs of blacks, women, and the elderly in contemporary America.

Dr. Solomon received her B.A. in psychology from Howard University, graduating *magna cum laude*, in 1954. At the University of California at Berkeley, she received her master's degree in Social Welfare in 1956. She earned a doctorate of Social Work at the University of Southern California in 1966.

Some of Dr. Solomon's most notable work has been published in major sociological publications such as *Social Service Review, The Gerontologist,* and *Social Work.*

DR. DAVID H. SWINTON
Director, Southern Center for
Studies in Public Policy
Clark College

Dr. David Swinton is recognized as one of the country's leading economists. As Director of the Southern Center for Studies in Public Policy at Clark College, he has written for national publications, including National Urban League publications.

Dr. Swinton has held positions as Assistant Director for Research, Black Economic Research Center; and as Senior Research Associate and Director of Minorities and Social Policy Programs at the Urban Institute.

Dr. Swinton received his undergraduate degree from New York University and his M.A. and Ph.D. degrees from Harvard University. He has served as a Teaching Fellow at Harvard and a lecturer at City College of New York.

DR. CHARLES V. WILLIE
Professor of Education and Urban Studies
Graduate School of Education
Harvard University

Dr. Charles Willie, an expert and noted author in education and sociology, served as the court-appointed master during the controversial Boston school desegregation case. President Carter appointed him a member of the President's Commission on Mental Health.

Dr. Willie received his B.A. degree from Morehouse College; a M.A. degree from Atlanta University; and a Doctor of Philosophy degree in Sociology from Syracuse University. He was a Professor and Chair of the Department of Sociology and Vice President of Syracuse University, and is currently Professor of Education and Urban Studies in the Graduate School of Education at Harvard University.

Dr. Willie is the author of several major publications on education and desegregation, including *Five Black Scholars* (1986); *Metropolitan School Desegregation* (1986); and *School Desegregation Plans that Work* (1984).

5

Black America, 1986:
An Overview

John E. Jacob
President
National Urban League, Inc.

1986 will go down in history as the year the nation staggered between the twin scandals of what have been called "Irangate" and "Boeskygate."

The first involved secret arms sales to Iran, illegal transfers of funds to the Nicaraguan Contras, and possibly illegal acts by high government officials. The second involved illegal financial manipulation of the stock market. Both have serious implications for the American political order and economic life, and both shed light on aspects of the black situation in ways most Americans have not considered.

The revelations of the secret dealings with Iran came on the heels of a series of events that shook the public's faith in the government's conduct of foreign policy. First came the news that our government had implemented a "disinformation" campaign about a possible attack on Libya, planting stories known to be untrue in the U.S. media. That was followed by the swap of a Soviet spy for an American journalist held by the Russians—a deal the government denied making, telling a disbelieving world that the two acts were separate and unrelated to each other. This was followed by a Summit meeting in Iceland that was sold to the public as not being a Summit, despite the fact that the two heads of state and their key staffs held intensive meetings. The Summit was then sold to the public as a success through a media blitz that sought to convert a foreign policy failure into a public relations triumph. Meanwhile, a plane supplying the Contras was shot down in Nicaragua and the pilot placed on trial, with subsequent reports of secret supply missions in apparent violation of Congressional mandates.

Finally, "Irangate" broke—an administration claiming to be neutral in the Iraq-Iran conflict and publicly refusing to deal with governments that sponsor terrorism was making massive arms sales to Iran in a failed effort to free U.S. hostages in Lebanon. Proceeds of the sale were placed in a Swiss bank account to buy arms for the Nicaraguan Contras. The tentacles of the secret operation reached high into the White House, and may have violated the Arms Export Control Act, the National Security Act, and laws related to misappropriation of government property.

The mushrooming scandal that ensued dealt a heavy blow to the administration's credibility, especially in the context of the other incidents that demonstrated the primacy of public relations over substantive policy.

The general picture was that of a government contemptuous of the laws of the land and of public opinion, obsessed by appearances, and devoted to "spin control," or shaping public perceptions rather than providing the public with the information it needs to make informed choices about policies.

What went virtually unnoticed in the public uproar over these foreign policy misadventures was the fact that they carried over into foreign policy patterns of behavior that have long typified the administration's domestic policies, and especially its policies directly or indirectly affecting black citizens.

What columnist David Broder called the "fatal blend of ignorance and arrogance" also describes the administration's civil rights policies. It tried to win tax exemptions for segregated schools, fought extension of civil rights laws, undermined affirmative action, destroyed the U.S. Civil Rights Commission, stacked the judiciary with right-wingers, and refused to budge from its support for South Africa's apartheid government—all the while implementing a public relations policy designed to convince Americans that we are now a color-blind, racially neutral society.

At the same time, it ignored mounting black poverty. In place of substantive domestic policy, it substituted demonstrably false statements designed to convince the public that unemployment was no longer a problem, that the poor don't want to work, and that social programs simply compound social problems instead of helping resolve them.

What our government did to all of its citizens in foreign policy it first did to black citizens in its domestic policies. The persistent disinformation campaigns and factual distortions characteristic of the administration's public relations thrust on domestic matters were simply translated to foreign policy. It is hard to determine which is more shameful—that the administration did all this, or that the public let it get away with it for so long.

The second major scandal, involving insider trading and financial manipulation, reflects the failure of a laissez-faire philosophy that encouraged greed, weakened our economy, and undermined public faith in the economic system, just as "Irangate" weakened public faith in government.

Some of the biggest names on Wall Street were implicated in the scandal. Financier Ivan Boesky was fined $100 million, young investment bankers earning six- and seven-figure incomes were guilty of criminal acts, and formerly respected financial organizations fell under a cloud of suspicion.

The scandal focused attention on the way sheer greed had become the prevailing creed of Ronald Reagan's America, and it shone a spotlight on the way short-term financial considerations have come to dominate American business, at the expense of long-term policies that increase productive capacity and create jobs.

As the prominent investment banker, Felix Rohatyn, stated in an address to the Urban League of Greater New York in December:

"Greed and corruption are the cancer of a free society. They are a cancer because they erode our value system. . .I have been in business for almost forty years and I cannot recall a period in which greed and corruption appeared as prevalent as they are today."

And Rohatyn went on to point out that insider-trading scandals go beyond a handful of bankers, brokers, and lawyers engaged in criminal behavior to undermine the integrity of the financial system and its institutions.

The scandal also focused attention on the wave of mergers and acquisitions that have been so widespread in recent years. The dominance of financial considerations, leading companies to stress short-term financial results in an effort to ward off mergers, may have undermined industry's ability to compete in world markets where our competitors implement long-term strategies to increase market shares.

The ideal image of corporations as socially responsible institutions mandated to produce goods and services the public wants and to create the jobs society needs was dealt a severe blow. The wave of asset-shifting, liquidations, plant-closings, and loss of markets to foreign competitors shook public confidence in the prevailing laissez-faire philosophy.

Liberal critics called for more and tighter regulation; conservative critics like Deputy Treasury Secretary Richard G. Darman issued populist calls for reordering corporate structures, and many business leaders criticized the way greed and the rush to get rich in a hurry have siphoned top talent away from creating products to creating deals.

So the twin scandals of "Irangate" and "Boeskygate" are not just politically titillating events—90-day wonders that produce headlines, gossip, and bad jokes. They are seismic tremors running through our political and economic systems that call into question the values and practices adopted over the past half-dozen years.

Nor can they be seen as excesses that mar otherwise satisfactory systems, for they are symptomatic of serious disorders that plague our society—disorders that stem from ideologies contemptuous of democratic processes and humane social considerations.

Black Americans have lived with those societal disorders and felt their effects in ways most white Americans have not, for disproportionate black disadvantage means blacks suffer most from undemocratic processes and from public and private policies that devalue humane mandates.

Typical of the moral blinkers donned by the nation in recent years is its indifference to the continued existence of racism and racial disadvantage that permeate our society and degrade national life and aspirations.

Racism continues to live on despite the pious pronouncements that we are now a color-blind society. It can be seen in the daily drumfire of local reports about racially inspired outrages that show old forms of racism thriving alongside the more subtle forms of discrimination that have become more popular.

Several incidents that made national news toward the end of the year suffice to demonstrate this. In one, the police chief of a New Orleans suburb announced that police officers would routinely stop blacks seen in white neighborhoods. This "anti-crime" measure was rescinded after protests, but similar policies prevail in other communities without benefit of formal announcements.

A second incident involved The Citadel, the South's historic military academy. White cadets in Klan dress invaded the room of a black cadet. Had they been using drugs, they would have been expelled. But racist violence is apparently considered a schoolboy prank by the institution's administrators, and the offenders' punishment stopped far short of suspension. The black victim resigned from the school in protest against continued harassment, and a persistent pattern of racist harassment of black cadets was revealed in subsequent reports.

Finally, a lynch mob in the Howard Beach section of Queens, New York, assaulted three black men for the "crime" of being in their neighborhood. One died after the attack, which followed similar incidents in recent years.

In addition, housing discrimination is commonplace, as has been documented time and again. Discrimination in other aspects of life is also documented in incidents ranging from blacks passed over for jobs and promotions to blacks discriminated against in voting procedures.

It is hard to avoid the conclusion that the continuation of illegal discrimination and the resurgence of racist feelings are fostered by the administration's refusal to admit that racism may still be a problem.

The Justice Department's war on affirmative action and the powerful disinformation campaign it wages to convince the public that affirmative action is actually reverse discrimination cannot but prejudice public attitudes and encourage hostility toward black citizens.

The department persists in narrow interpretations of the law that emasculate key protections, such as its insistence that it will not object to certain voting changes that have a discriminatory result despite the clear Congressional mandate requiring it to do so.

Its philosophy, as enunciated by the Attorney General in a highly publicized address at Tulane University, remains uncomfortably close to the states' rights philosophy of the old-line segregationists who held that public officials may defy Supreme Court rulings they disagree with.

The department which also spearheaded a year-long attempt to get the President to rescind a 20-year-old Executive Order promoting federal minority employment is laggard in enforcing civil rights laws, expends its energies in fighting civil rights goals, and demonstrates its attitudes toward blacks by not having a single black person among the department's top officers.

Conservative spokesmen are fond of pointing out that the real problems facing black Americans are those that may not be ameliorated by more aggressive civil rights policies—problems like unemployment, inadequate education, teenage pregnancy, and others. It is unconscionable to use these tragic circumstances as an excuse to avoid necessary civil rights strategies while at the same time refusing to implement policies that deal positively with black disadvantage.

The fourth consecutive year of economic prosperity found unemployment remaining at an unacceptably high seven percent level. What used to be labelled "recession-level unemployment" is now described as "full employment." For black workers, unemployment remained stuck at Depression-level rates of 15 percent, with rates for inner-city teenagers above the 50 percent mark.

The highly vaunted American "job-machine" was widely praised for creating some three million jobs over the course of the year, but less noted was the growth in part-time positions and the destruction of high-paying manufacturing jobs and their replacement by low-paying retail and service industry jobs. A study prepared for the Joint Economic Committee of Congress found that of the eight million new jobs created between 1979 and 1984, more than half paid less than $7,000 per year, indicating that the bulk of job growth has been in part-time and low-wage positions.

The U.S. Bureau of Labor Statistics estimates that nearly four million part-time workers want to work full-time, and almost 1.2 million discouraged workers have given up searching for jobs, an extraordinarily high figure for this stage of an economic recovery.

The Census Bureau reports that over 33 million people were poor in 1985—a rise of four million since 1980. More than one of every five American children are poor; for blacks, about half are poor. The rise in poverty has been accompanied by a widening gap between rich and poor. The Center for Budget and Policy Priorities states:

"The Census data show that from 1980 to 1985, the typical (or median) family in the poorest 40 percent of the population saw its income decline by $236, after adjusting for inflation. During the same five-year period, the typical family in the top 40 percent of the population saw its income rise $2,195, while the typical family in the richest 10 percent saw its income increase by $7,130."

Alongside the income gap is the wealth gap: the Census Bureau reports that the typical white family had a net worth twelve times as great as the net worth of the typical black family. Almost a third of all black families had no assets at all.

The growing gap between the rich and the poor cuts across racial lines, although it is most pronounced in white-black comparisons. The noted civil rights attorney, Joseph L. Rauh, Jr., summed up what he called "frightening signs of plutocracy" when he noted that:

"The net worth of the Forbes 400 richest went up in one year almost 20 percent compared to a 2.7 percent rise in the country's gross national product. While this was happening, the real hourly earnings for production workers was going down and the percentage of people living in poverty was rising."

Growing disparities in income and wealth are not accidental; they are the result of policies that encourage higher unemployment and lower levels of social spending and investment. Estimates of the cumulative effects of federal social spending cuts range from $114 billion to well over that figure, depending on the programs included. The most severe budget cuts have been in programs that invest in providing individuals with skills and opportunities, such as job training programs, which are a third smaller than they would have been had the 1981 law been kept in effect. Survival programs such as welfare and food stamps were also cut heavily, accounting for part of the rise in poverty and the added pressures burdening the poor.

The failure of current social welfare policies is most strongly dramatized by the plight of the homeless, now numbering some 3.5 million, according to the National Coalition for the Homeless. Despite the myth that the homeless are mentally disturbed individuals, the bulk of the homeless are individuals and families too poor to afford available housing. The administration has slashed federal funds for subsidized housing by 78 percent since 1980, and the gentrification of many urban areas coupled with the abandonment and destruction of low-income housing and the increased demand for such housing is primarily responsible for the shameful existence of widespread homelessness.

In the absence of sound social welfare policies, current programs expend large sums without alleviating problems. In late 1986 national attention was focused on a destitute New York family, which was placed in a two-room, rodent-infested apartment without a kitchen in a welfare hotel, at a cost to federal, state, and city authorities of $27,000 per year. Getting the figure for rent wrong, President Reagan told a news conference:

"I just read this morning in the paper about a needy family in New York that is being put up in a hotel, and the cost to welfare, just for the rent of the hotel, runs $37,000 a year. And I wonder why somebody doesn't build them a house for $37,000."

The President asked a good question, one that should be answered by his administration and the Congress through revived federal programs that increase the stock of low-income housing and reform the welfare system to provide education and job opportunities.

In lieu of broad-based national programs, however, the administration's task force on welfare recommended localization of social welfare programs and warned against sweeping reforms. Its disgracefully shallow report betrayed ignorance about the poor, the causes of poverty, and the potential of federal policies to encourage independence. While many states have implemented interesting experimental programs, including programs that place primary stress on providing education and training opportunities for welfare recipients, poverty is a national problem demanding national solutions, and a further withdrawal by the federal government can only worsen the situation.

While 1986 was yet another year of trial and tribulation for Black America, there were some signs that the tide may yet turn, and that the cause of black and poor citizens, invisible for so long, may return to the nation's consciousness and its conscience. The brief national fling with policies encouraging personal greed at the expense of the public good cannot obscure the powerful vein of idealism lying just beneath the surface. As historian Arthur Schlesinger, Jr., put it: "The political cycle is due to turn at the end of the 1980s, and private interest is scheduled to give way to public purpose as the guiding principle of our politics."

There is nothing mechanistic or deterministic about this process, however. National policies will change because the present ones demonstrably harm the national interest, and because they go against the grain of traditional American concepts of morality and fair play.

Such considerations were behind the startling reversal of the nation's South Africa policy—the result of grass-roots sentiment that rejected South Africa's racism and direct and indirect American complicity in the apartheid system. Americans saw that it was in their best interests to withdraw from even minimal interaction with the present South African regime, and their will was embodied by Congress and by the leaders of many corporations, who ended their business relations there.

A similar outcome will result from the feeling spreading among Americans that social and economic policies are encouraging a dangerous gap between the affluent and the poor, harming our economy and crippling our cities. The election results indicated that such a shift in national opinion is now under way. Despite the President's popularity in November 1986—before "Irangate" broke—voters rejected candidates that shared his ideology, and expressed their concerns about an economic recovery that excludes millions of Americans. The deterioration we have noted in jobs and incomes will spur a reconsideration of government's role as a creator of opportunities for all, and not just for a limited number of financial speculators.

There is also widespread concern about the ability of our economy to compete in the global marketplace, and the realization that America's future depends on national investment in human resources—in education and training that tap the potential of millions of disadvantaged people now excluded from full participation in our economy.

While white Americans remain largely ignorant of—or indifferent to—the plight of black citizens, there is a convergence of opinion among the races on some key issues. A national poll by the Gallup Organization conducted for the Joint Center for Political Studies found surprising agreement between blacks and whites on the major problems confronting the nation. Although white Americans continued to believe that civil rights was not a major problem, respondents of both races identified unemployment, drug abuse, and the high cost of living as the three most important issues, and both ranked crime, health care, and the quality of public education among the top ten. This suggests the possibility of increased interracial cooperation on issues that disproportionately affect the black population.

Another positive sign in 1986 was the final approval of the pastoral letter, "Economic Justice for All," by the National Conference of Catholic Bishops. "That so many people are poor in a nation as rich as ours is a social and moral scandal that we cannot ignore," the Bishops stated. They recommended an agenda similar to that supported by the National Urban League and other community-based organizations, including full employment policies, expanded job-training programs in the private sector, alternatives to welfare, job creation for the long-term unemployed, and others.

Perhaps the most positive development in 1986 was the intensification of the black community's effort to deal with such serious problems as crime, drugs, teenage pregnancy, family breakup, and public education. The National Urban League launched its nationwide Education Initiative in September to get the schools back on track, to motivate our young people, and to involve our communities in making the schools work better. It is a results-oriented program with a five-year time frame and concrete, achievable goals to improve the school performance of disadvantaged youngsters.

Each Urban League will mobilize the community to define key issues, maximize use of existing resources, build coalitions and support for change, and implement concrete action designed to target at-risk children and to have measurable results. Some of our affiliates have already developed action plans with five-year time frames designed to increase the number of black students in college-track classes and math and science courses. Others have programs to engage black adults and students in activities that have a positive impact on educational achievement, such as mentoring and guidance projects.

Other national and local community-based organizations are deeply involved in similar programs directly tackling internal community problems. The wave of community activism will counter the powerlessness that has impeded resolution of our problems, and will harness the tremendous resources and energies of black citizens to create brighter prospects for all black people.

So the black community enters 1987 in a hopeful mood, convinced it has weathered the worst and prepared to play its part in assuring a more hopeful future.

Within the following pages, we present major papers on a variety of subjects from outstanding scholars, whose independent evaluations are intended to inform and to stimulate. Their views do not necessarily reflect the official position or policies of the National Urban League. Our own summation and recommendations appear at the end of this report.

It is our hope that this publication will help increase an awareness of the reality of life within Black America and influence the decision-making process in 1987. We express our gratitude to the authors.

The Law and Black Americans: Retreat From Civil Rights

Julius L. Chambers

"Securing equality requires the attention, the energy, and the sense of justice possessed by all the well-intentioned citizens of the society. They need to be assured that the government, the law, and the courts stand behind their efforts to overcome the harm bequeathed to them by the past. They need to know that encouragement and support, not criticism and prohibition, are available from those who are sworn to uphold the law. Courts must offer guidance. . .to the attempts by individuals and institutions to rectify the injustices of the past. We must labor to provide examples of solutions that may work, and approaches that may be tried. If we fail, then we delay or postpone altogether the era in which, for the first time, we may say with firm conviction that we have built a society in keeping with our fundamental belief that all people are created equal."

> U.S. Supreme Court Justice Thurgood Marshall
> September 4, 1986

INTRODUCTION

Few would have thought that more than thirty years after *Brown v. Board of Education*[1] and twenty years after the Civil Rights Act of 1964,[2] black Americans and their supporters would today be committing most of their resources in an effort simply to preserve past gains. Yet, that has been the necessary focus of activity by most civil rights groups since the Reagan administration took office, and that remained true during 1986.

This administration, led principally by the U.S. Department of Justice, mounted vigorous efforts in a number of areas to halt civil rights progress and to reverse past gains. These efforts, to date, have met with only limited success. But the administration is in office for two more years. Despite setbacks, it has made clear that it plans no change from past efforts to turn back the clock on civil rights.[3] Because of this, a review and assessment of the administration's programs and efforts is appropriate.

What the present administration has done through its efforts (successful or unsuccessful) is to create a legal climate that encourages lack of enforcement of civil rights. Using the courts, the Justice Department has sought to undermine the principal requirements for effective enforcement. This has meant attacking established standards for defining illegal discrimination, such as its attempts to substitute an "intent" for an "effect" standard in determining if an act is

15

discriminatory. The department also consistently challenges the legality of effective remedies, specifically affirmative action and busing for the purpose of achieving desegregation. Another approach has been to undertake legal challenges to enforcement procedures embedded in statutes, executive orders, and administrative regulations. At the same time, the department litigates civil rights cases to the end and supports efforts to limit attorneys' fee awards available to lawyers who win private civil rights claims.

This chapter will focus on how the administration has handled the interpretation and enforcement of civil rights, how civil rights groups have responded, and what effect this has had on the law and black Americans. Several areas are examined including school desegregation, affirmative action, employment discrimination, voting rights, and attorneys' fees in civil rights lawsuits, as well as policies and practices of the Equal Employment Opportunity Commission (EEOC) and the U.S. Commission on Civil Rights. Brief discussions of the racial implications of recent Supreme Court decisions affecting the administration of criminal justice and of the administration's judicial appointments are also included.

SCHOOL DESEGREGATION LAW

An assessment of the current status of efforts to ensure equal education opportunities for blacks must begin with recognition of the federal government's active role in furthering educational equity for minorities—at least before the advent of the present administration. Decisive federal action was critical to many of the significant advances made by blacks in the past—whether the federal role was visible and public[4] or less apparent.[5] From 1961 to 1969 and again from 1977 to 1981, attorneys from the Department of Justice were allies of black parents and school children prosecuting desegregation suits, and they helped to win important court decisions furthering the cause of equal opportunity.[6] During the Nixon and Ford administrations, the federal government occasionally argued directly against black litigants in the Supreme Court,[7] but in general, once the court had made its decision, it was implemented by the Department of Justice.

Recent years have seen a considerable change in attitude and approach. Today in civil rights cases, the federal government not only argues against any *extension* of established legal principles, but it campaigns actively in the courts and in the arena of public opinion to turn the clock back and wipe out the gains of the past. Thus, in 1987 black Americans face a continued threat from the federal government aimed at halting the thrust for equity and equality which began in 1954 with *Brown v. Board of Education*[8] and at stripping them of effective legal protections against discrimination.

By far the most damaging example is the administration's argument that, once having implemented a court-ordered plan for desegregation, a school system becomes "unitary" and is then entitled (a) to have existing court orders withdrawn and (b) to implement new plans which, in effect, resegregate its schools. Recently, the Supreme Court declined to review lower court rulings which had permitted Norfolk, Virginia, to do just that: to end its busing plan and recreate ten all-black "neighborhood schools." Assistant Attorney General William Bradford Reynolds welcomed the Supreme Court decision not to get into the case, saying that Norfolk provides "a model for the future and for other school districts to follow."[9]

The administration has for some time been taking an even more perverse position in court suits. In Norfolk, at least, all of the parties agreed that while it was in effect, the busing plan imposed by court decree in 1972 produced actual school integration. But the Department of Justice has argued that whether or not integration is achieved, a school system should be declared "unitary" and released from court supervision so long as it has implemented a *plan* which was *expected* to work when it was first approved.[10] It opposed further desegregation in Denver, Colorado, on this basis,[11] for instance, and it negotiated a Consent Decree in its Bakersfield case which provides that even if enrollment goals at magnet schools are not achieved,

> If the District can demonstrate that it has implemented the plans, programs and policies approved by this Court and continued them in effect through the 1986–87 school year, a declaration of unitariness *shall* be entered, the Consent Decree terminated and this case dismissed.[12]

Moreover, the Department of Justice has also abandoned the only useful remedy in school segregation cases: mandatory pupil reassignment. In its place, the government urges the use of "magnet schools"[13] and other voluntary techniques which rely for their success on the good will of whites who were for years the beneficiaries of segregation. Although couched in "anti-busing" rhetoric, the obvious effect of the government position is to allow segregation to continue if white parents desire it. "We are not going to compel children who don't choose to have an integrated education to have one," Reynolds has stated.[14]

The federal government was equally aggressive in resisting black demands for equality that did not involve busing. The government argued strenuously in the Supreme Court that only judicial findings of past discrimination could justify a school district's conscious effort to hire and retain more black teachers.[15] In the longstanding suit to desegregate Tennessee's higher education institutions, despite drastic underrepresentation of the state's black population in graduate and professional schools, the Department of Justice refused to approve, and even appealed (unsuccessfully) an affirmative action plan worked out by the state and private lawyers that provides special counselling, training and early admission opportunities for black college sophomores identified as potential enrollees in professional schools. Reynolds argued that the plan was an unlawful racial preference unless the individual students who would benefit could show that they were the direct victims of discriminatory practices under the former dual system of higher education.[16]

The federal government is also trying to escape its obligation under litigation brought by the NAACP Legal Defense and Educational Fund in 1970 to ensure that funding and support of public systems of higher education is nondiscriminatory. The case, *Adams* v. *Bennett,* [17] has a dual purpose: nondiscriminatory admission and hiring practices in state systems of higher education and enhancement of traditionally black public institutions. *Adams* has resulted in a series of court orders requiring the Department of Education to promulgate criteria for desegregation plans, institute compliance procedures, and secure plans from the covered states.[18] These plans have increased in specificity over the years with respect to goals and timetables, measures, and financial commitments to achieve nondiscriminatory status and to provide enhancement of black schools. A number of states covered by *Adams* have made commitments to enhance traditionally black state schools, to bring black high school graduates into state colleges at the same rate as whites, to develop programs to keep black college students in school and graduating at the same rate as whites, to establish measures to accomplish the same goals for blacks in graduate and professional schools, and to employ black faculty members, administrators, and staff at state schools in proportion to their availability.

The *Adams* litigation has effected some changes, increasing minority enrollment and hiring and enhancement of some of the traditionally black institutions. Many problems remain, however, threatening not only opportunities for blacks in higher education but also the development and viability of traditional black colleges and universities.

Beginning in 1981, the Department of Education and the Justice Department began a concerted effort to undermine the validity and effectiveness of the *Adams* court orders. In its determination to get out from under the *Adams* decrees, the Department of Justice challenged the standing of black parents and students to sue as plaintiffs, asserting that the court orders violate the separation of powers. The challenge came after the NAACP Legal Defense Fund won two strong court orders in 1983.[19] A decision is pending in federal district court. In the meantime, the Office for Civil Rights in the Department of Education is dragging its feet on deciding whether the states have made good on their commitments.

In short, the federal government's activities concerned with civil rights in education remain consistent with the administration's position in the *Bob Jones University* controversy:[20] protestations of commitment to equality accompanied by actions directly contrary to black interests. This posture, especially when combined with the government's support for programs that would weaken public schools and the government's cutbacks in federal aid, threatens improved educational opportunities for blacks in 1987.

VOTING RIGHTS

Passage of the Voting Rights Act in 1965 resulted in black Americans making great gains in political participation. Registration among eligible black voters went from 25 percent in 1965 to over 50 percent in 1981. The number of black elected officials also rose dramatically. Nevertheless, entrenched political structures, erected during periods of blatant discrimination or in response to emerging black political power, continue as barriers to effective minority representation in the halls of government.

At-large elections and other electoral schemes that dilute the strength of black votes, and registration procedures that impose disproportionate informational, psychological, logistic, and sociological burdens on minorities deprive black Americans of the opportunity to participate equally with whites in the electoral process.

Congress has acted to remove these barriers by renewing and strengthening the Voting Rights Act. Additionally, Supreme Court decisions in voting cases have, for the most part, advanced the law in this area. From the beginning, however, the present administration has sought to block progress and deny blacks the opportunity to participate fully in the electoral process.

Since the Voting Rights Act was strengthened and extended in 1982 (over vigorous opposition from officials in the administration), the Department of Justice has initiated very few voting rights cases on its own. Moreover, the department argued (unsuccessfully) in opposition to a voting rights challenge brought by the NAACP Legal Defense and Educational Fund on behalf of black voters in North Carolina, contesting the state's reapportionment plan adopted in 1982 for elections to the state legislature.[21] (The department previously had found that aspects of the plan *were discriminatory.*)

In June of 1986 the Supreme Court rejected the state's (and the department's) claims in the case, when it unanimously affirmed the "results" standard incorporated in the 1982 amendments to the Act. (Section 2 of the Act, as amended in 1982, requires no proof of intentional discrimination, only discriminatory results, for voting requirements to be illegal.) The court held that the North Carolina plan, which called for large multi-member districts to elect members of the state legislature, had the effect of submerging black votes and of denying blacks an equal opportunity to elect candidates of their choice. The court also found that blacks were disadvantaged in majority-white districts because whites typically would not vote for a black candidate. Moreover, the court rejected the argument, made by the Solicitor General on behalf of the Department of Justice, that some electoral success, however limited—if, for example, even one black candidate had ever been elected from a voting district—showed that the system was fair. The court held that blacks were entitled to an electoral system that provided a full and equal opportunity to elect representatives of their choice, not merely "some" opportunity. The Justice Department's interpretation would have effectively gutted the 1982 amendments to the law and reinstated a standard as tough to meet as the "intent" requirement.

The department's involvement in voting rights cases on behalf of black plaintiffs occurs primarily in instances where private parties have already filed costly lawsuits. For example, although voting rights discrimination is and always has been outrageously blatant in Mississippi, the Department of Justice did not even begin to enforce the law in this state until forced to examine the evidence firsthand during a visit to Mississippi by the head of the Civil Rights Division, William Bradford Reynolds. The department's follow-up was minimal. Staff attorneys prepared eleven enforcement actions to enjoin local elections where discrimination was documented, but Reynolds refused to file all but one of these actions.

In October 1986, civil rights and public interest law groups wrote to Attorney General Edwin Meese protesting published reports that the department planned to weaken the enforcement standard for actions brought under section 5 of the Voting Rights Act. Section 5 requires that jurisdictions with a history of discrimination in voting practices submit all changes in election laws and procedures to the department for review and preclearance. Section 5 is crucial in preventing these jurisdictions from re-instituting discriminatory practices. In the past, section 5 has been highly successful in preventing proposed changes from being imposed on citizens who lack the funds to file lawsuits under section 2 of the Voting Rights Act.

In a speech at the American Political Science Forum[22] on August 30, 1986, Reynolds announced that the Justice Department would no longer consider a section 2 (results) standard in evaluating proposed voting changes for section 5 preclearance. Reynolds suggested that the department would preclear the change and, when appropriate, would file a section 2 civil action. Despite objections from Congress and the civil rights community, it appears that in at least one instance the Department has already begun to implement this new interpretation of section 5. In July 1986, section 5 approval was granted for at-large elections for the new Wilson County, North Carolina Board of Education; the following month, the department filed a *section 2* lawsuit challenging the change the department had just precleared.

This change in policy is a clear violation of the legislative history of the Voting Rights Act;[23] previous acts of the Justice Department;[24] and public testimony of Justice Department officials.[25] Failure to apply the section 2 results test to the section 5 preclearance process will inevitably lead to an increase in voting rights litigation, contrary to Congress's intent in enacting section 5.

Although voting is hailed as the "crown jewel" of American liberties, the United States—unlike other Western democracies—has implemented a system of registration which requires that voters assume the burden of identifying themselves to government authorities before being permitted to vote. Canada, for example, which also has a federal system of government, facilitates registration through household canvassing similar to census taking.

Registration procedures typically impose conditions that are more burdensome to blacks and other minorities and the poor. Persons who cannot register because they live in a rural area, far from the place of registration, without public transportation and no access to private transportation, are effectively denied the right to vote. Registration may also be a burden for hourly employees who cannot take time off during the day to go to the registrar's office without suffering loss of pay. In the case of black Americans, many millions among the voting age population have lived most of their adult lives in an atmosphere officially and pervasively hostile to their exercise of the franchise.

While many groups are working to increase voter participation among black Americans, they are doing so without any meaningful support from the Executive Branch, which has, in some instances, placed itself on the side of state officials whose actions are aimed at restricting the right to vote, and at preventing and discouraging blacks from exercising their franchise.

People who are registered tend to vote, unless they are denied the opportunity to vote for the candidate of their choice. Therefore, efforts to remove registration barriers must be combined with continuing legal challenges to electoral schemes that make black votes count less than white votes.

Although the Executive Branch has opposed the expansion of voting opportunities, the Legislative and Judicial Branches have firmly dedicated themselves to realizing the promise of the Constitution and the Voting Rights Act that blacks have an equal opportunity to participate in the electoral processes and to elect the representatives of their choice. The Supreme court's recent decision in *Gingles,* the participation in that case on the side of plaintiffs by a bipartisan leadership group of the House and Senate, and the recent efforts by legislators such as Senators Dole, Kennedy, and Biden, and Representatives Edwards, Fish, and Sensenbrenner to prevent the administration from gutting section 5 all testify to the widespread commitment to voting rights.

EQUAL EMPLOYMENT OPPORTUNITY

Title VII of the Civil Rights Act of 1964 was intended to eliminate entrenched patterns of racial discrimination in employment, to provide remedies for past discrimination, and to prevent future discrimination. Initially the courts interpreted the statute liberally with respect to procedures for filing a claim, defining what constituted a violation of the law, and determining adequate remedies. Implementation of Title VII also required effective enforcement. Despite reluctance by the Department of Justice and the EEOC to become involved in recent years in bringing suits under Title VII, an active private bar took up the mantle. Today, however, prodded by the administration, courts are interpreting Title VII far more strictly, limiting individuals' ability to establish a violation, limiting what can be obtained in relief, and limiting the ability of employees and public interest law groups to bring and maintain litigation under the statute.

Definition of Unlawful Discrimination

The administration has called into question some of the basic principles which allow persons to prove discrimination. One of these principles, the *Griggs* rule, requires employers to demonstrate that procedures or tests used to make employment decisions are job-related. This rule has been embodied since 1978 in the Uniform Guidelines on Employee Selection Procedures. Suggesting that the Guidelines impose too onerous a burden on employers, EEOC has proposed that they be modified to make it easier for employers to comply with Title VII.

To appreciate the importance of this proposed change one must view these Guidelines in the context of the overall federal enforcement scheme. There are three agencies which have the primary responsibility for the enforcement of the fair employment laws. Two[26] of these agencies act pursuant to Title VII of the

Civil Rights Act of 1964, as amended by the Equal Employment Opportunity Act of 1972: the Department of Justice, which has authority to sue state and local governments, and EEOC, which has authority to sue private employers. Title VII also allows private individuals to sue private and public employers for discrimination in employment. When Title VII was enacted in 1964, it prohibited intentional discrimination and made it unlawful for an employer "to limit, segregate, or classify . . . employees or applicants for employment in any way which would deprive or tend to deprive any individual of employment opportunities . . ." Section 703(h) of the Act allowed an exception for "professionally developed ability test(s) provided . . . [they were not] . . . intended or used to discriminate . . ."

In 1966 the EEOC adopted the first set of administrative guidelines interpreting these provisions. These guidelines defined "professionally developed ability test" to mean "a test which fairly measures the knowledge or skills required by the particular job . . ." In 1970 a more comprehensive set of guidelines was issued. These relied on standards developed by the American Psychological Association and set forth detailed requirements for test validation. It was these guidelines which the Supreme Court applied in 1971 in *Griggs v. Duke Power Co.*[27] Duke Power had required a high school diploma for its better jobs. Applicants who did not have the diploma could take and pass two tests used by the company. These requirements disqualified many of the black employees. The court ruled against Duke Power because the company could not show that either requirement bore "a demonstrable relationship to successful performance of the job for which it was used." Chief Justice Burger, writing for the court, observed:

> History is filled with examples of men and women who rendered highly effective performance without the conventional badges of accomplishment in terms of certificates, diplomas, or degrees. Diplomas and tests are useful servants, but Congress has mandated the common-sense proposition that they are not to become masters of reality.

Congress approved this principle when considering the Equal Employment Opportunity Act of 1972, which extended Title VII's coverage to federal, state, and local governments. The Supreme Court reaffirmed the principle in 1975 in *Albemarle Paper Co. v. Moody.*[28] However, within the federal government, it was not until 1978 that five federal agencies—the EEOC, the Civil Service Commission (now the Office of Personnel Management), and the Departments of Justice, Labor, and the Treasury—collaborated in adopting the Uniform Guidelines on Employee Selection Procedures. These Guidelines established a simple mandate for employers: If a test or other procedure used to make employment decisions has an adverse impact, the employer must demonstrate that the test or procedure is job-related. Adverse impact occurs whenever the test or procedure disqualifies or limits the employment opportunities of a disproportionate number of blacks or other protected groups.

Because of these Guidelines and numerous court decisions approving them, employers have attempted to develop job-related measures for employment decisions. Minority group members and women have been able to advance when evaluated by qualifications which meet the Guidelines' job-relatedness or validation requirements. Moreover, the *Griggs* principle has been used to attack other job "requirements" which employers have been unable to justify. For example, many employers had imposed prior experience requirements for more desirable jobs, such as supervisory or craft positions. These requirements excluded large numbers of minorities and women who had traditionally been unfairly denied such jobs and, therefore, had little or no experience. Because the use of the requirements had an adverse impact on minorities and women, employers could not legally retain them unless they were related to successful performance on the job.

Despite the success of the Guidelines, the Chair of the EEOC began in November 1984 to question the need for them or for the *Griggs* rule. This position was based, in part, on opposition to the use of statistical analyses to demonstrate that a particular requirement had an adverse impact on minorities and/or women.[29] This was part of a broader attack by the administration on statistical proof of discrimination, in which it contended that only overt, intentional discrimination should be actionable.[30]

As 1986 came to a close, however, the Uniform Guidelines appeared safe from change. EEOC has now acknowledged that the principles announced in *Griggs* and *Albemarle* are still the basis of the current law on selection procedures and that statistics serve an important purpose in establishing violations of Title VII.[31]

Race-Conscious Remedies

Rejecting a highly publicized assault by the Justice Department, the Supreme Court this past year reaffirmed the legality and necessity of affirmative action.[32] However, the Department of Justice continued its crusade against affirmative action, and cases to be decided by the court in the next year are likely to establish more specific standards governing the circumstances in which affirmative action is permissible. In addition, the Department of Justice has proposed revisions to Executive Order 11246 that would eliminate the requirement that federal contractors engage in affirmative action hiring.

Soon after the current administration took office in 1981, the Department of Justice commenced a campaign to overturn the victories of the prior three years, in which the Supreme Court upheld the validity of affirmative action under both the Constitution and Title VII of the Civil Rights Act of 1964.[33] The theory advanced by the Department was that Title VII limits relief to those actual victims of discrimination who can be located and brought into court and who are still eligible and interested in the job from which they were excluded.[34] This argument, if accepted, would have barred or substantially limited the availability of race-conscious relief to eliminate the pervasive effects of past discrimination.

The Justice Department's campaign reached the Supreme Court in the 1985-86 term, during which the court decided three cases raising the legality of affirmative action. One of those cases had been brought by the federal Equal Employment Opportunity Commission (EEOC) against the Sheet Metal Workers Union in New York City.[35] In the District Court and the Court of Appeals, the EEOC fought for imposition of affirmative goals and timetables to remedy the union's egregious, defiant refusal for more than ten years to comply with court orders to admit members on a nondiscriminatory basis.[36] Yet, when the case arrived at the Supreme Court, EEOC's position changed. The Solicitor General filed a brief on behalf of the EEOC arguing that "Title VII prohibits the award of relief such as union membership to persons who are not the actual victims of illegal discrimination."[37]

Another of the 1986 cases involved a consent decree entered into by the City of Cleveland and the Vanguards of Cleveland, a group of black firefighters.[38] In that decree, the city admitted that it had discriminated against black firefighters in hiring and agreed to temporary, numerical goals for future employment. The decree was challenged by the local firefighters' union, which was supported in the Supreme Court by the Department of Justice.

In the third case, *Wygant v. Jackson Board of Education,*[39] white teachers challenged a provision of the collective bargaining contract between their union and the City of Jackson, Michigan, which required that any layoffs be done in a manner that would not reduce the city's percentage of minority teachers. The Justice Department filed an *amicus* brief in support of the white teachers.

The Supreme Court upheld the affirmative action plans in the *Sheet Metal Workers* and *Cleveland Firefighters* cases, and invalidated the *Jackson* layoff provision. In all three cases the court held that affirmative action benefiting individuals who are not the actual victims of discrimination may be used in appropriate circumstances.[40] It appears that voluntary affirmative action, including that incorporated into Title VII consent decrees, may be used by private and governmental employers to increase the number of minority workers in jobs where there is a large difference between the percentage of minorities employed and the percentage of minorities available for such jobs in the labor market.[41] Furthermore, in the public schools, voluntary affirmative action may be used to achieve the benefits of a racially diverse faculty.[42]

Following the decisions in *Sheet Metal Workers* and *Cleveland Firefighters,* the EEOC again reversed itself and apparently now supports affirmative action remedies at least in some circumstances.[43] However, the Justice Department continues to challenge the legality of affirmative action, using extremely strained legal reasoning in an attempt to limit the impact of the 1986 rulings. For example, the department is challenging an affirmative action remedy for housing discrimination by arguing that the *Wygant* decision means that an affirmative action remedy is never "narrowly tailored."[44] In a challenge to the hiring goals of the District of Columbia Fire Department, the Justice Department asserted that only "an employer's discriminatory conduct of an egregious, flagrant or pervasive nature" may justify race-conscious affirmative action.[45]

The Supreme Court has agreed to hear two other affirmative action cases in the 1986–87 term. In *Paradise v. Prescott,*[46] the District Court held that one minority for each nonminority must be promoted to each of the upper ranks of the Alabama State Patrol until each rank has achieved 25% minority representation or until the department has developed an unbiased procedure for filling vacancies in each rank. The Justice Department originally brought this lawsuit against the State Patrol and concedes that the Patrol engaged in "pervasive past discrimination."[47] Nonetheless, the department argues that these violations do not justify the current promotion goals because the violations involved hiring and not promotion discrimination.[48] The department also asserts that affirmative action may not be used as a "catch up" measure to remedy "longstanding racial imbalances in the upper ranks," even though such imbalances are the result of past discrimination.[49]

In *Johnson v. Transportation Agency of Santa Clara County*,[50] a white male challenged the promotion of a white female to the position of road dispatcher. The promotion was made pursuant to a flexible, case-by-case approach, under which affirmative action was one of many considerations in each hiring and promotion decision.

The woman who was selected for the dispatcher job scored only two points below the male plaintiff in a panel interview. No woman had ever been employed by the Agency as a road dispatcher or in any other skilled craft job. Nonetheless, the Department of Justice argues that there is insufficient evidence that the total absence of females from these skilled craft jobs is caused by prior discrimination.[51] The Supreme Court's decisions in both *Paradise* and *Johnson* will serve as extremely important tests for the future of effective, feasible affirmative action.

The Department of Justice has also launched an attack upon the affirmative action requirements of Executive Order 11246, which governs federal contractors. The principle that it is fair to obligate those who do business with the United States government to make special efforts to hire qualified women and minorities has been approved by Congress[52] and the courts[53] and is supported by both business[54] and labor organizations.[55] Under the Executive Order, government contractors are required to analyze their work force and to adopt goals and timetables where the facts show a need for such action. Regulations implementing the Executive Order specifically preclude "inflexible quotas," providing only for "good faith" efforts to reach "reasonably attainable" goals.[56]

In 1985 the Department of Justice drafted a replacement for Executive Order 11246, which eliminates the affirmative action requirement.[57] The Secretary of Labor, whose department is responsible for enforcement of the Executive Order, opposes the replacement Order.[58] So far, this internal disagreement and the strong support for the current Order voiced by Congress, the business community and others have resulted in no change. However, the threat to Executive Order 11246 remains a very real one; newspaper reports have suggested that ongoing negotiation between the Justice and Labor Departments could result in a compromise which would still undermine the affirmative-action provisions.[59]

Despite persistent challenges, affirmative action has survived. The Supreme Court shows no inclination to depart from the moderate, flexible approach to affirmative action established in the 1970s.

Resources for Enforcement

A crucial aspect of enforcement is the ability to bring and maintain lawsuits under civil rights statutes. Congress has recognized that attorneys' fees and costs of litigation can impose enormous burdens on victims of discrimination. As civil rights law becomes more complex, it also becomes more costly to implement; a typical class action employment discrimination suit, for example, can involve expenses of at least $100,000 wholly apart from attorneys' fees. Congress sought to encourage private enforcement of civil rights law, along with federal efforts, by providing that civil rights plaintiffs who prevail can recover reasonable attorneys' fees and costs from defendants.

As early as 1968 the Supreme Court interpreted the attorneys' fees statutes broadly to give plaintiffs the right to recover fees as a matter of course when they win.[60] In general, the courts have continued to interpret the fees statutes liberally in order to carry out the intent of Congress to encourage and facilitate the enforcement of civil rights.

Prior to the Reagan administration, the federal government supported the broad interpretation of these statutes and filed *amicus curiae* briefs on the side of civil rights plaintiffs in a number of cases. This administration, however, together with the past leadership of the Senate Judiciary Committee, has embarked on a concerted effort to undermine the fees statutes and thereby seriously interfere with the enforcement of civil rights by private parties. By weakening the private enforcement of civil rights and making it more difficult for organizations and individuals to vindicate their rights in court, the administration will be freer to carry out its program of eviscerating the civil rights laws.

The administration has advanced on two fronts. In Congress it has introduced the so-called "Legal Fees Equity Act." Although this bill has not, to date, been reported out of subcommittee, it contains a number of provisions that would seriously cut back on the availability of fee recoveries. The effort in Congress has been paralleled by attempts to convince the Supreme Court to adopt a number of rules that would weaken the existing civil rights statutes. Over the past three terms of the Supreme Court, the Department of Justice has filed *amicus* briefs or has otherwise participated in virtually every civil rights attorneys' fee case in the court and has in every instance taken a position contrary to that of the civil rights plaintiffs. This effort has included briefs signed by the head of the Civil Rights Division of the Department of Justice.

Thus, the government has urged the court to deny fees for work done in federal administrative proceedings where civil rights have been vindicated,[61] to limit fees to a proportion of money damages recovered;[62] to limit fee recoveries in employment discrimination cases against federal agencies;[63] to restrict the amount of fees that may be recovered by attorneys working for civil rights organizations;[64] and to permit defendants, through a number of procedural devices, to deny fees completely to plaintiffs who have won their suits.[65]

The government's efforts in the Supreme Court have met with only mixed success to date. In two crucial cases, however, *Evans v. Jeff D.* and *Marek v.*

Chesny, the court has agreed with the government and has announced rules that can have a serious impact on private civil rights enforcement.

These two decisions give defendants in civil rights litigation powerful weapons to drive a wedge between plaintiffs and the attorneys who are working to vindicate their rights, and they seriously undermine the purpose of the statutes— to encourage litigation that Congress knows is necessary to vindicate constitutional and civil rights. Congress's mandate remains clear, and the vigorous pursuit of civil rights cases will continue to be one of the most important ways of achieving justice.

U.S. COMMISSION ON CIVIL RIGHTS

Since its reconstitution in 1983, the United States Commission on Civil Rights has violated its statutory mandate as an independent, bipartisan, fact-finding agency; has committed serious violations of its own internal administrative procedures; and has committed numerous irregularities in financial management and personnel practices. In response to these abuses, the 99th Congress reduced the Commission's appropriations and placed restrictions on expenditures for fiscal year 1987.

From its inception in 1957, the Commission on Civil Rights had as its mission to collect information on discrimination and the denial of equal protection of the laws because of race, sex, national origin, age, and handicap; appraise the laws and policies of the federal government; and investigate allegations of the denial of the right to vote. But in the last three years, the Commission has instead provided a prominent public platform for the views of those who seek to turn back the clock on civil rights gains. A majority of the eight commissioners consistently align themselves with virtually all of the administration's positions on civil rights. Instead of serving as the civil rights conscience of the nation, the Commission has attacked the very laws and remedies which have been enacted by Congress and approved by the federal courts to advance equal opportunity for minorities, women, the disabled, and senior citizens.[66]

The Commission is no longer a collegial body which initiates studies and fact-finding in order to make recommendations to Congress and the President. Rather, it has become a platform from which Commissioners try to muster support for positions that undermine and attack affirmative action, comparable worth, minority business set-asides, and other civil rights issues. What passes for fact-finding, comes *after*, not before, the Commission has announced its position. Furthermore, the number of studies, clearinghouse reports, and state advisory committee reports has fallen off sharply—since 1983 the Commission has not issued a single report on federal civil rights enforcement.

THE FEDERAL JUDICIARY

A grave threat to established gains—one that will affect all of us far into the future—is the administration's effort to appoint to the federal bench judges who have views that show a lack of sympathy for the plight of blacks and other disadvantaged groups. To date, the administration has appointed 289 of the authorized total of 648 federal district and appellate court judges. All but five are white.[67] Typically, they are young as well as conservative; many will be sitting for the next three or four decades.

Recently the Senate has begun to resist some of the administration's nominees. The Senate Judiciary Committee refused to send the nomination of Jefferson B. Sessions 3d from Alabama to the full Senate. Opponents had provided ample evidence of Sessions' gross insensitivity to issues of concern to black Americans.

Moreover, the selection and appointment of federal judges, under the Reagan administration, has changed profoundly from what it was during the Carter administration. The number of blacks, Hispanics and women who were Federal judges at the time the Congress passed the Omnibus Judgeship Act in 1978 was appallingly low. Out of 399 district court judges, less than 20 were black; of the 97 appeals courts judges, five were black. The bill created 152 additional federal judgeships, 117 for the district courts and 35 for the appeals courts, thereby expanding the judiciary by approximately 29 percent. [68]

After passage of the bill, the Carter administration set in motion procedures to open up the selection process in order to increase the numbers of qualified minorities and women appointed to the federal bench, including selection commissions with members drawn from different backgrounds and racial groups as well as some non-lawyers. Civil rights groups were invited to recommend persons for appointment to the commissions, as well as to suggest potential nominees for the newly created vacancies.

Not surprisingly, the names of many qualified blacks, Hispanics, and women began to appear among the nominees, with the result that by the time Mr. Carter left office, his record in appointing blacks, other minorities, and women to the bench was singular and exemplary. Mr. Carter appointed a total of 258 federal judges. Among a total of 202 appointed to district courts, 29 were women, 28 were black, and 14 were Hispanic; of the 56 appeals courts appointments, 11 were women, nine were black, and two, Hispanic.[69]

All of this changed when the Reagan administration took office. The innovative and successful experiment in "democratizing" the nomination and confirmation process came to an abrupt end, and the process once more became a closed one. Moreover, the administration still has more than 50 vacancies to fill—*not including* additional vacancies bound to occur through attrition, resignation, death, and retirement. By the end of his term, according to estimates by the Department of Justice, the President will have appointed to lifetime positions more than 45 percent of the entire federal judiciary.

ADMINISTRATION OF CRIMINAL JUSTICE

A number of significant cases before the Supreme Court during 1986 have seriously challenged persistent racial bias in the administration of criminal justice. One of these cases, *McCleskey v. Kemp,*[70] involves the most comprehensive research ever conducted on capital sentencing patterns — a meticulous study of how the State of Georgia has administered its death penalty statutes during the 1973–79 period. What the study reveals is a clear, unshakable pattern of discrimination based upon race: black defendants, especially those whose victims have been white, are many times more likely to receive death sentences than are white defendants, or those whose victims are black. Indeed, even after hundreds of legitimate sentencing considerations besides race have been taken into account, those who have killed white victims are over four times more likely to receive death sentences than those whose victims have been black. Black life — whether that of the defendant or the victims—simply counts for less in Georgia's capital punishment system.

This is an old and unmistakable pattern in virtually every state examined. Discrimination in sentencing dates back to well before the Civil War, when separate, harsher penal codes were reserved for slaves and for free blacks alike. Warren McCleskey has argued to the Supreme Court that Georgia's present discriminatory use of its capital statutes *in practice* is no less acceptable in the 1980s than were pre-Civil War statutes specifically requiring a dual system of punishment.

The implications of the ruling in *McCleskey,* which is expected in early 1987, will be significant not only in Georgia, but in other states with capital statutes. Indeed, its potential reach could extend to states which impose *non-capital* penalties in a discriminatory manner as well.

One way in which the criminal justice system has long permitted discrimination against blacks has been the well-established practice of prosecutors using "peremptory" challenges without explanation to remove blacks from juries. The Supreme Court upheld the practice in 1965 in *Swain* v. *Alabama.*[71] The court reversed *Swain,* however, in 1986, in *Batson* v. *Kentucky,*[72] and declared that, henceforth, prosecutors may be challenged to demonstrate that peremptory removals of black jurors rests on nonracial grounds. Although the decision in *Batson* leaves many practical details for further elaboration, it will provide the first real check against prosecutors' use of all-white or overwhelmingly white juries to try black defendants in criminal cases.

Another significant victory in jury selection came during 1986 in *Vasquez v. Hillery,*[73] where a majority of the court strongly reaffirmed its condemnation of racial discrimination in the selection of grand juries which meet to consider whether to return criminal indictments. The court first considered this practice in 1880, but efforts have continued to undercut the force of that decision. In *Vasquez,* the Supreme Court rebuffed those efforts and insisted that blacks may not be systematically excluded in grand jury selection. Also in 1986, the Supreme Court, in *Turner v. Murray,*[74] increased the ability of black defendants — at least in capital cases—to probe potential white jurors about possible racial biases.

Together *Batson, Vasquez,* and *Turner* will do much to free our jury system from the lingering effects of racial bias — guaranteeing fairer trials to black persons accused of crimes. Although *McCleskey* still hangs in the balance, and much work remains to be done in the future, the past year demonstrates that the federal courts have not closed their doors to claims of racial discrimination in the criminal justice system.

CONCLUSION

The discussion above documents attempts of the administration to carry out an agenda of undermining effective enforcement of civil rights laws. To date, those efforts have met with only partial success. In general, the courts, including the Supreme Court, have rejected the most important arguments of the administration and have continued to interpret broadly the civil rights statutes. With a new Senate, the administration's efforts to fill the judiciary with rigidly ideological judges, as well as to press for legislation that will limit opportunities for minorities, should be more difficult.

The failure of the administration to achieve its goals to date has not been an accident. The determined opposition of civil rights organizations and their allies who represent blacks, other minorities and disadvantaged Americans, and women has been a major factor.

The administration, however, has two more years in office. Its agenda is still clear, and recent pronouncements by the Attorney General make clear the Administration's continued ideological commitment to that agenda. Civil rights groups and their supporters must continue their vigilance and active opposition to efforts to turn back the clock on civil rights progress.

With the continued cooperation of this coalition, Black America can look forward to holding the line for the next two years and, hopefully, to a new agenda that will move us further along toward a free and equal society. The change in the leadership of the Senate in 1986 was due largely to the votes of black Americans in the South and elsewhere. That vote, achieved through years of vigorous enforcement of the Voting Rights Act, along with continued vigorous enforcement of existing civil rights law and precedents, can continue to make a real difference in the direction America will take.

Taking Charge:
An Approach to Making the Educational Problems of Blacks Comprehensible and Manageable

Sharon P. Robinson

In all fairness the major education reform reports have given some attention to the myriad of problems revolving around black access, achievement, status, and other concerns at both the core and perimeter of American educational issues. Yet for the overwhelming majority of the reports the problems intrinsic to black participation and involvement in the public education process have not been adequately addressed.

In general the reports fail to integrate minority concerns within the mainstream of their recommendations. And where attention is given, it is broad rather than specific, vague rather than clear, and lacking the sharpness of focus, intensity, and sense of priority necessary to initiate programs grounded in the urgency of the moment.[1] Somewhere lost in the shuffle of education reform has been firmness regarding the notion and commitment that both equity and excellence cannot only co-exist but are vital and critical components of education in a multi-cultural, pluralistic, and democratic society.

It is ironic and unfortunate that the energy and enthusiasm that have grown out of the Department of Education's pivotal report, *A Nation at Risk,* have resulted in the virtual ignoring of the nation's "at risk" black children. To be sure, education reports from minority related organizations and groups such as the Urban League, Children's Defense Fund, and National Alliance of Black School Educators, among others, have stressed this point.[2] Speaking to the plight of "at risk" children — those who are poor, nonwhite, handicapped, or female — a spokesman for the report *Barriers to Excellence* says that, "Policymakers at many different levels talk of bringing excellence to schools and ignore the fact that hundreds of thousands of youngsters are not receiving even minimal educational opportunities guaranteed under law."[3] In the rush by politicians and educators to reform American schooling, the problems of black students continue to expand in alarming and threatening proportions.

The full and complex range of crucial issues involving black students, parents, and institutions cannot be overstated. In fact, the sheer massiveness of the problems may have become a source of intimidation to policymakers and educators who might otherwise have more sensitivity to "at risk" blacks and minorities. A review of indicators such as levels of student achievement, dropouts, teenage pregnancies, passing rates on various teacher examinations, environmental role models, and family income, to list a few, indicate the extent of the predicament. These indicators are intricately interwoven into a contextual fabric of political and economic urgency. Study after study has shown that black students, particularly those in inner-city school districts, have not demonstrated academic achievement at a rate and level consistent with their white public-school counterparts.[4] This discrepancy in achievement is also apparent when black inner-city students are compared to both white and black students educated in suburban school districts. While the effective schools movement and other demonstration projects have brought about isolated and provocative pockets of successful academic achievement under what could be considered adverse circumstances, the significance of such projects is often overlooked. The "success" of such demonstrations is important as a source of evidence to reinforce the contention that the education of black students is possible.

In his recent book, *The Black Elite,* Daniel Thompson describes the impact of what might well be called the black community's historic effort in "effective schools." *The Black Elite* discusses the role of the historically black colleges and universities, in a former time, in preparing black students for work in some of the country's most prestigious graduate programs and for productive lives in American society. This tradition of success was never questioned or threatened until competition for resources and students resulted in the redistribution of both, which now threatens the survival of the historically black colleges and universities.[5] Creating opportunities and conditions for legitimate educational attainment of all black students is the real challenge facing Black America.

The student dropout problem is a national social problem crossing all ethnic and geographical boundaries but is most acute among urban minority youth. Hispanics are more likely to drop out than are blacks or whites; in turn, blacks are more likely to drop out than whites.[6] According to Mary Hatwood Futrell, President of the National Education Association, whose "Operation Rescue" hopes to reverse this trend, the national dropout rate of 30 percent is costing the country $45 billion every year, money which could be used to eliminate the federal budget deficit in three years.[7]

There are multiple causes of dropping out and dropouts often report more than one reason. The causes and reasons fall into categories: those related to student experiences in school, those related to conditions of the student's family, and those related to economic factors.[8] The problem with the reform movement in this regard is that "across the board" raising of standards without consideration of the means to help all students achieve the higher standards may have an adverse impact on potential dropouts.[9] Thus it is important to understand the aggregate consequences of the current climate of rising standards for public school students.

The increase in teenage pregnancies is both dramatic and alarming. As educational analyst Harold L. Hodgkinson has pointed out:

The U.S. is confronted today with an epidemic increase in the number of children born outside of marriage — and 50 percent of such children are born to teenage mothers. Indeed, every day in America, 40 teenage girls give birth to their THIRD child. To be the third child of a child is to be very much "at risk" in terms of one's future . . . . There is a particular aspect of this situation that is vital — teenage mothers tend to give birth to children who are premature. Prematurity leads to low birth weight, which is a good predictor of major learning difficulties when the child gets to school. This means that about 700,000 babies of the annual cohort of around 3.3 million births are almost assured of being either educationally retarded or "difficult to teach." This group is entering the educational continuum in rapidly increasing numbers.[10]

Each year more than a million American teenagers become pregnant. Four out of five of them are unmarried. Some 30,000 of those who become pregnant are under age thirteen. Both the pregnancy and birth rates for black teens are over four times higher than among white teens.[11] Black adolescents also begin childbearing at younger ages than whites, increasing the likelihood of subsequent births during teenage years. If present trends continue, researchers estimate that 40 percent of today's 14-year-old girls will be pregnant at least once before the age of twenty.[12] If that trend is anywhere close to accurate for the general teenage population, it is frightful to imagine the percentages of black teenagers that will be affected. While the cost of these pregnancies for the nation exceeds $16.6 billion annually in social, welfare, and administrative services, the loss in human potential is incalculable.[13]

While the black girls are having babies, increasingly young black men have dropped out of school, deserted all vestiges of the work ethic, developed false notions of manhood, become heavily involved in drugs, and resorted to careers in crime. Taken together, the pregnancy rates of young black females and the "social drop-out" rates among black males pose real threats to the hope of a stable black community. But it is this lack of hope, not potential, which is most debilitating for today's black youth.[14]

Somewhat different but inextricably linked to the educational problems of black students are those of black teachers. Because of increased opportunities in other professions, low teacher compensation, status and prestige, and the abysmally low passing rates of blacks on teacher pre-service and in-service examinations, the most important role model for blacks in the education enterprise may be virtually eliminated. In 1980 black teachers represented 8.6 percent of all teachers, K-12. But if the observable impact of competency testing on in-service and potential black teachers continues along with normal rates of attrition through retirements and teacher burnout, black teacher representation in the national teaching force could be reduced to less than five percent by 1990.[15]

In higher education the number of black faculty is equally dismal as the last decade has witnessed drastic declines in the numbers of black faculty at predominantly white universities and, ironically, an increase in white faculty at historically black institutions. Lower numbers of blacks in Ph.D. programs as compared to the numbers enrolled in the 1970s will only aggravate this situation.[16] Additionally, the positive black role models and economic viability that existed in practically every neighborhood when nearly all black Americans lived

in segregated areas have all but vanished as middle class blacks have geographi-
cally segregated themselves from the "underclass." Churches, schools, businesses, and other institutions which blacks of all classes once attended and
patronized are now the sole territory of the black poor. The physical conditions
of these neighborhoods and institutions are worse than ever. As Nicholas
Lemann points out in a recent *Atlantic Monthly* article, this problem is widespread but more acute in large urban environments.[17]

If the problems thus far reviewed are a cause for concern, then their long-range
implications are a legitimate cause for panic. Unless there is intensive and
comprehensive intervention to address these problems, they will only intensify,
and bad matters will become worse. Consider, for example, that the National
Center for Educational Statistics indicates that minority public school enrollment presently exceeds 50 percent in New Mexico and Mississippi. Minority
public school enrollment is projected to approach 50 percent in California,
Louisiana, South Carolina, and Texas by 1990. By the year 2000, Alabama,
Arizona, Georgia, Florida, and North Carolina, which currently have minority
public school enrollments ranging from 30 percent to 40 percent, are likely to
approach the 50-percent mark.[18] Most important, by around the year 2000,
America will be a nation in which one of every three citizens will be nonwhite.
These trends suggest that what is coming toward the educational system is a
group of children who will be poorer, more ethnically and linguistically diverse,
and who will have more handicaps that will affect their learning.[19]

It is, therefore, critical that the nation moves swiftly to develop policy which
acknowledges and addresses this challenge of creating public schools that will
deliver a quality education for the black students of today and tomorrow. At first
glance this challenge may appear staggering, but a closer analysis indicates that
intervention, which is targeted to where the problems are most acute, is manageable.

Consider the fact that over 80 percent of the black children in this country are
educated in fewer than four percent of the school districts. In Wisconsin, 84.8
percent of black students are educated in one school district; Arkansas, 98
percent in two; California, 47 percent in 13; Connecticut, 41.2 in one; District of
Columbia, 100 percent in one; Florida, 49 percent in five; Illinois, 67.3 percent
in 12; Kansas, 58.2 percent in two; Louisiana, 43.6 percent in four; Maryland,
46.2 percent in two; Minnesota, 99 percent in four; Nevada, 92.8 percent in two;
New York, 74.3 percent in six; Rhode Island, 67.6 percent in one; Pennsylvania,
67.4 percent in four; and Nebraska, 69.2 percent in two.[20] This means that
though the number of students in need of intervention is large, their concentration in urban school districts is extraordinarily high. *A policy for these "at risk"*
students needs only to be targeted to four percent of the nation's school districts to
have national impact.

With the understanding that the "at risk" can be targeted, it is then necessary
to organize and advocate an agenda for access and success as it relates to
educational opportunities for Black America. The politics of education at the
local, state, and national levels must feel the pressure of renewed commitment to

hold the public and the politicians accountable for creating universal conditions for successful educational attainment among black students. The research is replete with examples of "what works." Now "what works" must become the reality for every black child in America.

Black America must reunite and organize a political coalition which transcends economic status, geographic residence, and other distinctions that may separate one black person from the plight of another. For additional political leverage, every effort must be made to bring the parents of "at risk" students into the center of the action. These parents are potentially the most explosive and powerful component to the coalition; they could become the vanguard of one of the most significant movements in American education. Though black parents care deeply about the educational issues affecting their children, they have largely been ignored. The disaffection of black parents with quality of education offered their children may be measured, in part, by the rapid growth of private schools for blacks. According to the Institute for Independent Education, 220 such schools now exist, the vast majority serving poor families in inner-city neighborhoods. These schools are characterized by their emphasis on academics and discipline and are staffed, attended, owned, and operated almost entirely by members of minority groups. Academic achievement runs higher than in public schools.[21] But it is neither likely nor desirable that a system of private schools adequate to meet the need can be sustained. The political coalition suggested here must organize for the purpose of securing conditions for success through the public schools of the black community.

The goals of this renewed political coalition can be achieved by organizing a variety of initiatives and support programs, some of which are set forth below:

(a) Community-based programs to assist black parents to be effective advocates for their children as they negotiate the public educational establishment, and to assist black parents to establish conditions in the home to support student achievement.

(b) The establishment of early childhood development programs in every community. Such programs are essential if black children are to realize the full advantage of traditional elementary school experience.

(c) Redefine compensatory education from remediation to acceleration. The old paradigm of remediation assumes deficiency rather than lack of opportunity. Black students deserve the assumption of potential and success as the guiding principles of curricular and funding decisions.

(d) Community-based efforts to work with the local schools of black students to define the standards of accountability, and to work with local school staff to achieve the conditions necessary to meet such standards.

(e) Community-based efforts to work with and support the teachers of black students such that these schools become attractive and desirable places to teach. Along with competitive salaries and real opportunities for post-secondary education, this approach represents an important aspect of efforts to recruit minorities to teaching as a career.

(f) Legitimate vocational education programs which provide an adequate academic foundation and viable, employable skills.

(g) Reconsideration of school finance plans such that resources required for the quality education of black students will be available.

The development of a coalition to advocate the education agenda for black students is in the best interests of the nation. There are long-range political and economic benefits to be gained by halting discrimination against children on the basis of their race, sex, origin, or handicap. The failure to educate properly millions of children will turn the potential for social profit and well-being into a grave deficit and unrest. Perhaps now more than ever, the future state of Black America depends on the ability and the will of today's black community to organize and realize the political and financial support required to give black children a real chance at success through education.

The author gratefully acknowledges the assistance of Al-Tony Gilmore, Program Specialist, National Education Association, and Linda Darling-Hammond, Education Director, Rand Corporation. By sharing valuable data, insights, and criticism, they both contributed significantly to the timely completion of this project.

The Future of School Desegregation

Charles V. Willie

The American education system is under scrutiny from many interests and forces. No educational issue has generated more controversy and intense reaction than the debate over school desegregation. The noble goal of desegregation has been an active part of the national consciousness for only a generation—since the United States Supreme Court's landmark *Brown v. The Board of Education of Topeka, Kansas* decision of 1954, in which the high court overturned the accepted doctrine of "separate, but equal."

In *Brown,* the Supreme Court exposed the basic inequality of dual educational systems, thus setting in motion a chain of events that challenged longstanding precepts and propelled an often reluctant nation into the midst of dramatic changes.

Simply defined, the school desegregation movement is fueled by the belief that racial segregation in public schools is inherently wrong and counter to the equal protection guarantees of the Constitution.

School desegregation efforts achieved momentum toward the end of the 1960s, continued during the 1970s, and experienced retrenchment with the emerging prominence of the radical right-wing movements of the 1980s.

While it is difficult to isolate totally the impact of school desegregation within the total context of social change, a reasonable assessment of school desegregation efforts confirms that school desegregation has contributed to the enhancement of education in this nation probably more than any other experience in recent years: it has resulted in changes that have been beneficial to the nation as a whole, white America as well as Black America. Yet politicians, professors, pupils, and parents alike have an ambivalence about the real accomplishments of school desegregation and whether the successes have been and continue to be worth the effort. The national memory tends to forget what the nation was like before *Brown*—a segregated system of unequal opportunity.

Too often images of school desegregation include the most dramatic instances of resistance such as the Boston school controversy. However, the National Review Panel on School Desegregation Research discovered that "school desegregation does not lead to significant increases in school violence." To the contrary, the increased interracial contact resulting from school desegregation is "friendly" more often than not (Hawley, 1981).

There is evidence that the quality of education has also improved during the era of desegregation. The National Institute of Education has recorded that effective school programs are "currently in use in 1,750 school districts." These programs, which began in inner-city elementary schools, have expanded into some secondary schools and into suburban and rural districts (National Institute of Education, 1985). During the height of school desegregation activity in 1976, our bicentennial year, 50 percent of the parents of public school children rated the performance of their local schools at A and B levels. Only five percent said that their local schools had failed (Elam, 1978). This opinion still prevails one decade later. The proportion of parents who give the public school A or B ratings for performance has increased to 55 percent. While the proportion of blacks who rate schools as performing at these higher levels is slightly lower, only five percent of blacks and other minorities believe the public schools have failed (Gallup, 1986).

Without a clear understanding of what desegregation has achieved, many people find it difficult to read aright the educational signs of the time. Moreover, they are confused by misleading assessments of the educational system, such as that by the National Commission on Excellence in Education, which declared that "the average graduate of our schools and colleges today is not as well-educated as the average graduate of 25 or 35 years ago (National Commission on Excellence in Education, 1983)."

But the U.S. Census Bureau, in its 1986 report *How We Live: Then and Now,* offers an assessment of education that differs from that of the National Commission on Excellence in Education. According to the Census Bureau, Americans today are better educated than their forebears were; each generation has achieved more education than the one before (*Atlanta Journal*, 1986).

Evidence supporting this conclusion derives from Census Bureau studies during the 1980s: these studies showed that 90 percent to 95 percent of all school-age children are registered as matriculating students in school and that of the adults in this country over age 25, two-thirds are high school graduates, one third have attended college, and one sixth have graduated from college (U.S. Census Bureau, 1982–83). These educational benefits were experienced by the total population, blacks and other minorities as well as whites.

Census records also reveal that minority students are staying in school longer. In 1950, before the era of school desegregation, the median number of school years completed by white adults over age 25 was 9.7 years. This figure was 40 percent greater than the median of 6.9 years recorded for blacks and other minorities at that time. Today the difference in the median school year for these racial populations is less than one percent (U.S. Census Bureau, 1983–84).

Willis Hawley believes that such gains in education are associated with the school desegregation movement, which had its greatest impact, according to Karl Taeuber and Franklin Wilson, between 1968 and 1976. Taeuber and Wilson discovered a 50-percent decrease in the segregation of whites and minority groups occurred during this period. Also, Hawley reported a 50-percent decline in the dropout rate of black students for this period. In recent years the rate of desegregation has slowed but continues (Hawley, 1981).

On the basis of these data, one may conclude that a high proportion of all racial populations continues to believe in public education, that many are inclined to give public schools high marks for performance, and that the performance of public schools has benefited blacks and other minorities as well as whites.

In the early 1980s, a poll conducted in Boston indicated that 73 percent of the blacks were concerned that an end to court-ordered school desegregation would be a setback for them. Moreover, 71 percent of blacks reported that if they could choose an integrated over a segregated school, they would choose integration. In 1985, a decade after court-ordered desegregation began in Boston, the superintendent of schools said, "Black, white, Asian and Hispanic students are going to school together, becoming sensitive to each other, and developing an appreciation of pluralism and learning to judge individuals on the basis of their character and not on the basis of race, religion or ethnicity " (Willie, 1985).

In 1958 when the Gallup Poll first asked whites if they would object to their children attending a school in which half of the children were black, 50 percent said they would not. During the peak of the school desegregation movement, the proportion of whites who said they would not object to a racially balanced learning environment for their child increased from 60 percent in 1965 to 70 percent in 1975 (Schuman, Steeh, and Bobo, 1985). Among blacks, 78 percent favored general desegregation in 1964. By 1974 (the period when desegregated education had its greatest impact), this proportion had fallen to 62 percent (Schuman, pp. 144–5). Although a large majority in the black population still favored desegregation, their interest had diminished.

With continuing support for desegregated education from blacks nationwide, and even in communities like Boston that have experienced some violence, one is hard-pressed to explain the increasing pessimism among some blacks regarding school desegregation as a desirable goal.

The Boston data give a clue that is confirmed by the analysis of blacks nationally. While seven out of every 10 blacks in Boston said that they would choose desegregated schools if given an option, they were unsure about whether court-ordered busing had been a good thing. Boston blacks were about equally divided on the issue (Willie, p. 153). The same discrepancy is seen in the national survey that compared the attitudes of blacks about school desegregation with their attitudes about busing. The survey found that at the height of the desegregation movement in 1972, a majority of blacks favored desegregated schools, but only 46 percent liked busing as a way of achieving desegregation (Schuman, pp. 144–5).

The future of desegregation in the black community, therefore, depends a great deal on how desegregation is implemented. The resistance of blacks, which is sometimes interpreted as resistance to the concept of desegregation, would appear to be resistance to the way desegregated schooling has been implemented. As pointed out by Mary von Euler, formerly of the National Institute of Education, "Minority groups, as plaintiffs, usually provide the impetus for legal action" (von Euler, 1981). Yet, the group that has experienced the greatest amount of desegregation has been the white majority, who usually are not the plaintiffs in desegregation cases. An anomalous outcome is that the group that has benefited the most from school desegregation plans is the group that predominantly white school boards represent as defendants in school desegregation litigation.

A few examples will demonstrate how whites have experienced desegregation more often than blacks or the other minorities who won the court cases. The student desegregation plan for Atlanta, Ga., required little movement of whites to achieve desegregation. However, black students were assigned to all predominantly white schools so that they represented at least one-third of a school's student body. The Atlanta plan, therefore, permitted many schools to remain all black, but none were all white (Willie, 1984). Thus whites experienced the beneficial effects of a desegregated education in Atlanta, but an overwhelming majority of Atlanta's blacks did not.

The situations in Dallas, Texas; Milwaukee, Wisc.; and St. Louis, Mo., were similar. Initially, the court-ordered plan in Dallas, a plan appealed by the local branch of the National Association for the Advancement of Colored People (NAACP), desegregated white schools but left half or more of the black students in racially segregated all-black schools (Alpert, White, and Geisel, 1981). Again, whites—who were not plaintiffs in the Dallas school desegregation case—received the benefits of a desegregated education; but most of the blacks, who were members of the plaintiff class, continued to attend segregated schools (Alpert, pp. 170–2). Milwaukee, like Atlanta, prohibited all-white schools by requiring at least a 25-percent black population in each school (Willie, 1982), but left 20 of its 120 schools with all-black student bodies. In Milwaukee all whites experienced a desegregated education, but some blacks did not. The blacks, of course, in Milwaukee as elsewhere, were members of the plaintiff class that won the court case seeking a desegregation remedy. St. Louis desegregated its white schools but left several schools with all-black student bodies (Willie, p. 89).

In Louisville, Ky.; Charlotte-Mecklenburg, N.C.; and Milwaukee, the implementation of school desegregation plans was grossly unfair to blacks. Desegregation in Louisville was achieved by busing a majority of black students two of their 12 schools years and busing a majority of black students eight of their 12 school years. Clearly, a racial discrepancy existed that favored whites, who had to use transportation the least number of years to go to and from school (Arnez, 1978). In the Charlotte-Mecklenburg desegregation case, equal numbers of black and white elementary children were bused, although each black child was bused four years, while his or her white counterpart was bused only two years (Finger, 1976). Milwaukee transported nine times as many blacks as whites in its school desegregation plan. This differential rate constituted a disproportionate burden that blacks carried to achieve desegregation. If the Louisville, Charlotte-Mecklenburg, and Milwaukee plans are representative of other school desegregation plans, one can understand the increasing belief among blacks that they are treated unfairly in the desegregation implementation process. John Finger, a desegregation planner for several communities, admitted that some plans may be "inequitable" (Finger, p. 61), but he did not indicate what should or could be done to overcome this injustice.

Despite the recommendation of some desegregation planners, such as Derrick Bell, that communities should devise plans in the future that contain the potential for "improving educational opportunities for blacks without the cost and disruption of busing," blacks have not given up on integration. Data presented in this study demonstrate that a majority of blacks believe that blacks and whites should attend the same schools. These data also indicate that black parents are inclined to choose a desegregated over a segregated school when options are available. What has discouraged blacks and could affect their future support of desegregation is the unjust and inequitable way that desegregation has been implemented.

One suspects that blacks continue to support the concept of school desegregation because they are subdominant participants in the national power structure, and subdominants tend to be inclusive rather than exclusive in their orientation. The Atlanta experience is instructive. There, blacks were in control of the school system in terms of numbers of members on the school board, and implemented a school desegregation plan in 1970 that initially offered whites 50 percent of the administrative positions in a system that had a two-thirds black student population.

Also, despite the dwindling proportion of white students in the system, Atlanta blacks maintained their belief in inclusiveness and retained a proportion of white teachers in the Atlanta public schools that was twice the proportion of white students in the systemwide student body. As final proof of its inclusive orientation and belief in desegregation, the Atlanta school board elevated a white member to president when the term of office expired for Benjamin Mays, an esteemed black educator (Willie, 1984, p. 191).

It is possible that blacks continue to support the concepts of integration and inclusiveness because many remember when the school desegregation court cases were initiated. As long as blacks were educated separately from whites, they could be and were treated differently, a treatment that was unequal to that for whites. From 1938 through 1954, blacks, under the leadership of NAACP attorneys, won several victories in federal courts that demonstrated the inequality of separate facilities (Willie, 1983). Blacks therefore are not about to risk a return to separate facilities sanctioned by a state, even if promised that separate schools will be more effective. They know that "the reason for separating the races in the first place (was) to accord them differential treatment" and that "communities unwilling to desegregate their (black) population have been unwilling to upgrade it economically" or educationally (Willie, 1964). In an inclusive system one racial population—for example, blacks—cannot be harmed without also harming other populations, such as whites. Blacks who understand this principle are likely to continue to choose integration, or at least, desegregation.

The record shows that effective schools, even if they can be implemented as segregated units, are too few, and are likely to continue as a limited option. The National Institute of Education commissioned the preparation of a document that contained an "up-to-date" directory of school improvement programs being implemented around the country. The document was particularly designed to synthesize and disseminate research and practical information about "successful school effectiveness programs" (Kyle, 1985).

This up-to-date sourcebook listed effective school programs in 1,750 school districts out of a 1982 total of 15,840 school districts. Thus the study commissioned by the federal government found unique school improvement programs, commonly labeled "effective schools" in only 11 percent of the school districts nationwide. This finding is not a good omen for blacks and other minorities in 89 percent of the school districts if the effective schools approach that supposedly is not dependent on desegregation is used as the chief school improvement method.

If the school is accepted as the basic educational unit, the statistics are even more disappointing for the widespread development of effective schools. The effective schools sourcebook found such programs in only 5,228 (nine percent) of the nation's elementary and secondary schools (Kyle, p. 1; National Center for Education Statistics, 1983). For a nation that has been obligated by its Supreme Court to provide an effective education for all children, including blacks and other minorities, the effective schools model does not appear to be a comprehensive and thus constitutionally effective approach.

Some of the inequities in the implementation of school desegregation have been mentioned. In addition to the disproportionate burden of busing they have suffered to achieve desegregation, blacks have been denied the opportunity to be a majority in some multiracial schools, as if such a balance would not be in the public interest. The commonwealth of Massachusetts passed a public law in 1965 known as the Racial Imbalance Act. The act declared that any school with a student body more than 50 percent black was racially imbalanced (Smith, 1978). A public law defines what is and what is not in the public interest legally. A principle inferred from this law is that it is in the public interest for a school to have a white majority (51 percent) but not a black majority. Although the intent of the Racial Imbalance Act was to foster desegregation for blacks, it did not prevent segregation of whites. It also offered a racist interpretation of "not in the public interest" for any clustering of blacks that constituted a majority.

The public interest is an important concept in community life. The Supreme Court in *Brown II* (1955) stated that district courts could "take into account the public interest" in fashioning school desegregation remedies. For this reason, the Massachusetts law that prohibited a black critical mass of 51 percent but did not prohibit a white critical mass of 51 percent in public schools must be classified as arbitrary, capricious and, ultimately, racist.

That the Massachusetts Racial Imbalance Act represented a general attitude of whites when it was passed is indicated by the results of a 1965 public opinion poll. Gallup Poll revealed that while most whites would not object to sending their children to schools that were racially balanced—50 percent white and 50 percent black or other minority—nearly two-thirds would object to sending their children to schools that had a black majority (Schuman, p. 106).

Massachusetts encoded into public law the prejudice and fear of whites against being a minority, and several school desegregation plans throughout the nation adopted this guideline. Seattle adopted a definition of racial imbalance that permitted the racial ratio in a school to vary not more than 20 percent above the districtwide ratio, provided a single minority group was not greater than 50 percent (Siqueland, 1981). Although 77 percent of school-age children in St. Louis were black, St. Louis defined a legally desegregated school as one in which blacks were 30 percent to 50 percent of the student body (Willie, 1982, p. 89). In 1977 Milwaukee declared a school to be legally desegregated if its black student population was 25 percent to 50 percent, although the ceiling for minorities was increased later. The assumption in all of these definitions of desegregation is that "whites always ought to be the majority" (Willie, p. 89).

John Finger revealed the purpose of many school desegregation planners: to be more concerned with developing plans that are satisfactory and acceptable to children and parents. In fact, Finger said that the reactions of this group may be more important than "complete equity" (Finger, p. 61). Since black and other minority children and their parents usually provided the impetus for litigation to avoid being "misused by the educational system," according to Mary von Euler, they were clearly seeking equity and peaceful social change through court action (von Euler, xv). Finger, therefore, must have been referring to whites when he asserted that the satisfaction and acceptance of the desegregation plan by parents and children were more important than the plan's equitability. Finger's attitude about desegregation planning and that of other planners with similar systems of belief are contrary to the Supreme Court order in *Brown II* (1955). That order states that "constitutional principles cannot be allowed to yield simply because of disagreement with them." Thus white parental satisfaction with a school desegregation plan should have been of less concern to desegregation planners than the achievement of constitutional desegregation. But it was not. Many planners gave precedence to public interest concerns or the concern of white parents in the development of school desegregation plans. This was probably true because most school desegregation planners were white.

Since "self-interest is the basic motive for human action" (Willie, 1983),most white planners considered first the interests of the group with whom they were affiliated. A review of the desegregation concerns of white and of black planners reveals a real difference in what members of dominant and subdominant racial populations emphasize. Barbara Sizemore, a black educational planner, claims that the planning priorities of many desegregation experts appear to be wrong:

She sees desegregation as concerned with "education equality and equity," and in that order. She believes that desegregation should fulfill the needs of black people "for recognition and respect" and that educational policy to achieve these ends should focus specifically on grouping practices, testing procedures, curriculum development, multilingual-multicultural models, disciplinary practices, in-service training, promotion standards, extracurricular activities, and counseling services (Sizemore, 1978). To Sizemore and other blacks, these are first-generation problems that should have been but were not addressed in desegregation plans. Reports prepared by Gordon Foster (1973); John Finger (1976); Larry Hughes, William Gordon, and Larry Hillman (1980); and the Vanderbilt University Center for Educational and Human Development Policy (Hawley, et al., 1981) indicate the prevailing interests of school desegregation planners who are associated with the majority group. In summary, most white educational planners are primarily concerned with "the practicalities of assigning pupils so that schools are desegregated" (Foster, 1973), and with ensuring that residential areas remain stable without massive change in the racial composition of the population.

Social location in society as dominant or subdominant in the power structure, as a member of the majority or minority group, may be associated with the planning strategies emphasized and the priorities given to different components of a desegregation plan. If increased racial diversity with enhanced educational opportunities is the two-fold goal of the Supreme Court *Brown* decision, then a diversified planning group is essential in achieving this goal. Otherwise, only one aspect of the goal may be emphasized at the expense of the other.

A review of planning strategies by educators who identify with different racial populations reveals that minority-group planners tend to be more concerned with educational outcomes, and majority-group planners tend to focus more on the racial balance of student bodies (Willie, 1984, pp. 44–45).

Barbara Sizemore and Nancy Arncz claim that minorities in general have been excluded from the desegregation planning and policymaking process, and their exclusion has resulted in plans that have been "deleterious" for black children (Sizemore, p. 63; Arnez, pp. 28–29).

Of the many court-ordered school desegregation plans in operation, the Boston Plan (*Morgan v. Hennigan,* 1974, later named *Morgan v. Kerrigan,* 1974) has probably been the most comprehensive. An explicit goal of this plan was to "improve the quality of education in the city of Boston" as well as to desegregate the public schools. As stated in the plan, "The *linchpin* of effecting educational improvement . . . is the involvement of the city's colleges, universities, cultural institutions, and businesses." The court order matched colleges and universities with particular schools. The purpose of these pairing arrangements was to "enable participating institutions of higher learning to share in the direction and development of curriculum and instruction with the School Department" (Smith, pp. 101-2).

The invitation to more than 20 colleges and universities in the Boston metropolitan area to participate in the education of Boston school children was a unique feature of the Boston Plan. The invitation was extended first by the court-appointed masters and the court-appointed expert educational planners who assisted the judge in formulating the school desegregation plan.

The masters and the experts in the Boston case were multiracial groups, which may explain why their plan emphasized both educational quality and desegregation (Smith, pp. 83–85). A multiracial group of educational planners is something of value. But few courts or school boards or plaintiffs have retained such groups. Frequently, a single expert or master is retained to assist the court. Usually this person is white, middle-class, middle-aged, and male and is expected to recommend or oversee the development of a plan of remedy for the grievances of the plaintiffs who, in most school desegregation cases, are children and parents of black and brown racial minorities (Willie, 1978).

The three-person, multiracial Compliance Assistance Panel was appointed by the court during the early 1980s in the Denver school desegregation case (*Keyes v. School District No. 1*), but was given insufficient authority to formulate a school desegregation plan. The multiracial, four-person panel of masters and two-person panel of experts in Boston had sufficient authority to review the various plans submitted by the parties to the school desegregation case and to recommend a plan that gathered up the best features of all plans and included their own ideas. The Boston District Court's approach to obtaining assistance in designing a school desegregation plan recognized the value of diversity. Such recognition is a manifestation of the wisdom of Judge W. Arthur Garrity who had responsibility for the Boston case.

Rather than ask the question that Barbara Sizemore asked—"How can black educators assume a position of leadership in desegregation when (they) formulate none of the theory, . . . construct none of the definitions, design none of the models, and negotiate none of the decisions?" (Sizemore, p. 63)—black and other minority planning, legal service, social service, advocacy and action agencies in the future should insist that groups of desegregation planners, advisers and consultants be multiracial, including planners, advisers, and consultants who are retained by plaintiffs or defendants or the court. Blacks and other minorities should insist on a multiracial body of planners both for designing and implementing school desegregation plans, since the fulfillment of self-interest is the basic motive for human action, and since it is difficult for individuals of one social segment, such as members of a majority group, to understand fully the personal and social needs of individuals of another social segment such as members of a minority group. There is greater probability that a multiracial group of educational planners will consider issues of educational quality as well as issues of equitable student placement, as illustrated by the Boston experience. With a diversified panel of desegregation planners, blacks are more likely to continue to win court cases mandating desegregation and will cease losing out on the planning and implementation stages.

In this connection, a promising school desegregation model plan designed by a multiracial team of planners is under consideration for implementation in Little Rock and Seattle. Called "controlled choice" and prepared by Michael Alves of the Massachusetts Bureau of Equal Educational Opportunity and this author, the plan "ensures that both majority and minority students . . . have equal or genuine proportional access to all schools . . . of choice and that all . . . assignments will be made irrespective of where a child lives . . . . " Controlled choice further provides "a self-correcting mechanism that prevents resegregation while facilitating the more efficient use of existing school facilities, thus ensuring both stability of assignment and continuity of education for all students during the life of the plan." Moreover, "controlled choice (stimulates) the development of improved instructional practices . . . (by way of) the reputational method of school choice" and guarantees desegregation (Alves and Willie, 1986). Controlled choice is implemented by eliminating individual school attendance boundaries (or consolidating individual schools into larger zones of heterogeneous populations), adopting a definition of desegregation that is more or less similar to the districtwide ratio of racial and ethnic populations (which guarantees proportional access to all schools), allowing parents and students to make multiple school selections but without guarantee of receiving the first choice (although most persons will), operating effective parent information centers, and maintaining complete honesty and integrity in the student assignment process. This has been a brief summary of a more detailed analysis presented elsewhere (Alves and Willie).

Finally, in the future more attention must be given to the composition of the educational authority and chief policy-making body in the local community—the school board. It is this group that ultimately implements school desegregation plans. Even if the litigation for school desegregation is successful and the plans are appropriate and equitable, the authority to implement such plans is that of local educational agencies. By serving as members of the board of such agencies, blacks and other minorities may ensure that interests of others accommodate and are in harmony with their interests. When blacks are not members of local community decision-making bodies, these groups seldom recognize the full range of interests found among local citizens.

A chapter entitled "The Continuing Significance of Race" in *A New Look at Black Families* makes these observations:

Lee Sloan and Robert French (Sloan and French, 1977), who prepared a case study entitled "Black Rule in the Urban South?," state that "holding the line against black power seems to be a growing problem for metropolitan white America." They state that "it is becoming increasingly evident that whites moving out may be forfeiting political control to the blacks who are left behind." Whites attempt to regain control, according to Sloan and French, by "redefining political boundaries so that the proportion of blacks within the new political unit is decreased drastically." Sloan and French say that this method of regaining control "can assume the forms of gerrymandering or annexation." Also, they classify the at-large election as another way of retaining control as numbers of a majority population began to dwindle (Willie, 1981, p. 32).

The Boston School Committee is more responsive to the interests of blacks and other minorities now that they are members of this decision-making group. Boston is guaranteed of a diversified, local, educational decision-making authority because its school committee members are elected by single-member districts and at-large. When the school desegregation case was filed in federal court in 1972, the school committee was all white, its members were elected at-large only, and such a committee was not inclined to accommodate the interests of blacks and other minorities. As evidence of the responsiveness of the present School Committee, whose membership comes from single-member districts, the twenty-first superintendent of the Boston School Department (appointed in 1985) was the first black person to serve in that capacity since the office of superintendent was created in 1851 (Willie, 1985, p. 175).

To guarantee participation in local decision-making in the future, blacks throughout the nation should push for a change in voting arrangements for local lawmakers from at-large arrangements to single-member districts or single-member districts in combination with at-large elections.

A specific way to deal with "establishment" control was seen in Houston in the late 1970s. Houston became the nation's fifth largest city and continued to be managed by a network of businessmen and developers, despite the increase in black and Hispanic populations that contributed to growth over the years. As a result of political pressure, Houston adopted a new voting arrangement in which local policy-makers are elected by districts and at-large. Previously, all policymakers were elected at-large, an arrangement that diluted the voting strength of blacks and Mexican-Americans. Under the at-large arrangement, the minorities (40 percent to 45 percent of the Houston population) had only one representative on the city council. Under the new voting arrangement of single-member districts, three to four black or Hispanic policymakers are guaranteed election. These racial and ethnic lawmakers elected from single-member districts are, of course, more beholden to the constituents in their districts than are establishment-controlled policymakers elected at large (Willie, 1981, pp. 32–33).

Following desegregation litigation in several cities, blacks have continued the reform movement by pressuring for change in the method of electing local lawmakers, including school board members who have authority to block or to approve and implement school desegregation plans. Without a diversified policy-making and implementing group, communities throughout the United States will continue to experience what Ralph McGill observed during the first decade after *Brown*—a dishonest distortion of court decisions that could elevate inadequate school systems if they are honestly implemented (McGill, 1964).

McGill said that history is already drawing a harsh indictment of white political leaders who distorted the "wise proportion and meaning" of the *Brown* school desegregation decision (McGill, p. 246). The same may be said of blacks who dishonestly use the defective manner in which school desegregation plans have been implemented in the past as the basis for turning against desegregation as a viable concept today.

School desegregation deserves to continue, with appropriate modifications, so that its promise may be fulfilled for black students.

When the side benefits that were stimulated by and have emerged because of the school desegregation movement are considered—such benefits as the Education for All Handicapped Children Act, governmental requirements for transitional bilingual education for children who cannot benefit from instruction in English, and the educational amendments of 1972 that prohibit exclusion of persons from educational programs on the basis of sex, one must conclude that the school desegregation movement has been the greatest contribution in this century to educational reform. We should therefore press on with school desegregation and its spirit of inclusiveness for the direct and indirect benefits it promises for majority as well as minority children in years to come.

Economic Status of Blacks 1986

David Swinton

INTRODUCTION

The deep recession that has gripped the black community throughout the Reagan era has continued, despite modest improvement in the economic conditions of black Americans during 1985 and 1986. In fact, the four-year-old Reagan recovery has had such weak impact on blacks that their current labor market conditions are still more depressed than they were at the bottom of all previous postwar recessions. Most standard indicators of economic life continue to record the highest levels of racial inequality since the mid 1960s. There is no escaping the conclusion that a major impact of six years of Reagan administration leadership on the economy has been to increase racial inequality and exacerbate the economic difficulties of blacks. The black community is definitely not better off under Reagan than in the pre-Reagan era.

National data on income, poverty rates, and labor market status show the extent of economic distress in the black community. Since the advent of the Reagan administration, black family income has declined, poverty rates have increased, and the labor market difficulties of blacks have intensified. Moreover, racial inequality in income, employment, and wages has also increased. On the national level, six years of Reagan policies have produced no gains for blacks.

The impact of Reagan administration leadership on the economic status of blacks has differed across the regions. The economic status of blacks has deteriorated more and racial inequality has increased more in the Midwest region. In fact, it would be more accurate to describe the current economic status of blacks in the Midwest as a depression than a recession. The recovery has had its most favorable impact on the status of blacks in the South and the West. In fact, in the South some but not all aspects of the economic status of blacks have improved to above their pre-Reagan levels in the past two years.

Many questions can be raised about the trends in the economic status of the black population in the Reagan era. However, the key issue is why has there been so little progress towards the attainment of economic parity during the past six years. Is the lack of economic progress for blacks a result of black failures in motivation, behavior, morals, or preparedness; or does the lack of progress result from failures in the economy or Reagan administration policies? The evidence suggests the blame for the persisting economic difficulties of blacks should be placed squarely on Reagan administration policies.

The gaps which must be closed for blacks to achieve the goal of economic parity are still relatively large. Significant increases in employment and gains in wage rates are among the more important changes required. In order for these gains to occur, however, the economy will have to improve. This change would require a reversal in the decline of the manufacturing sector and an improvement in the wages of the service sector. Finally, it will also be necessary to eliminate the remaining human capital gaps between blacks and whites. It is clear to us that it is unlikely that these types of changes will occur without a significant change in federal government policies.

This paper will provide evidence to document the relatively low economic status of blacks and show that little overall progress has been made in improving this status after six years of Reagan policies. It will show that the economic difficulties of blacks are not primarily the result of black shortcomings but result primarily from factors external to the black community which have not been adequately addressed by Reagan administration policies. Finally, this paper concludes with a discussion of how far blacks have to go to achieve economic parity and the policies required to bring this about.

PATTERNS AND TRENDS IN RACIAL
INEQUALITY IN ECONOMIC LIFE

An evaluation of the impact of the Reagan administration on the economic status of blacks depends on prior expectations about what should be accomplished by successful federal policies. At the start of the Reagan administration, the economic status of blacks reflected a high level of economic problems and was still very unequal. Although modest progress had been made in reducing some of these problems and narrowing some aspects of racial inequality since the civil rights revolution of the 1960s, the pace of progress was slowing down in the few years preceding the Reagan administration. Indeed, there already existed widespread dissatisfaction among many advocates of greater economic progress for blacks at the slow rate of progress.

Advocates of racial parity in economic life should expect that during the 1980s more progress would be made in bringing blacks fully into the economic mainstream if the Reagan administration approach is valid. Indeed, if the policies are truly successful, we should expect continued improvement in income, poverty rates, labor market status, wealth, business ownership, and dependency levels. We should look for a faster rate of progress than had been attained prior to 1980. From this perspective, the appropriate standard for evaluating the results of Reagan policies is whether or not these policies have resulted in a significant acceleration of the rate of economic progress for Blacks. With this standard in mind we examine the record of the Reagan years.

Income Trends

The most recent year for which income data are available is 1985—five years after the start of the Reagan administration and three years into the recovery. In the discussion which follows we will use Census Bureau data for 1985, and we will also compare the first five years of the Reagan administration with the five years preceding Reagan. All dollar amounts used in the discussion have been adjusted for price changes.

The per capita income for both blacks and whites reached all-time highs in 1985 at $6,840 and $11,671, respectively (see Table 1). However, since per capita income generally attains new heights each year this is not an overwhelming achievement. For blacks, 1985 marked the first year under Reagan that per capita income regained the level that had been attained at its pre-Reagan peak. Income in per capita terms has thus been somewhat lower for blacks for the last five years than it was during the previous five years. The average per capita income for the first five years of the Reagan administration was $6,319 vs. $6,413 in the five years preceding the Reagan administration.

Table 1

Per Capita Income During and Before
the Reagan Administration
(In Constant 1985 Dollars)

	Blacks	Whites	Blk/Wht
1985	$6,840	$11,671	58.6
5 Reagan years	6,319	11,034	57.2
5 Pre-Reagan years	6,413	10,902	58.8

Source:
Bureau of the Census, *Current Population Report, Consumer Income*, Series P-60, No. 154 and 149, table 1; No. 146, 142, and 137, table 22; No. 132, table 24; No. 129, table 18; No. 123, 118 and 114, table 17.

The gap between black and white per capita incomes had increased under the Reagan administration. However, the smallest gap of the Reagan years was attained in 1985 when blacks received 58.6 cents for each dollar attained by whites. Nonetheless, even in 1985 the ratio of black-to-white per capita income was lower than it was in all but one of the five years preceding Reagan. That year was the recession year of 1980. The average per capita income received by blacks was 57.2 cents for each dollar received by whites during the five Reagan years vs. 58.8 cents in the five years preceding Reagan. Thus, racial inequality in per capita income has clearly increased during the Reagan years.

A similar pattern is revealed by an examination of the more familiar median family income indicator in Table 2. However, even though black family income reached its Reagan peak of $16,786 during 1985, its level was still lower than at any time during the ten years prior to 1980. The average median family income for blacks during the five Reagan years was only $15,867 vs. $17,216 for the five years preceding. Thus, in constant purchasing power terms, the typical black family has lost about $1,349 on the average or 7.8 percent of its purchasing power in each year since the start of the Reagan administration. This is particularly distressing since family income is generally expected to gain rather than lose ground from peak to peak during a recovery.

Racial inequality in family income has also increased during the Reagan years. Again, the administration achieved its best performance during 1985 when black median family income was 57.6 percent of white family income. This ratio, however, still remains lower than it was in most years between 1970 and the start

Table 2

Median Family Income During and Before the
Reagan Administration by Race
(In Constant 1985 Dollars)

	Blacks	Whites	Ratio
1985	$16,786	$29,152	57.6
5 Reagan years	15,867	27,992	56.7
5 Pre-Reagan years	17,216	29,651	58.1

Source:
Bureau of the Census, *Current Population Report, Consumer Income,* Series P-60, No. 154
and 149, table 1; No. 146, 142, and 137, table 22; No. 132, table 24; No. 129, table 18; No.
123, 118 and 114, table 17.

of this administration. In the five years immediately preceding Reagan, the average ratio of black to white median family income was 58.1 percent vs. 56.7 percent in the first five Reagan years.

As Table 3 shows, the family income distribution worsened in general under Reagan. The proportion of families receiving very low income increased while the proportion in middle- and upper-income categories declined. For example, the percentage of black families receiving less than $5,000 was 13.5 percent in 1985. This number had improved somewhat from the earlier Reagan years but was still substantially higher than it had been in the peak pre-Reagan year of 1978 when only 9.6 percent of black families had incomes less than $5,000. In fact, the percentage of blacks with so little income was only 9.9 percent in 1970. On the other hand the percentage of blacks with incomes over $35,000 had rebounded from 14.5 percent in 1982 to 18.8 percent in 1985. However, this was still lower than the 1978 level of 19.0 percent. Generally, blacks have been more likely to be very poor and less likely to have high incomes under Reagan than in the preceding five years.

The racial differences in the income distributions have also increased—especially at the lower ends. For example, a 6.9 percent difference between the percentage of black and white families with incomes lower than $5,000 in 1978 had increased to a 9.8 percent difference in 1985, despite the improvement recorded in that year. On the other hand, the percentage of whites with incomes over $50,000 was 12.6 percent greater than the percentage of blacks in 1985, compared with only 11.1 percent greater in 1978. The deterioration in the distribution of family income started before the Reagan administration. However, the situation has continued to worsen since President Reagan took office.

There continues to be regional variations in the level of black income (see Table 4). In 1985 median family income increased in all regions compared to 1984. However, the increase was least in the South, which resumed its place as the

Table 3

**Proportion of Families Receiving Incomes Within Specified
Range by Race for Selected Years
(In Constant 1985 Dollars)**

	1985		1983		1978		1970	
	Black	White	Black	White	Black	White	Black	White
Under $5,000	13.5	3.7	14.3	3.9	9.6	2.7	9.9	3.2
Under $10,000	30.6	11.2	34.4	11.6	28.3	9.6	27.3	10.3
Over $35,000	18.8	39.3	17.9	36.1	19.0	40.2	15.2	34.1
Over $50,000	7.0	19.6	5.7	16.8	7.1	18.2	4.5	13.9

Source:
Bureau of the Census, *Current Population Report, Consumer Income,* Series P-60, No. 154,
p. 10.

region with the lowest median family income ($15,816). Black family income was highest in the West at $24,453. Despite gains in 1985, black family income in the Northeast ($18,085) and Midwest ($15,956) census regions continues to be below their pre-Reagan levels. However, family income in the South and the West have recovered much of the ground lost in the last recession. Indeed, while income levels for blacks in the Midwest and the Northeast in 1985 were still substantially below the levels attained in the early 1970s, income in both West and the South exceeded their early 1970s levels in 1985. The Reagan era has clearly had regionally differential impacts on the economic status of blacks. However, for the period as a whole in every region except the West, black income has been lower than in the five years preceding Reagan.

Racial inequality in income levels continues to persist in all regions. However, compared to the first four Reagan years, 1985 saw a large jump in the ratio of black-to-white family income in the West and modest improvements in the other regions. In all regions except the West, blacks received less than 60 cents for each dollar received by whites. In the West black median family income was 80 percent of white median family income. In general, racial inequality in income has been greater during the Reagan years in the Midwest and the Northeast and less pronounced in the South and West. Even in 1985, racial inequality in the Northeast and the Midwest is substantially higher than it was in the pre-Reagan era. In fact, during the Reagan years inequality, as measured by the ratio of black-to-white median family income, has become more pronounced in the Northeast and the Midwest than it is in the South.

Poverty Rates

The low income levels of the black population are reflected in high black poverty rates (see Table 5). During 1985, nearly one of every three blacks (31.3 percent) had incomes which placed them below the poverty level. While this

Table 4

Median Family Income by Region and Race During and
Before the Reagan Administration
(1985 Constant Dollars)

	Northeast		Midwest	
	Black	White	Black	White
1985	$18,085	$31,491	$15,956	$28,964
5 Reagan years	16,693	29,877	15,168	28,087
5 Pre-Reagan years	18,002	30,197	19,753	30,313

	South		West	
	Black	White	Black	White
1985	$15,816	$27,104	$24,453	$30,239
5 Reagan years	14,960	26,319	20,301	28,795
5 Pre-Reagan years	15,709	27,875	18,981	29,523

Ratio: Black to White

	Northeast	Midwest	South	West
1985	.574	.551	.584	.809
5 Reagan years	.559	.540	.568	.705
5 Pre-Reagan years	.596	.652	.564	.643

Source:
Bureau of the Census, *Current Population Report, Consumer Income,* Series P-60, No. 154 and 149, table 1; No. 146, 142, and 137, table 22; No. 132, table 24; No. 129, table 18; No. 123, 118, and 114, table 17.

proportion was down from the earlier Reagan years it was still somewhat higher than in the pre-Reagan period. Poverty rates have generally been higher during the Reagan years. The average percentage of blacks in poverty for the five Reagan years was 34.1 percent whereas the average for the five years immediately preceding Reagan was 31.3 percent.

Racial inequality as measured by racial differences in poverty rates remains high. However, white poverty rates have also increased during the Reagan years. As a consequence, the ratio of black-to-white poverty rates has actually declined during the Reagan years. Indeed, while the actual black poverty rate in 1985 (31.3 percent) is slightly lower than the 1980 and 1970 rates for blacks (32.5 percent and 33.1 percent, respectively), the actual white rate in 1985 of 11.4 percent is higher than the 1980 and 1970 rates of 10.2 percent and 8.1 percent, respectively.

As was the case with income, the national data represent somewhat diverse regional experiences as shown in Table 6. Poverty rates for blacks in the

Table 5

Percent of Persons With Income Below the Poverty Level by Race Before and During the Reagan Administration

	Black	White	Blk/Wht
1985	31.3	11.4	2.75
5 Reagan years	34.1	11.6	2.94
5 Pre-Reagan years	31.3	9.2	3.40

Source:
Bureau of the Census, *Current Population Report, Consumer Income,* Series P-60, No. 154, p. 27.

Northeast, the Midwest, and the South have been higher under Reagan than in the five years preceding Reagan. Black poverty rates have increased most in the Midwest during the past five years. In fact, black poverty rates in the Midwest have overtaken black poverty rates in the South. On the other hand, black poverty in the West has not increased during the Reagan era. Moreover, the improvement in 1985 lowered black poverty in all regions except the Midwest to below the average for the five years preceding Reagan.

During 1985 the black poverty rate in the South of 32.7 percent was at an all-time low while the black poverty rate in the Midwest of 35.3 percent was still substantially above its pre-Reagan levels.

Table 6
Poverty Rates by Region and Race Before and During the Reagan Administration

	Northeast		Midwest		West		South	
	Black	White	Black	White	Black	White	Black	White
1985	28.0	9.8	35.3	11.4	20.1	12.1	32.7	11.9
5 Reagan years	31.7	10.4	36.9	11.1	24.0	12.3	35.7	12.5
5 Pre-Reagan years	28.8	8.5	29.9	7.9	24.0	9.2	33.9	10.9

Ratio: Black-to-White				
	Northeast	Midwest	West	South
1985	2.86	3.10	1.66	2.75
5 Reagan years	3.05	3.32	1.95	2.88
5 Pre-Reagan years	3.39	3.78	2.61	3.11

Source:
Bureau of the Census, *Current Population Report, Consumer Income,* Series P-60, No. 154, p. 27.

Racial inequality in the regions as measured by the ratio of, or differences in, black and white poverty rates was also varied. In general, during the five Reagan years, racial inequality by this measure has been greater in the Northeast and the Midwest than in the West and South. In comparison to the immediate pre-Reagan period, the ratio of black-to-white poverty rates has declined in all regions. This is because the increase in poverty rates that has occurred during the Reagan years has hit whites as hard as blacks in all regions, but especially in the South and West. Thus, in general, the racial gaps in poverty rates have narrowed in relative terms during the Reagan years in all regions in comparison to the immediate pre-Reagan years.

The increase in poverty rates during the five Reagan years was relatively less for blacks than for whites in all regions. However, the increase for blacks was absolutely larger in all regions except the West.

On the average a poor black family is poorer than a poor white family. In 1985, the median black family would have needed an extra $4,424 to escape poverty as compared with $3,582 for the median white family. The poverty deficits are much more equal for the single individuals at $1,871 for blacks and $1,802 for whites. In the aggregate $9.7 billion would have been required to eliminate poverty for black families and $3.1 billion would have been required to eliminate poverty for single black individuals in 1985.

Labor Markets

One of the principal reasons for the high rates of black poverty and low levels of black income is the substantial labor market difficulties of blacks. In 1984, for example, blacks earned $5,103.13 per person from wage and salary and self-employment. This was about 59 cents for every dollar per person earned by whites in the labor market. The black disadvantage arises from several factors:

- There are proportionately fewer blacks of working age.
- There are proportionately fewer males among the working-age black population.
- Black male and black teenage participation rates are lower than white male and white teenage participation rates.
- Blacks have higher rates of unemployment.
- Blacks have poorer occupational distributions.
- Blacks have lower wage rates.

All of these factors existed before the present administration. However, over the last five years some of the factors have worsened and few if any have improved.

Working Age Population and Male Composition

The first two factors are demographic. Smaller proportions of the black than white population are of working age. In 1985, for example, only 72 percent of the black population over 15 compared to 79 percent of the white population. Thus, blacks had roughly two million fewer working-age individuals in proportion to their population size than did whites. This increases the burden on the fewer blacks of working age. If everything else were equal, this factor by itself could reduce black per capita earnings by 10 percent and account for almost 25 percent of the per capita earnings gap.

The ratio of black males to black females among the over 15 population was 8,115 per 10,000 vs. 9,161 per 10,000 for whites in 1984. The smaller number of black males accounts for over half of the black/white difference in working age populations. These missing black males clearly add a significant burden to the black population—especially since males in our society continue to work more often and earn more than females.

These two demographic factors clearly existed prior to the Reagan administration. During the past five years, the percentage of blacks of working age continued its long-term upward drift. However, the ratio of black males to females among the adult population continued its long-term decline. The disappearance of black males thus continues to be a significant problem for the black community.

The Participation Rate

Given the size of the working age population, the labor supply depends on the participation rate (see Table 7). The past five years have essentially seen a continuance of longer term trends in the labor force participation rate. The participation rate for black women has moved up while the rate for black males has drifted downward. There may also be a slight upward movement in black teenager participation.

The participation rate for black females reached new all-time highs during each year of the Reagan administration. The average participation rate for black women over the first eight months of 1986 was 58.7 percent. Over the first six Reagan years, the participation rate for black females over 20 has averaged 57.3 percent as opposed to 54 percent in the six years preceding Reagan.

The participation rates for black male adults continued its downward slide. In 1986 the rate continued its recovery from the deep recession levels but still stood at only 75 percent. In comparison with the six years preceding Reagan, the average participation rate during the six Reagan years has fallen slightly from 75.8 percent to 74.8 percent.

The participation rate for black teenagers has edged up slightly during the Reagan years to stand at 40.8 percent in 1986. The six-year average of 39.1 percent is slightly higher than the 38.9 percent average of the previous six years.

Overall total black participation rates have been slightly higher during the Reagan years than in the six years immediately preceding Reagan. Thus, blacks have increased their efforts to obtain jobs during the Reagan years.

Trends in labor force participation for white male and female adults paralleled those for blacks. During the Reagan years there was a moderate decline in white male participation and a relatively sharp increase in white female participation. The average participation for the Reagan years was 78.9 percent for white males and 53.0 percent for females as compared with 80.2 and 48.0 percent, respec-

Table 7

Labor Force Participation Rates by Race, Gender and Age
Before and During the Reagan Administration

	Total		Men 20+		Women 20+		Both Sexes 16-19	
	Black	White	Black	White	Black	White	Black	White
1986[1]	63.4	65.4	75.0	78.5	58.7	54.8	42.1	57.7
6 Reagan years	62.0	64.7	74.8	78.9	57.3	53.0	39.1	57.6
6 Pre-Reagan years	60.3	62.9	75.8	80.2	54.0	48.0	38.9	59.2

Ratio: Black-to-White

	Total	Men 20+	Women 20+	Both Sexes 16-19
1986[1]	.969	.955	1.071	.730
6 Reagan years	.958	.948	1.081	.679
6 Pre-Reagan years	.959	.945	1.125	.657

[1]Average for first 8 months, seasonally adjusted.

Source:
Bureau of Labor Statistics, *Employment and Earnings,* September 1986, p. 38; *Handbook of Labor Statistics,* June 1985, pp. 20 and 21.

---

tively, during the pre-Reagan period. The convergence that has been evident for black and white females since the early 1970s continued into the Reagan years as white women continued to narrow the gap, while the relative gap between black and white males remained essentially unchanged. The participation rates for white teenagers actually fell slightly during the Reagan years, causing a slight narrowing of racial gaps.

Unemployment

As shown in Table 8, unemployment has generally been higher during the Reagan administration. In 1986, after a four-year recovery, black unemployment was still higher than it was in the six years immediately preceding Reagan. Unemployment during the Reagan years has been higher for black adults and black teenagers. However, the sharpest increases in unemployment rate has averaged 15 percent during the Reagan years compared with 10.9 percent in the six years immediately preceding Reagan. Even during the first eight months of 1986, black male unemployment averaged 12.9 percent. The unemployment rate for black women has averaged 14.1 percent under Reagan compared with 11.8 percent in the six years prior to Reagan, while the average unemployment rate for black teenagers increased from 38.9 percent to 43.6 percent.

Table 8

Unemployment Rate by Race, Gender, and Age
Before and During the Reagan Administration

	Total		Men 20+		Women 20+		Both Sexes 16-19	
	Black	White	Black	White	Black	White	Black	White
1986[1]	14.7	6.1	12.9	5.3	12.4	5.5	40.8	15.6
6 Reagan years	16.6	7.1	15.0	6.3	14.1	6.2	43.6	17.4
6 Pre-Reagan years	13.7	6.3	10.9	4.8	11.7	6.1	38.9	15.6

Ratio: Black-to-White

	Total	Men 20+	Women 20+	Both Sexes 16-19
1986	2.41	2.43	2.25	2.62
6 Reagan years	2.34	2.38	2.27	2.51
6 Pre-Reagan years	2.17	2.27	1.92	2.49

[1]Average for first 9 months, seasonally adjusted.

Source:
Bureau of Labor Statistics, *Employment and Earnings,* November 1986; *Handbook of Labor Statistics,* June 1985, pp. 71 and 72.

Unemployment was also higher for whites during the past six years but not nearly as high as it has been for blacks. The overall white rate was only 6.1 percent in 1986 in contrast to the 14.7 percent rate of blacks. Thus, black unemployment was more than 2.4 times while unemployment during the past year. Each black demographic group had unemployment rates that were well over two times the corresponding white rate. For the six years of Reagan's presidency, the racial gap in the unemployment rates has increased for all the demographic groups.

Employment Population Ratios

The net result of these participation and unemployment trends is reflected in the employment population ratio or employment rates shown in Table 9. For all demographic groups, 1986 was the best employment year since Reagan took office. However, black men and black teenagers have generally had lower employment rates under Reagan than in the pre-Reagan period. Black women have generally had higher employment rates under Reagan. For black men the 1986 rate of 65.3 percent was still below the pre-Reagan average of 67.5 percent. For the six-year Reagan period as a whole, the rate of 63.6 percent is 3.9 percent below the average for the pre-Reagan period. While the black teenager employment rate in 1986 exceeds the pre-Reagan average, the black teenager employment rate for the period as a whole of 21.9 percent is also less than the 23.7 percent attained in the 6 years before Reagan. The employment rates for black women have generally gone up under Reagan despite their higher employment rates because of the increase in participation rates among black women. The average employment population ratio for black women under Reagan was 49.3 percent compared with 47.7 percent in the pre-Reagan period.

Table 9

Employment to Population Ratio by Race, Gender, and Age
Before and During the Reagan Administration

	Total		Men 20+		Women 20+		Both Sexes 16-19	
	Black	White	Black	White	Black	White	Black	White
1986[1]	54.1	61.5	65.3	74.3	51.5	51.8	24.9	48.7
6 Reagan years	51.7	60.1	63.6	73.9	49.3	49.8	21.9	47.6
6 Pre-Reagan years	52.0	58.9	67.5	76.4	47.7	45.1	23.7	50.0

Ratio: Black-to-White

	Total	Men 20+	Women 20+	Both Sexes 16-19
1986[1]	.880	.879	.994	.511
6 Reagan years	.860	.861	.990	.460
6 Pre-Reagan years	.883	.884	1.058	.474

[1]Average for first 8 months, seasonally adjusted.

Source:
Bureau of Labor Statistics, *Employment and Earnings,* September 1986, pp. 38 and 39; *Handbook of Labor Statistics,* June 1985, pp. 46 and 47.

There was a slight increase in racial inequality in employment rates during the Reagan years. Comparing the six Reagan years with the six years immediately preceding Reagan, the racial gaps increased slightly for all the demographic groups. For black males and black teenagers the relative declines in black employment rates were greater than they were for whites whose employment rates also declined under Reagan. For black females the relative increase was smaller. In fact, for the first time on record, the employment rates of white females surpassed the employment rates of black females.

Regional Variation In Employment and Unemployment
    Tables 10 and 11 show that there is considerable variation in the labor market status of blacks across the different regions of the country. Black unemployment

rates in the Midwest have been over 30 percent in every year of the Reagan presidency. During the first five years, the unemployment rate of blacks in this region averaged 23.7 percent. In all the other regions, black unemployment has averaged between 15.1 and 15.8 percent.

The employment population has also been lowest for blacks in the Midwest during the past six years. The 1985 average employment rate was only 47.2 percent in the Midwest, and the five-year average is only 46 percent. The Northeast has had the second lowest employment rates at 50.2 percent. The highest employment rates have been in the West with 54.7 percent and the South with 52.9 percent.

Table 10

Unemployment Rate by Region and Race
During the Reagan Administration

	Northeast		Midwest		South		West	
	Black	White	Black	White	Black	White	Black	White
1985	12.0	5.6	22.2	6.7	14.0	5.7	13.0	6.9
5 Reagan years	15.1	6.9	23.7	8.1	15.6	6.3	15.8	7.6

Ratio: Black-to-White

	Northeast	Midwest	South	West
1985	2.14	3.31	2.46	1.88
5 Reagan years	2.19	2.93	2.48	2.09

Source:
Bureau of Labor Statistics, *Geographic Profile of Employment and Unemployment,* 1981-1985, Table 1.

Table 11

Employment to Population Ratio by Region and Race
During the Reagan Administration

	Northeast		Midwest		South		West	
	Black	White	Black	White	Black	White	Black	White
1985	52.3	59.9	47.2	61.9	55.5	60.5	57.0	61.8
5 Reagan years	50.2	58.3	46.0	60.1	52.9	59.7	54.7	61.1

Source:
Bureau of Labor Statistics, *Geographic Profile of Employment and Unemployment,* 1981-1985, Table 1.

The region that has had the greatest racial inequality during the Reagan era has been the Midwest, both in terms of the gap between black and white unemployment and employment rates. The black unemployment rate was over three times the white unemployment rate in the Midwest during 1985 and over 2.9 times during the entire five-year period. The gap in employment population ratios was 14.7 percentage points in 1985 and 14.1 percentage points for the five-year period. The ratio of black-to-white unemployment rates for the five-year period was 2.48 in the South, 2.19 in the Northeast, and 2.09 in the West. The employment population ratio differences were 8.1 percent in the Northeast, 6.8 percent in the South, and 6.4 percent in the West. Thus, inequality was clearly greater in the Midwest.

We might also note that the data also suggest that the marked sex differences that exist in the national data also show up in the regional data. In general, the racial gaps in employment proportions are much larger for males than they are for females. To a lesser extent this is also true of the racial gaps in the unemployment rates.

Table 12
Employment to Population Ratio for
25 Large SMSAs for 1985 by Race

	Black	White
Denver-Boulder, CO	72.8	73.2
Washington, D.C.	67.9	73.7
Atlanta, GA	67.4	67.9
Kansas City, MO/KS	65.7	68.6
Boston, MA	65.3	66.4
Dallas-Fort Worth, TX	64.1	72.2
Houston, TX	62.7	67.8
San Francisco-Oakland, CA	60.5	66.2
Minneapolis-St. Paul, MN	59.9	73.9
Miami, FL	56.8	62.1
Nassau-Suffolk, VA	56.0	62.7
Indianapolis, IN	55.7	67.3
Newark, NJ	53.9	64.3
Baltimore, MD	52.8	62.0
Los Angeles-Long Beach, CA	52.6	61.8
New York, NY	51.0	53.7
Cincinnati, OH	50.1	63.2
Philadelphia, PA	48.5	61.4
Milwaukee, WI	47.8	62.4
Chicago, IL	46.0	64.1
St. Louis, MO	45.6	62.3
Cleveland, OH	42.9	59.2
Detroit, MI	39.6	62.2
Pittsburgh, PA	39.1	51.8
Buffalo, NY	32.7	55.7

Source:
Bureau of Labor Statistics, *Geographic Profile of Employment and Unemployment,* 1985, Table 23.

Variation Across Largest SMSAs in Employment and Unemployment

The data for the 25 largest standard metropolitan statistical areas (SMSAs) in 1985 shown in Tables 12 and 13 reveal even more clearly the wide variance in the labor market position of blacks across the country. The employment rates for blacks vary much more widely than they do for whites. The highest black employment to population ratio is 72.8 percent in Denver-Boulder while the lowest is 32.7 percent in Buffalo, New York. The white range is from 73.7 percent to 51.8 percent. Blacks have lower employment proportions than whites in every one of the 25 SMSAs. In general, the lowest black employment rates are found in the Midwest and Great Lakes region; i.e, the old industrial heartland.

Similar wide-ranging variation is found in 1985 unemployment rates. Black unemployment rates vary from a low of 4.5 percent in the Boston SMSA to a

Table 13

Unemployment Rate for 25 Large SMSAs
1985

	Black	White	Blk/Wht
Boston, MA	4.5	3.4	1.32
Nassau-Suffolk, VA	6.8	3.9	1.74
Washington, D.C.	7.9	2.1	3.76
Miami, FL	6.8	3.9	1.74
Denver-Boulder, CO	9.1	4.3	2.12
Atlanta, GA	9.9	3.1	3.19
San Francisco-Oakland, CA	10.5	5.3	1.98
Dallas-Fort Worth, TX	10.8	4.0	2.70
New York, NY	11.1	6.6	1.68
Newark, NJ	11.4	4.2	2.71
Los Angeles/Long Beach, CA	12.3	6.6	1.86
Philadelphia, PA	13.8	4.6	3.00
Baltimore, MD	13.9	3.3	4.21
Indianapolis, IN	14.2	6.6	2.15
Kansas City, MO-KS	14.4	3.1	4.65
Houston, TX	14.6	5.9	2.47
Cincinnati, OH	15.8	7.8	2.02
St. Louis, MO	17.4	4.9	3.55
Minneapolis-St. Paul, MN	19.9	4.5	4.4
Cleveland, OH	21.5	6.7	3.21
Pittsburgh, PA	23.5	9.6	2.45
Chicago, IL	24.5	5.6	4.38
Buffalo, NY	27.8	7.5	3.71
Milwaukee, WI	27.9	6.0	4.65
Detroit, MI	29.9	6.5	4.60

Source:
Bureau of Labor Statistics, *Geographic Profile of Employment and Unemployment,* 1985, Table 23.

high of 29.9 percent in Detroit. Blacks had unemployment rates about 10 percent in 19 of 25 SMSAs whereas there was no SMSA in which the white unemployment rate was above 10 percent. The black unemployment rate was greater than the white unemployment rate in every SMSA; the size of the differential varied across SMSAs. However, the differential was greater than two to one in 19 of 25 SMSAs and greater than three to one in twelve SMSAs. Finally, the pattern of variation across the sexes was in all respects similar to the pattern noted earlier; that is, black males experienced the greatest disadvantages in all SMSAs.

Industry and Occupational Utilization Rates

There have been no marked trends in utilization of blacks by industry and occupation under Reagan. Industry statistics show that blacks continue to be utilized at lower rates than whites in some significant industries, while they have equal or greater rates of employment in other industries (see Table 14). The industries which underutilize black workers are agriculture, mining, construction, durable goods manufacturing, wholesale and retail trade, and finance insurance and real estate. Collectively, these industries employed 20.3 percent of the black working age population vs. 31.0 percent of the white population: Their overall rate of employing blacks is 34.5 percent less than the rate of employing whites. The industries which employ blacks at a higher rate than whites are nondurable goods manufacturing, transportation and public utilities, services, and public administration. Collectively, these industries employ 33.1 percent of the black working age population vs. only 30 percent of the white population. However, this offsets only about 29 percent of the disadvantage from low employment in the other industries. Thus, after five years of Reagan policies, major American industries continue to underutilize blacks. However, it should be noted that the distribution of blacks across the industries is not in itself a disadvantage. The primary disadvantage blacks have is from their lower levels of employment.

Inspection of occupational utilization rates shown in Table 15 reveals that the familiar patterns of black underutilization in better paying, higher status occupations and overutilization in the lower paying, less prestigious occupations have persisted during the Reagan administration. There appears to be only slight movement in the pattern during the Reagan years. Black males are employed at about 40 percent of the rate of whites in managerial, professional, and sales occupations. Altogether these occupations employed about 10 percent of working age black males and 27 percent of working age white males. They employed about 60 percent of the rate of whites in technical and craft occupations which employ roughly 13 percent of working age blacks vs. 21 percent of white males. They are employed from 1.2 to 1.4 times as often as whites in protective service, operative, and clerical occupations. These occupations employ 21 percent of black and 16 percent of white males. Finally, they are employed from 1.7 to 1.9 times the rate of whites in private household, other service, and laborer occupations, which employ 16 and nine percent of white and black males, respectively. There has been a slight tendency for black males to lose slightly

Table 14

1985 Industry Utilization Rate*
By Race

	Black	White	Blk/Wht
Agriculture	.010	.019	.526
Mining	.002	.006	.333
Construction	.024	.042	.571
Manufacturing	.106	.119	.891
Durable goods	.055	.072	.764
Nondurable goods	.051	.046	1.109
Transportation & Public Utilities	.048	.042	1.143
Wholesale & Retail	.084	.130	.646
Wholesale Trade	.012	.026	.462
Retail Trade	.072	.104	.692
Finance, Insurance, and Real Estate	.028	.041	.683
Services	.197	.185	1.065
Private Household	.018	.006	3.000
Other Service industries	.179	.180	.994
Professional Service	.125	.120	1.042
Public Administration	.035	.027	1.296

*Industry utilization is calculated using the employment-to-population ratio times the percent of employed in each category.

Source:
Bureau of Labor Statistics, *Employment and Earnings, January 1986,* pp. 183 and 197.

more representation in low-benefit occupations during the Reagan years than they have gained in high-benefit jobs.

The occupational distribution of black males is disadvantageous. A rough calculation shows that if blacks had equal pay within occupations and equal total employment, their occupational distribution would lower their average wage by about 13 percent. This accounts for roughly 30 percent of the existing earnings differential between black and white males.

Similar occupational utilization patterns exist for black females, who are more heavily utilized in the least desirable female occupations—although the degree of occupational dissimilarity is not as great. Five occupational groups—managerial, professional, sales, clerical, and agricultural—employ black females at substantially lower rates than white females. Together these five occupations employ about 25 percent of black and 35 percent of white women. The

Table 15

1985 Occupation Utilization Rate By Race

	Males			Females		
	Black	White	Ratio	Black	White	Ratio
Executive, Admin & Managerial	3.96	9.98	.40	2.79	4.92	.57
Professional Specialty	3.42	8.68	.39	5.15	7.40	.70
Technical & Related	1.26	2.10	.60	1.64	1.62	1.01
Sales	3.0	8.39	.36	3.99	6.84	.58
Administrative & Clerical	5.04	3.90	1.29	12.46	15.21	.82
Private Household	.12	.07	1.71	2.60	.81	3.21
Protective Service	2.46	1.74	1.41	.38	.20	1.90
Other Service	8.52	4.41	1.93	11.26	7.61	1.48
Craft & Precision	9.24	15.18	.61	1.25	1.17	1.07
Machine Operations	6.66	5.42	1.23	4.91	3.09	1.59
Transportation Operations	6.54	4.77	1.37	.38	.41	.93
Laborers & Helpers	6.96	4.12	1.69	1.06	.76	1.40
Farming, Forestry, & Fishing	2.76	3.5	.79	.24	.66	.36

Source:
Bureau of Labor Statistics, unpublished tabulations from the Current Population Survey, annual averages, Table MQ-2, pp. 217-240.

technician, craft, and transport operative groups all employ black and white women at roughly equal rates (3.25 percent of black and 3.2 percent of white women). The remaining occupations—private household, protective, and other service, machine operatives, and laborers—all employ black women at a higher rate than white women. Together they employ about 20 percent of black and 12 percent of white women. Utilization of both black and white women has increased during the Reagan years; however, the utilization of white women has increased more.

The basic occupational patterns for black and white women have not changed appreciably during the Reagan years. Although the black female distribution is disadvantageous, the net impact on black female earnings is much smaller than is the net impact of occupational dissimilarity for black males. A rough calculation shows that black female earnings may be reduced by about six percent because of the occupational distribution.

Wage Rates and Earnings

The data in Table 16 show that during the Reagan years the constant dollar wages of full-time wage and salary workers have declined. In 1985 the median usual weekly wage for full-time black workers was only $304 compared to $342

Table 16

**Median Weekly Earnings of Full-Time Wage and Salary
Workers by Race and Gender Before and
During the Reagan Administration
(Constant 1985 Dollars)**

	Males			Females		
	Black	White	Ratio	Black	White	Ratio
1985	$304	$417	.729	$252	$281	.897
5 Reagan years	311	416	.748	245	271	.904
5 Pre-Reagan years	342	441	.776	250	270	.926

Source:
Bureau of Labor Statistics, unpublished tabulations from the Current Population Survey, annual averages, Table MQ-2, pp. 217-240.

in the five years preceding the Reagan administration. For the five-year period, this wage averaged $311 for black males. The constant dollar usual weekly wage for black males declined in both 1984 and 1985. The median usual weekly wage for black women has also been lower during the Reagan period, averaging $245 vs. $250 in the five years preceding Reagan. However, since 1982 the constant dollar wage for black women has risen moderately to $252 by 1985, but this is still below the real wage levels attained from 1976 to 1978.

Racial inequality is wages also increased during this period as measured by the ratio of black-to-white wage rates. Although white male wage rates declined during the past five Reagan years, they did not decline as much as black male wages. The ratio of average male wages in the pre-Reagan period was .776 and this had declined to .748 for the five-year Reagan period. By 1985 the ratio of usual median weekly earnings for full-time black workers was only .729. The degree of inequality of full-time female workers also increased, as the wages of whites have gone up more than the wages of black females. The ratio of black to white female wages dropped from .926 in the five years preceding Reagan to .904 during the five Reagan years. By 1985 this ratio had dropped to .897.

Conclusions About The Labor Market Status of Blacks Under Reagan

The above discussion can only lead to one conclusion: The general labor market position of blacks has been lower under the Reagan administration. By each measure of outcome—whether it is employment rates, unemployment rates, occupational standings, or wage rates—there has been no improvement since Reagan took office. Indeed, for each measure of labor market status, results on average have been worse for blacks during the five- or six-year Reagan presidency than in the five- or six-year period before Reagan. Even after three or four years of the Reagan recovery, black unemployment rates are higher, and earnings rates are lower than they were before the Reagan presidency.

The labor market status of black males has deteriorated most seriously during the past few years both absolutely and relative to whites. And, despite marginally high employment rates, the labor market position of black females has also deteriorated relative to the position of whites. Thus, by most standard indicators, racial inequality in the labor market has clearly increased under Reagan.

Furthermore, although the black situation is unequal in all regions, the situation is particularly bad in the Midwest, and the deterioration has been the sharpest in that region. In certain cities in the old industrial north, the current labor market status of blacks is at deep recession levels. The rather anemic recovery to date has had little impact on the labor market status of blacks in these areas. Moreover, although the labor market status of whites has also been lowered in these areas, the level of racial inequality has increased to scandalous levels. In cities such as Detroit, Buffalo, Chicago, and Cleveland, the gap between the labor market position of blacks—especially black males—and whites probably exceeds the highest levels that ever existed in the most racist of the South's cities.

The high level of labor market problems that has plagued blacks throughout the Reagan administration is very costly. The following examples illustrate the economic loss that the excessive disadvantages cost blacks, estimating costs for 1984.

The higher unemployment rates of both males and females and the lower participation rates of black males and teenagers result in larger proportions of blacks having zero earnings. In 1984 16 percent fewer black males than white males and four percent fewer black females than white females had no labor market earnings. This factor by itself reduced black male earnings by 12.9 billion dollars and black female earnings by 2.3 billion dollars. Altogether the black community lost about 15.2 billion dollars in 1984 because of this factor.

Black males who worked in 1984 also earned less on the average than did whites. This is caused by three factors. First, black males who work, work less than their white counterparts because of greater unemployment and greater rates of part-time employment. Second, as we have seen, black males have less favorable occupational distributions. Finally, black males have lower wages within any given occupational category. The net impact of these three factors was estimated to have reduced black male earnings by 30.8 percent, or 37.4 billion dollars.

Black females also are more likely to be employed in lower paying occupations and also receive lower wages within many occupations. However, black women are more likely to work full time and more likely to work all year round. The net impact of these factors on the earnings rates was favorable to black women during 1984. We estimated that black women earned 1.7 billion dollars more than they would have with equal average earning rates.

The combined impact of lower average earnings and higher proportions with zero earnings for black males totaled about 60 billion dollars in 1984. The combined impact of these factors on female earnings was about 464 million dollars during 1984. Thus, the net impact of the total labor market disadvantages experienced by blacks in 1984 was about 60.2 billion dollars, or 49.5 percent of the existing earnings.

The estimate for 1984 is an estimate of the cost of existing labor market inequality to blacks. Of course, all of this cost did not derive form the Reagan administration. Extensive inequality existed before then. Moreover, costs such as the general decrease in male employment and the general decline in male wages are not accounted for in the above calculation. Taking these factors into account, we estimate that on the average black labor market earnings have been reduced by about 10.1 billion dollars per year for the first four Reagan years. This total was derived as follows:

Black Males

Increased wage inequality	1.5 billion
Greater employment inequality	1.5 billion
Lower male employment	.9 billion
Lower constant dollar wages	7.2 billion

Black Females

Increased wage inequality	.9 billion
Greater employment inequality	1.2 billion
Higher female employment	-1.2 billion
Higher female wages	-1.5 billion
Net Lost	10.1 billion

It is likely that this estimate would be somewhat lower for 1985 and 1986. Nonetheless, the cumulative cost of the Reagan years is probably at least another additional 50 billion dollars about the high cost blacks were already paying because of labor market inequality.

EXPLAINING BLACK ECONOMIC PROBLEMS

The discussion to this point has pointed out some of the facts concerning recent trends in the economic status of blacks. We have seen that black economic status is low and unequal as measured by income levels or poverty rates. We have also seen that there has been little improvement in these measures during the Reagan years. Similar results were found when we reviewed the trends concerning black labor market status. Moreover, if we had looked at data on wealth or business ownership, the degree of inequality would have been even more glaring.

We acknowledge that while the economic and labor market status of blacks has worsened slightly since the start of the Reagan administration, the situation was already bad and deteriorating in the years immediately preceding the Reagan presidency. The problem of racial inequality was not created by Reagan policies.

However, the policies of the past few years have permitted a further worsening of an already serious problem.

In order to fully understand the recent economic difficulties of the black population, it is necessary to appreciate the position of the black population in the United States and the nature and functioning of the U.S. economy. The black population is and throughout its history has been an economically and socially disadvantaged population. In particular, four historic disadvantages have plagued the black population. First, blacks own, manage, or control few businesses or other important economic or job-creating institutions. Second, blacks have historically had limited accumulations of wealth. Third, blacks have traditionally experienced racial discrimination in gaining equal access to opportunities owned, managed, or controlled by non-black groups. Finally, blacks have traditionally had lower levels of formal education and training.

These four factors have historically generated the lower economic status of blacks given the nature of the American capitalist system in which the principal means of production are owned and operated in the interest of private individuals. Most individuals and almost all blacks do not own businesses and are thus primarily dependent on working in order to earn their living. But, how many jobs exist, how much income the jobs pay, and who is hired are determined by the interest of the capitalist owners and mangers. It is generally maintained that under capitalism, these decisions are made primarily on the basis of private profit considerations.

Historically, the limited black ownership and control of businesses and other institutions have meant that black economic achievements have depended on their ability to attain opportunities or resources from non-blacks. Blacks must generally compete with some non-blacks for scarce opportunities and resources which are owned, managed, or controlled by other non-blacks. How well blacks have done at different times depended on the nature and extent of economic opportunities, the extent of racism and discrimination by non-blacks, and the extent of black competitive disadvantages.

Finally, in our mixed capitalist system, at least in recent times, the policies of the government play an important role in determining the final outcomes of the capitalist market process. Government has at least five major ways of influencing economic outcomes. First, government economic and regulatory policy can influence the overall level and structure of economic activities. Second, government may regulate the labor market to influence the level of wages and terms of employment. Third, government may influence the distribution of both human and non-human capital. Fourth, government may regulate the amount of discrimination. Finally, government may redistribute income. Since at least the time of Franklin Roosevelt, the American government has participated to some extent in all of these types of interventions.

However, the first major effort to address explicitly the problem of racial inequality did not take on any significant scope until the 1960s. This effort consisted primarily of attempts to reduce discrimination against blacks through regulatory activities, efforts to reduce the historic human capital disadvantages, and an effort to redistribute income to the poorest blacks. Each of these efforts had some success, and they did result in some moderate attenuation in racial inequality. However, these efforts were limited, and by the early 1970s progress in reducing racial inequality had ceased. At that point, conditions were still very unequal, and all of the historic disadvantages, though attenuated somewhat, still continued to exist.

With this as background, we can now turn our attention to explaining recent trends in black economic status. The key dynamic factor that has operated in the private market since the early 1970s is an increasing relative scarcity of jobs in general and an increasing scarcity of high wage jobs in particular. This situation was brought about by developments on both the labor supply and the labor demand sides of the market.

On the labor supply side, the key factors were the tremendous expansion in the labor market participation of women during the past twenty years and tremendous increase in the average level of education and training among the workforce. The increased participation among women would have required an additional 8.4 million jobs between 1972 and 1984 above and beyond the normal job growth required to maintain constant employment rates without this expanded participation. The increasing level of education of the workforce is also relevant to understanding the developing shortage of good jobs because the numbers of individuals at least nominally qualified for better jobs have grown a lot faster than the number of better jobs. Between 1970 and 1984, the proportion of jobs which have traditionally required some college education increased by 28 percent while the proportion of the workforce with some college increased by 65 percent. It seems clear that more and more educated people are competing for a relatively smaller number of good jobs.

Several demand factors have also played an important role in increasing the relative scarcity of jobs. First, the rate of job growth since the early 1970s has not been great enough to accommodate the greatly increased labor supply. A simple calculation shows that between 1970 and 1980 job growth was roughly 4,000,000 jobs short of what would have been required to maintain 1970 male employment levels and accommodate the additional female workers without increasing the female unemployment rate. Moreover, job growth has slowed during the Reagan years relative to the growth which occurred during the 1970s. In fact, the job shortage that existed in 1980 had increased to 5,275,000 by the end of 1985.

Second, there has been a structural shift in jobs away from the higher paying and more male-intensive goods - producing sector to the lower paying more female-intensive service sectors. During the first five Reagan years, for example, total employment increased by about 8.1 percent while employment in the non-service sector declined by about two percent. In fact, between 1970 and 1985, the share of jobs in manufacturing dropped from 33 percent to 23.8 percent while the share of jobs in the retail trade and service sector increased from 38.7 to 48.2 percent. In 1984 32.4 percent of those employed in the manufacturing sector were women and the average weekly pay of all workers was $373. In contrast, 52.2 and 60.7 percent of the workers in retail trade and services, respectively, were women. The average weekly earnings of workers in these two industries were $176 in retail trade and $249 in services.

Third, there has been a general decline in the level of wages paid within each sector. Between 1972 and 1980, the average earnings in constant dollars declined in every major industrial sector except mining. Overall wages fell by about 13 percent. Wage stagnation continued from 1980 to 1985. Overall constant dollar wages fell by less than one percent. Slow improvement has occurred in a number of sectors. However, earnings in every section are still below their late 1960s levels.

Fourth, the value of the minimum wage has been allowed to erode substantially. The minimum wage has lost over 16 percent of its purchasing power since the beginning of the Reagan presidency. Moreover, the value of the minimum wage both absolutely and in relationship to the average wage in private industry is at a historic low point.

The combined impact of the demand and supply developments has created a relative scarcity of jobs in general and of high paying and high status jobs in particular. The working class as a whole has been made worse off. Of necessity, unemployment rates overall had to increase. Moreover, the decline in the general level of wages also meant that real earning levels had to decline. However, in our market economic particular individual workers bear most of the burden by getting no job or low-paying jobs. The lack of jobs has produced intensified competition among workers for scarce employment opportunities and scarce good jobs in particular. Some workers lose under these circumstances.

The increased difficulties that blacks have experienced since the mid-1970s are a result of the increased worker competition for jobs. Blacks have been disproportionate losers in this increased competition primarily because of racial discrimination and the legacy of historic disadvantages.

CONCLUSIONS

Recent trends in black economic status cannot be satisfactory to those concerned about ending the long-standing conditioning of excessive racial inequality in the United States. Over the last few years we have retrogressed. There is no region for which racial parity has been achieved. In many parts of the country, racial inequality has increased sharply.

The economic status of black males in particular is in serious disarray in every region and in most major cities. Blacks are losing hard-won ground throughout the Midwest and in many parts of the Northeast. If present trends continue or if the current anemic recovery should slip back into another deep recession, we can expect all of the gains of the civil rights revolution to be lost for the masses of the black population. Only the most highly educated and the most successfully employed will have a chance of holding on to these gains.

The economic difficulties confronting blacks are traceable to economic trends that are lowering the standard of living for American workers in general. The economic policies of the current administration are at best passively accepting this turn of events in the name of the supremacy of laissez-faire. The government's willingness to tolerate the decline of our major industries is a primary factor generating the current labor market malaise. The willingness and even encouragement of the assault on the wages of American workers is a further exacerbating factor. Indeed, the current belief that market forces left to themselves can bring about a satisfactory solution to our current economic problems is the major barrier to mounting an effective campaign to save the living standards of American workers.

This administration's abandonment of the effort to bring blacks into the mainstream at the very time when the increasing job scarcity puts blacks at a more severe disadvantage has permitted a disproportionate share of the burdens generated by the current negative economic trends to be concentrated among blacks. Most of the special efforts to reduce the longstanding human capital disparities have been curtailed or completely abandoned, although a substantial part of the inherited disadvantages has never been removed. The miniscule efforts at business and economic or community development have been allowed to wither. But most cruel of all are the cutbacks and emasculation of the spirit, if not the letter, of equal opportunity and affirmative action efforts just when economic events make it more likely that discrimination will occur.

A solution to the longstanding economic difficulties of the black community will require two major changes in public policy. First, there must be a more effective national economic policy to end the erosion of the American industrial structure. The living standards of American workers must be preserved and improved . The economy must also be strong enough to provide equal and adequate opportunities to all citizens who are willing to work. A complete reconstruction of economic policies is required to achieve these goals. We cannot afford to sit back and hope that the magic of market forces will suddenly reverse a decade-old trend of decline. Rather, we must take the offensive and design and experiment with rational interventions to save our industries and the American standard of living.

Second, black Americans must insist on a major commitment from the federal government as the representative of the American people to make the effort to repair once and for all the damages of centuries of exploitation and mistreatment. The failure of past policies stems directly from their failure to go far enough in repairing the damages of the historic legacy of discrimination. The repair of these damages cannot be considered complete until the black population is able to attain the same economic outcomes as whites.

In conclusion we would suggest that a failure to reverse current policy directions will result in a continued slow deterioration in the strength of America and a more rapid decline in the economic state of Black America.

Blacks, Budgets, and Taxes: Assessing the Impact of Budget Deficit Reduction and Tax Reform on Blacks

Lenneal J. Henderson

INTRODUCTION

" . . . a Black American struggle for *rights* in the 1940s through the 1960s had not yet been fully understood in terms of inevitable demands to come in the form of a struggle for *resources*."[1]

Charles V. Hamilton

"Since the budget represents conflict over whose preferences shall prevail, the . . . implication is that one cannot speak of 'better budgeting' without considering who benefits and who loses or demonstrating that no one loses. Just as the supposedly objective criterion of 'efficiency' has been shown to have normative implications, so a 'better budget' may well be a cloak for hidden policy preferences."[2]

Aaron Wildavsky

Hamilton and Wildavsky go right to the center of black concerns about budget and tax reform: The struggle over rights and resources and policy preferences inherent in budget reform. These concerns were thriving in 1986, the year when two of the most monumental fiscal policies in the twentieth century were enacted. The first was the Balanced Budget and Emergency Deficit Control Act of 1985, popularly known as Gramm-Rudman-Hollings, and the Tax Reform Act of 1986.

The Balanced Budget and Emergency Deficit Control Act mandates a budget process guided by a "sequestration" process of automatic spending reductions if Congress fails to meet deficit targets clearly indicated in the law. Reductions occur in all federal programs except those specifically exempted by the law.[3] Although a special three-judge panel of the federal District Court for the District of Columbia ruled that the sequestration process is an unconstitutional violation of the principle of separation of powers, the general mandate for deficit reduction remains intact.[4]

The Tax Reform Act of 1986 represents the most comprehensive overhaul of the federal tax system since World War II. The objectives of this reform included tax simplification, moving toward a more equitable system, economic growth, and increased tax yields. Increased tax yields is an objective clearly related to budget deficit reduction.[5] By reducing the number of tax brackets for individual and corporate taxpayers, radically reforming categories of itemizable deduction, and shifting more tax burden to corporate taxpayers, Congress hopes to match budget deficit reduction with increases in revenues from the federal income tax.

Both budget and tax reform profoundly affect black individuals, households, and institutions. These fiscal reforms have some negative and some positive short- and long-term impacts on black economic and social processes and aspirations. The key question is: When negative and positive impacts on blacks are considered, how much more are blacks helped rather than hurt by fiscal reform? Answers to this question include significant economic, social, institutional, and political dimensions.[6] These dimensions are best understood in a political economy framework. In such a framework, *resources* are the key element of exchange and decision for all actors in the economy and body politic, including blacks.

FISCAL REFORM AND THE THEORY OF POLITICAL ECONOMY

To assess best the impact of budget and tax reform on blacks, this paper adopts a modified version of the political economy model developed by Warren Ilchman and Norman Uphoff.[7] Ilchman and Uphoff interrelate economic and political decisions through a framework of *resources*.

A resource is anything that has intrinsic value and can, therefore, be exchanged. Money, material goods, and services are but a kind of resource. Other resources such as status, legitimacy, authority, coercion, information, and infrastructure are more social and political in nature. A social or political resource such as status or legitimacy may be exchanged for an economic resource such as money or commodities. Resources may also be sorted, saved, or given away. Depending upon their value, storing or saving them may appreciate or depreciate them in value. Giving a resource away without some reciprocation or compensation is considered a net loss to the group possessing the resource. Most importantly, *power* in this framework is not necessarily the result of how much of a resource base a group has, or even what combination of resources they possess, but how *strategic* the group is in utilizing and exchanging those resources they own. Strategic use of resources includes cultivation and development of the net value of the group's resources following exchange.

Each major fiscal reform involves a distribution and redistribution of both economic and political resources for every actor in the economy and political system. How do blacks affect and how are they affected by such reforms? How do the reforms reflect the present state of black economic and political resource endowments prior to and following the enactment of reform measures? These are empirical questions Hamilton suggests fall into the resources category. They are closely related to but distinct from traditional and more normative "rights" questions posed by the black community. Once empirical questions are answered, normative inferences can be made.

This paper will, therefore, discuss the basic provisions of both Gramm-Rudman-Hollings and Tax Reform laws; identify key indicators in the black political economy affected or likely to be affected by these laws; identify key indicators in the black political economy affected or likely to be affected by these laws; discuss cross-impacts of these reforms on blacks; and draw conclusions about the strategic implications of these reforms for the development of the black political economy.

BASIC PROVISIONS OF GRAMM-RUDMAN-HOLLINGS AND OF THE TAX REFORM ACT OF 1986

Both the Balanced Budget and Emergency Deficit Control Act of 1985 (hereinafter referred to as Gramm-Rudman-Hollings or GRH) and the Tax Reform Act of 1986 reflect fiscal imbalance in American government. GRH resulted from congressional frustration with its inability to reduce substantially the federal deficit. Since 1980, the federal deficit has grown from $60 billion to $220.5 billion at the end of 1985, increasing from 2.3 to 5.3 percent of the gross national product of the United States. Deeply concerned about the implications of deficits on aggregate economic performance; about the failure of the Economic Recovery Tax Act of 1981 and other measures to stimulate economic growth; and about the impact of these failures on upcoming 1986 congressional elections,[8] Congress assigned a high priority to deficit reduction in 1985.

Despite considerable efforts to reduce the budget, Congress and the President accomplished little. The President's budget proposed a 5.9 percent real growth in defense, no tax increases, and massive domestic spending reductions, including termination of federal school lunch, Job Corps, Work Incentive Program (WIN), Urban Development Action Grants, revenue sharing, and mass transit assistance programs. Congress found these proposed cuts both economically and politically unacceptable. Both economic and political resources of many political constituencies — both Republican and Democratic, regional, racial, gender, labor, and business — were jeopardized. Congress knew that these constituencies would use remaining economic and political resources against incumbents if the President's program was adopted.

The Senate budget proposed a three-percent real growth in defense and somewhat smaller reductions in domestic programs, largely by providing no increase in defense over inflation. After months of compromise, conflicts, and confusion, Congress reached a compromise providing for no real growth in defense and a still substantial $171.9 billion deficit, only eight billion dollars less than the President's proposed deficit.[9]

By the end of calendar year 1985, with economic performance languishing and the budget progressing quickly through the authorizing and appropriations committees, it became increasingly clear that the fiscal year 1986 deficit would exceed $200 billion. Despite awareness of the magnitude of the deficit, its potential for economic damage, the protests of hundreds of interest groups, and the approaching 1986 congressional elections, Congress and the President failed to agree on deficit reduction. The House and Senate were split largely along partisan lines on deficit reduction strategies. The President refused to concede deep real-dollar reductions in defense spending, more moderate reductions in spending for domestic programs, and pressures for tax increases.

GRH was formulated in an attempt to force Congress and the President to agree on a budget which directly and substantially reduced the deficit. GRH sets a series of deficit ceilings designated to eliminate the deficit by fiscal year 1991 and provides a framework for across-the-board reductions (sequesters) in controllable domestic programs if the President and Congress cannot agree to a budget within the prescribed ceiling. Senators Gramm, Rudman, and Hollings and their cosponsors in the House of Representatives hoped that the unpalatable possibility of widespread, mandatory reductions would encourage the President and Congress to agree to some combination of program cuts and revenue increases to reduce the deficit. However, given the President's insistence on three-percent real growth in defense, no reductions in Social Security, and no tax increases, and the Congress' past resistance to deep reductions in domestic programs, the prospect of mandatory cuts in the 1987 fiscal year seemed almost imminent.[10]

GRH classifies federal programs into four categories: (1) Exempt; (2) Category I (indexed); (3) Health Services; and (4) Category II (controllable). The first category, titled "Exempt," does not allow mandatory reductions for: Social Security, interest on the federal debt, the earned income tax credit, prior year obligations, and judicially-ordered claims against the federal government, as well as antipoverty programs such as Aid to Families with Dependent Children (AFDC), Food Stamps, child nutrition programs, WIC, community health centers, and Medicaid.

Category I designates a series of indexed programs and calls for up to half of all required savings to come from reductions in cost-of-living adjusted increases in these programs. Cuts in the base of these programs are prohibited. In essence, GRH freezes Category I programs at fiscal year 1985 levels. Of these programs, civil and military retirement and Special Milk programs, for example, would experience a direct reduction and real-dollar reductions due to inflation resulting from direct reductions.

In the Health Services category, GRH provides for reductions of up to one percent in fiscal year 1986 and two percent thereafter in five health services programs, including Medicare. Given rapid increases in health care costs and failures in many health services areas to contain such costs, the real impact of these reductions is closer to five percent.

Category II, the controllable category, subjects all other defense and domestic programs to across-the-board reductions if deficit targets specifically identified in the statute are not met.[11] The absolute size of these reductions would be determined by the relationship of proposed budgets to budget targets established in the law.[12] This process, known as "sequestration," automatically executes across-the-board spending reductions in Category II programs.

In determining whether to trigger these reductions, the Congressional Budget Office (CBO), the President's Office of Management and Budget (OMB), and the General Accounting Office (GAO) play key roles and assume major new responsibilities in the original statute. CBO and OMB were to estimate jointly the size of the deficit for the upcoming fiscal year and to determine whether the deficit exceeded the specified limit by more than $10 billion. If it did, CBO and OMB were required to calculate the two uniform percentages — one for defense and one for domestic programs — by which affected programs would have to be reduced in order to close the gap. This so-called "snapshot" of the federal budget situation was to take place on August 15 of each year. It would then be sent to the GAO for verification and transmitted to the President and Congress by August 25.

The President is required to issue an emergency sequestration order if CBO, OMB, and GAO predict a deficit in the upcoming fiscal year that exceeds the GRH limit by more than $10 billion and Congress and the President have not enacted an alternative deficit-reduction plan to meet the limit. The sequestration order must be issued on September 1 to take effect in final form on October 15. The sequestration order automatically reduces spending in all federal programs with certain important exceptions. Half of the total dollar spending reductions must come from defense and half from non-defense spending. In each of these areas, all affected programs would be reduced by a uniform percentage.[13] For fiscal year 1986, these reductions were 4.3 percent and for fiscal year 1987, estimates of automatic reductions were as high as 20 percent. Table I identifies the deficit targets for fiscal years 1986 through 1991. These targets guide decisions about sequestration for all federal programs affected by GRH.

Table I.

**Deficit Targets Under Gramm-Rudman-Hollings
Fiscal Years 1986 to 1991**

Fiscal Year	Deficit Level
1986	$171.9 billion
1987	$144 billion
1988	$108 billion
1989	$ 72 billion
1990	$ 36 billion
1991	$0

Source: Balanced Budget and Emergency Deficit Control Act of 1985 (P.L. 99-177).

Many interests were immediately and profoundly affected by GRH. Their status, legitimacy, authority, and economic resource base was conspicuously threatened by the process and anticipated outcomes of GRH. Many interests sought, unsuccessfully, to persuade Congress to repeal or significantly amend the statute. Others sought immediate judicial remedies. The President's proposed fiscal year 1987 budget sought to reduce many programs beyond the GRH targets to allow more room for incremental increases in defense spending, despite interest group discomfiture with both GRH and large increases in defense budgets.

The President's proposed 1987 budget would cut 14 percent from domestic programs while increasing military spending from $286 billion to $320.3 billion (12%). At the same time, federal aid to public education would drop from $10.9 billion to $5.6 billion; guaranteed student loans would be cut from $3.2 billion to $2.5 billion. Some programs would be eliminated altogether: Legal Services, which provides poor citizens with access to the justice system; the Community Service Block Grant, which helps cities provide social services to the poor; housing assistance; emergency food and shelter programs; the Job Corps; and the Small Business Administration (SBA).[14]

Many of these programs directly or indirectly benefit the black community. For example, Richard Greenstein, the Director of the Center on Budget and Policy Priorities, has concluded that blacks would suffer disproportionately from cuts originally proposed by the President and inspired by GRH. Greenstein noted that 24 percent of those using Legal Services were black, as were 37 percent of those receiving food stamps, and 45 percent of the youths involved in the Job Corps.[15] Moreover, because grants-in-aid to state and local governments comprise a major portion of controllable domestic programs subject to sequestration under GRH, state and local governments — particularly those with substantial numbers of black citizenry or elected officials — would be significantly damaged.[16]

However, on February 7, 1986, a special three-judge panel of the federal District Court for the District of Columbia, in the case of *Synar v. United States*,[17] found the sequestration process to be an unconstitutional violation of the principle of separation of powers. Because it gives executive branch authority to the Comptroller General, who is in some respects part of the legislative branch, the panel argued that Congress had delegated too much of its constitutional responsibility to make budget decisions. However, spending cuts that took effect on March 1, 1986, and for the subsequent fiscal years indicated in the statute were left intact. On July 7, 1986, the U.S. Supreme Court ruled similarly.[18] However, only the automatic sequestration process was ruled unconstitutional. The remainder of the statute remains in effect but places the onus of budget responsibility back on the shoulders of Congress and the President.

The distributive effects of GRH are essentially negative. Beginning with a budgetary base already insufficient for most human needs, including priority concerns for blacks identified in the Congressional Black Caucus Alternative Budget,[19] GRH reduced Category I and II programs by 4.3 percent in fiscal year 1986, and will further reduce such programs in fiscal year 1987. When increases in the needs of the black community resulting both from absolute population increases and increasingly needy populations are combined with increases in the cost of goods and services paid by diminishing federal dollars, the actual GRH reductions range from 8.6 to 11 percent of the 1985 base budget.

Almost concurrent with the economic and political forces that resulted in GRH were pressures to transform significantly the federal tax code. In 1981,

President Reagan introduced and Congress passed the Economic Recovery and Tax Act (ERTA). Designed to stimulate economic growth by increasing disposable income and capital available for investment, the Economic Recovery and Tax Act lowered tax rates for all taxpayers by 25 percent (five percent in the first year and 10 percent in each of the next two years). ERTA included a substantial investment tax credit and accelerated depreciation aimed to induce business development. However, the basic assumption underlying ERTA was faulty; that is, reducing taxes makes available disposable income and capital that can be saved and/or invested; therefore, increased savings and investment will automatically stimulate business. What made this assumption particularly faulty was the unprecedented inflation in the period 1978-81. Double-digit inflation and interest rates exceeding 20 percent artificially inflated incomes without increasing standard of living. Most items in the Consumer Price Index accelerated beyond increases in earnings. The result was that both households and corporations tended to use ERTA tax benefits to catch up with inflationary impact rather than to save or invest. As Burbridge indicates, the result was the loss of billions of dollars to the Treasury and an exacerbation of the deficit.[20] Clearly, the impact of ERTA and the emergence of the GRH option are inextricably intertwined.

Consequently, President Reagan's tax reform proposals to Congress four years later focused on the following policy objectives: fairness, growth, and simplicity.[21] These proposals guided the work of House Ways and Means Committee Chairman Dan Rostenkowski (D-Ill.) and Senate Finance Committee Chairman Bob Packwood (R-Or.).

Concerns with fairness focused on the need to have corporations and wealthy individuals pay their fair share of taxes while providing some relief for middle- and low-income taxpayers; the need to have taxpayers in similar income circumstances paying about the same amount of federal taxes; and the need to address taxpayers, both individuals and companies, receiving major tax breaks that far exceed those enjoyed by average taxpayers and cannot be justified in terms of equity or economic efficiency.

Concerns with growth focused both on real economic growth and more efficient and effective tax yields. Ironically, the President's proposals were critical of ERTA provisions he had advocated. He argued that some tax provisions stimulate investments in areas and projects that would not make economic sense in their absence. He also argued that high tax rates discourage work and saving and that loopholes distort economic activity.

Concerns with simplicity were focused on how to streamline the tax system, make it "payer friendly," and on demystifying many of its labyrinthine provisions.

Both the House of Representatives and the Senate also were concerned with fairness, growth, and simplicity but placed greater stress on the role of tax reform in both deficit reduction and improved macroeconomic performance.[22]

Once enacted, key provisions of the Tax Reform Act of 1986 include:

(1) *Bracket simplification.* When fully effective in 1988, tax reform reduces the number of tax brackets for individual taxpayers to two rates of 15 percent

and 28 percent. The 28-percent rate kicks in for singles above $17,850 of taxable income, for heads of household above $23,900, and for married-filing-jointly above $29,750. In addition, a five-percent surcharge will be imposed starting in 1988 on income at the $43,150 level for singles, $71,900 for married-filing-jointly, and $61,650 for heads of household. The surcharge, which is designed to phase out the benefit of the 15-percent rate for higher income taxpayers, will have the effect of a 33 percent marginal rate. These provisions replace the current 14 to 15 distinct brackets of marginal rates ranging from 11 to 50 percent. New tax brackets are indexed for inflation. However, limited, staggered relief is provided for 1987 by means of a five-rate structure of 11 percent, 15 percent, 28 percent, 35 percent and 38.5 percent. In addition, there is no phase-out of the lower rates or personal exemption at the higher income levels in 1987.

(2) *Elimination of many tax shelters for those itemizing.* The new law limits or eliminates many tax shelters in the old law, including deductions for contributions to charitable institutions, interest on consumer debt, state and local sales taxes, and deductibility of mortgage interest payments for those who own more than two homes.

The adverse impact of tax reform law on beneficiaries of charitable contributions results from changes to the non-charitable provisions of the law which indirectly affect the after-tax cost, or price, of making charitable gifts. There are two leading causes of these indirect effects on giving. One, the reduction in the marginal tax rates for most individuals contemplates collapsing the current rate schedule of some 14 marginal rate brackets mentioned earlier. The other is the prospective reduction in the number of taxpayers who will itemize their tax returns.[23]

(3) *Increased taxes on capital gains,* the money earned on the sale of property.

(4) *Removal of more than 6 million, poverty-level households from the tax rolls.* This results from increases in standard deductions for workers, personal exemptions for each member of the household, and earned income tax credits for low-income workers with children. However, it is important to emphasize that these households contributed a range of $25 to $750 dollars per household to federal revenues and that their elimination from the tax rolls not only enhances fairness but also makes tax law enforcement more efficient and productive.

(5) *A separate standard deduction for households headed by a single parent.* With the growth in households consisting of a single adult with children, the addition of this category with standard deductions was long overdue. Given the large percentage of female-headed households among blacks, this change will benefit working families.[24]

(6) *Low-income housing.* The new tax law attempts to tighten rules governing real estate tax shelters and housing development schemes. Depreciation periods of all housing have been considerably reduced, including low-income hous-

ing. Thus, at a time when demand for housing, particularly among blacks, is increasing, the incentives to invest in the development of such housing will decrease. Moreover, income losses sustained by those making rental housing available is sharply curtailed, thus reducing incentives to make low-income housing available by current methods. Limitations on the issuance of tax-exempt industrial development bonds for low-income housing also promise to frustrate investment in low-income housing. Although the new law allows a nine-percent credit on investments in low-income housing, subject to more stringent criteria, it remains to be seen whether this credit will offset clear disincentives to invest in low-income housing.

(7) *Retroactive repeal of the investment tax credit (ITC).* A key provision of the new tax law is the repeal of the investment tax credit for businesses, retroactive to January 1, 1986. A key provision of the ERTA, the repeal of this tax credit is likely to have a significant effect on new equipment purchases and retrofitting of plant equipment, particularly for capital-intensive or manufacturing industries.[25]

(8) *Continuation of the deductibility of state and local income and property taxes.* Strongly opposed by the President, continuation of state and local income and property tax provisions was a hard-fought victory for House conferees. However, sales taxes are no longer a deductible item. This provision is particularly important to black state and local elected and appointed officials.[26]

Although these provisions are but part of the total universe of tax reform provisions, they are essential to black Americans. Many of these provisions will be phased into the law over a two- or three-year period, but they require significant adjustments in tax mentality and practice. Since the law is very recently enacted, it is not completely clear how all provisions of the law will impact on any Americans, particularly black Americans. However, the next section of this paper attempts to identify key anticipated impacts of both GRH and Tax Reform on blacks.

ANTICIPATED IMPACTS OF FISCAL REFORM ON THE BLACK POLITICAL ECONOMY

Both GRH and Tax Reform will have significant effects on the distribution and redistribution of economic and political resources among blacks and between blacks and other Americans. As these impacts are assessed, it is important to keep in mind both the criteria for good fiscal policies and their compatibility with the economic and political goals of blacks. Fiscal policies should maintain the principles of *productivity, equity,* and *elasticity.* Both budget and tax policies should adhere to these principles.

A productive fiscal policy generates sufficient revenues to meet governmental needs on the tax side and makes investments in human needs, economic development, and defense on the spending side.[27] If tax policies fail to generate adequate revenue, more public monies must be spent on borrowing with a subsequent effect on interest rates and economic growth.

An equitable fiscal policy is fair to both taxpayers and to specific public constituencies benefiting from public expenditures.[28] In tax policy, economists refer to two kinds of equity — *horizontal* and *vertical*. Horizontal equity means that taxpayers who have the same amounts of income should be taxed at the same rate. Vertical equity implies that wealthier people should pay more taxes than poorer people. A related principle is that tax policies should be *progressive*. Taxes increase as income increases. *Proportional* principles of taxation increase tax in exact and direct proportion to increases in income. *Regressive* taxes impose greater burdens on taxpayers less able to pay or taxes increase as income decreases.[29]

Although applied traditionally to taxes, notions of progressivity, proportionality, and regressivity also have a budgetary counterpart. Fiscal policies that tend to benefit the least needy and deprive the most needy are budgetarily regressive. Generally, GRH is regressive in its impacts on blacks because it utilizes budget bases that were already retrenched before 1985 as baselines for GRH-mandated cuts. Even exempted programs will not experience significant increases in expenditure.

On the other hand, the Tax Reform Act is generally progressive in that it seeks to eliminate the working poor from the tax rolls, to impose greater taxes on those able to pay, and to shift tax burden to income-generating corporations.

Finally, the principle of *elasticity* suggests that the fiscal system be flexible enough to address its revenue and spending needs regardless of macroeconomic changes in economic conditions. Taxes and spending make a contribution to the stabilization of the economy. An additional principle, somewhat at odds with the elasticity principle, is that taxes be *neutral*. Neutrality suggests that tax laws should not affect taxpayers' spending, saving, investment, and other financial decisions. Not all experts agree that this is a realistic or desirable policy.[30]

As we review the anticipated impacts of GRH and the Tax Reform Act on blacks, these fiscal principles are essential. Generally, they are compatible with black economic and political aspirations, particularly with regard to the need to have more affluent and able taxpayers pay their share of the tax burden; to promote fiscal policies that encourage economic development and, hence, employment; to support human services and education in the black community; and to foster successful minority business development.

Three levels of impacts on the black community require examination: the individual/family/household level, the institutional level, and the macrocommunity level. The levels are intimately interrelated.

Household/Individual Impacts

When GRH and Tax Reform provisions are considered together, they are fiscally regressive for black individuals and households. Tables 2, 3, and 4 provide the context for this assertion. Although the Tax Reform Act is generally positive for low-income black families and households, anticipated reductions in

84

GRH Categories I and II, miniscule growth in exempted programs, and increased demands for both exempt and retrenched programs erode most of the benefits of tax reform for the lowest-income blacks.

Table 2, developed by Lynn Burbridge, an economist at the Urban Institute, describes basic provisions of tax reform by income group. Even though more than six-million low-income individuals will be subtracted from the federal tax rolls, only the lowest income individuals in the black community will benefit. According to Table 3, approximately 25 percent of all black households are likely to be affected by elimination from the tax rolls. Tables 3 and 4 describe median income and family characteristics by race. While black wives are less likely to participate in the labor force than white wives, black female heads-of-household are more than three times likely to exist than white females. Thus, the significance of both the standard deduction for single heads-of-households and the earned income tax credit is particularly high for black females heading a household.

Table 2. Selected Tax Provisions Affecting Low-Income Households

	CURRENT LAW	NEW LAW*
TAX RATES		
Individual	14 brackets — 11–50%	2 rates: 15% and 28%; with phase-out for high income: 33% top rate
Corporate	15–40% on first $100,000; 46% thereafter	15–30% up to $75,000, 34% thereafter
Capital Gains	20% top rate	28% top rate
Minimum Tax	20% individuals, 15% corporate	21% with fewer loopholes
INCOME TAX THRESHOLD		
Standard Deduction		
Single	$2,480	$3,000
Joint	$3,670	$5,000
Head of Household	$2,480	$4,400
Exemption (per person)	$1,080	$2,000 (by 1989, phased out for high incomes)
Earned Income Tax Credit	$550 maximum	$800 maximum
LOW-INCOME HOUSING		
Depreciation	more favorable for low-income housing	same for all housing

Rental Loss Limitation	none		$25,000 in deductions or $7,000 in credits (phased out after $200,000 income)
Industrial Development Bonds	volume cap excludes multi-family housing		volume cap includes multi-family housing
Low-Income Housing Credit	No credit		9% for rehabilitation and new construction, 4% if other subsidy
Criteria for IDB and Credit	For IDB: 20% of tenants below 80% of area median		For IDB and credit: 40% below 60% or 20% below 50% of area median.

*Some provisions are subject to transition rules and may not take full effect immediately.

Source: Lynn Burbridge, Urban Institute, 1986

Table 3. Median Income and Family Characteristics by Race, 1984

Characteristic	Number of Families				Median Income	
	White		Black		White	Black
	(millions)	(%)	(millions)	(%)	($)	($)
All families	54,400	100	6,778	100	27,686	15,432
Type of family						
Married couple families	45,643	83	3,469	51	30,058	23,418
Wife in paid labor force	23,979	44	2,221	33	35,176	28,775
Wife not in paid labor force	21,664	40	1,248	18	24,246	14,502
Male householder no wife present	1,816	3	344	5	25,110	15,724
Female householder, no husband present	6,941	13	2,964	44	15,134	8,648

Number of earners						
Total	53,777	100	6,671	100	27,752	15,337
No earners	7,674	14	1,376	21	12,941	5,277
One earner	15,219	28	2,312	35	22,050	11,809
Two earners	23,303	43	2,237	33	32,260	25,334
Three earners	5,317	10	527	8	40,374	32,984
Four earners or more	2,263	4	218	3	51,309	38,143

Source: U.S. Department of Commerce. Bureau of the Census. Money Income and Poverty Status of Families and Persons in the United States: 1984. Current Population Reports, Series P-60, No. 149. Washington, D.C., Government Printing Office, 1985.

Table 4. Family Income Distributions, 1984

Family income class	White		Black	
	Class (%)	Cumulative (%)	Class (%)	Cumulative (%)
Under $2,500	1.6	1.6	4.7	4.7
$2,500 to $4,999	2.2	3.8	10.1	14.8
$5,000 to $7,499	3.7	7.5	10.2	25.0
$7,500 to $9,999	4.4	11.9	9.0	34.0
$10,000 to $12,499	5.3	17.2	8.3	42.3
$12,500 to $14,499	5.0	22.2	6.6	48.9
$15,000 to $19,999	10.7	32.9	12.3	61.2
$20,000 to $24,999	11.0	43.9	9.4	70.6
$25,000 to $34,999	19.8	63.7	13.1	83.7
$35,000 to $49,999	19.4	83.1	10.5	94.2
$50,000 and over	16.9	100.0	5.8	100.0
Median income	27,686	[1]	15,432	[1]
Mean income	32,422	[1]	18,347	[1]

[1] Not applicable

Source: U.S. Department of Commerce. Bureau of the Census. Money Income and Poverty Status of Families and Persons in the United States: 1984. Current Population Reports, Series P-60, No. 149. Washington, D.C. Government Printing Office, 1985.

Many of the benefits to black households and individuals from tax reform are likely to be overshadowed by the economic impacts of GRH. Since blacks depend more upon direct government support than whites, their income and occupational status are particularly sensitive to reductions in government spending, even in defense. Raises in the income tax threshold may shift more tax burden to middle- and upper-income groups, but the offsetting effects of deficit-reduction measures should also be considered in calculating net benefits from the new tax provisions.

Tax reform is particularly beneficial for middle-income Americans, including blacks. Increasing the standard deduction and personal exemptions, and across-the-board reduction in income tax rates are identified as major aspects of tax relief to this group. The retention of deductions most relevant to middle-income working families in the black community is another. These deductions include the exclusion of employer-provided health benefits and other fringe benefits, deductibility of state and local taxes, and the continued deduction for home mortgage interest.[31]

But, returning to the budget side, much of these benefits depends upon continued levels of employment in middle-income families and households, particularly since a disproportionate number of middle-income blacks works in government-related or government-sponsored occupations and institutions affected by GRH. Federal government support for agencies with substantial black employment — the Postal Service; the Labor Department; the Departments of Health and Human Services, Housing and Urban Development, and Education — and for state and local government has been and will continue to be directly affected by GRH and other efforts to control the deficit.[32]

Another basic concern under both GRH and Tax Reform is the status of children and youth. Table 5 describes the reductions in children and youth-oriented programs described by the Children's Defense Fund. In almost every category, including exempt programs, absolute funding levels for these programs declined. These spending reductions immediately affect family structure and integrity, particularly in the absence of a cost-effective alternative outside of government.

A key concern for black individuals and households is housing. As indicated earlier, discouragement of real estate investments, curtailment of capital gains, and stricter rules on income losses for rental property tend to discourage the development of low-income housing in the black community, just as GRH reductions in the housing and Community Development Block Grants under GRH are occurring.[33] Since blacks tend to occupy rental housing to a much greater extent than whites (Table 6), it is not likely that tax credits for investors in low-income housing can offset disincentives combined with steadily increasing operating costs. Moreover, the National Association of Home Builders predicts a

Table 5.
Children's Survival Bill Programs Cuts Under Gramm-Rudman FY 1986

	FY 1985	FY 1986	G-R FY 1986 Red.	FY 1986 Appr. - G-R Red.
		($ in millions unless noted)		
Child Welfare				
Child Welfare Services	200	207	9	198
Child Abuse	26	26	1	25
Juvenile Justice	70	70	3	67
Runaway Youth	23	23	1	22
Family Violence	6	2.5	.1	2.4
Foster Care and				
Adoption Assistance	552.6	549.6	b	
Child Care				
Head Start	1.075 bill.	1.087 bill.	47	1.04 bill.
Title XX Social				
Services	2.75 bill.	2.7 bill.	116	2.58 bill.
School Age Child Care	0	5	.2	4.8
Health				
Maternal and Child				
Health Block Grant	478	478	21	457
Family Planning	143	143	6	137
Immunization				
Stockpile	42.3	47.4	2	45
Grants	4	4	.2	3.8
Community Health				
Centers	383	400	4[c]	396
Migrant Health				
Centers	44.3	45.4	.5[b]	44.9
Mental Health				
Alcohol, Drug Abuse				
and Mental Health				
Block Grant	493.6	491	21	470
Community Support	10.5	12.5	.5	12
(includes Child and				
Adolescent Services				
Program)				
Education				
Chapter I	3.69 bill.	3.69 bill.	159	3.53 bill.
Education of the				
Handicapped	1.32 bill.	1.41 bill.	61	1.35 bill.
Magnet Schools	75	75	3.2	71.8
Bilingual Education	173	173	7.4	166
Employment				
Job Training				
Partnership Act	3.75 bill.	3.46 bill.	149	3.31 bill
Summer Youth	825	665	29	636
Job Corps	617	640	28	612

[a] Cuts in the listed programs under Gramm-Rudman in FY 1986 are 4.3%.

[b] Special rules apply.

[c] Cut limited to 1% in FY 1986.

Source: Children's Defense Fund

rent increase of 28 percent in new developments as a result of tax reform.[34] Whether for new or existing housing, it is not clear that the combination of GRH and Tax Reform will encourage rapid development of low-income housing and, consequently, accommodation to the needs of urban blacks.

Table 6
Total Firms and Black-Owned Firms in the U.S. by Industrial Category

Industry	Total industry no. firms 1981 (thousands)	No. black-owned firms 1982 (thousands)	%firms black-owned (%)	Annual gross receipts black-owned firms, 1982 ($ millions)	% annual gross receipts black-owned firms (%)
Total all U.S. industries	13,858	339	2.4	12,444	0.2
Agricultural services, forestry, & fishing	466	5	1.1	129	0.2
Mining	208	1	3	37	4
Construction	1,444	23[1]	1.6[3]	995	0.3[4]
Manufacturing	538	4	0.7	988	4
Transportation & public utilities	565	24	4.2	795	0.1
Wholesale trade	647	4	0.6	859	4
Retail trade	2,728	84	3.1	4,119	0.4
Finance, insurance, & real estate	2,059	15	0.7	748	4
Selected services	4,969	147	3.0	3,249	0.8
Industries not classified	2	33	3	526	3

[1] Less than 1,000.
[2] Not indicated in data used.
[3] Not applicable.
[4] Below 0.1%.

Source: U.S. Department of Commerce. Bureau of the Census. Statistical Abstract of the United States, 1985. Washington, D.C., Government Printing Office, 1984. U.S. Department of Commerce. Bureau of the Census. 1982 Survey of Minority Owned Business Enterprises. Washington, D.C., Government Printing Office, 1985.

GRH/Tax Reform Impacts On Black Institutions

As Ellis and Calbert indicate, the social institutions and processes within which individuals live and work are important determinants of their earning potentials, safety, health, and overall quality of life. The effects of projected budget and tax policy changes on black businesses, black education and educational institutions, municipal bureaucracies under black influence, black participation in the legal and medical professions, and black churches are all essential to continued resource development and cultivation in the black political economy.[35]

Three major institutions are essential: black businesses, black-managed municipalities, and black charitable and community-based institutions. As Table 6 indicates, black businesses are a small proportion of both the total number of businesses in the United States and the proportion of total gross receipts generated by such businesses.[36] Black-owned firms tend to be comparatively small, with average annual gross receipts in the range of $35,000 to $40,000. Key provisions of both GRH and Tax Reform impacting on black business include:

(1) *Changes in the capital cost recovery provisions.* Transformation of the Accelerated Cost Recovery System (ACRS) into shorter term economic depreciation deeply affects firms, including black businesses, with significant investment in machinery and heavy equipment.

(2) *Retroactive repeal of the investment tax credit.* Although most black businesses have relatively little capital investment, retroactive repeal of the investment tax credit on equipment, machinery, and other productive technologies does not affect black businesses in the aggregate as much as other large and small U.S. businesses. However, relatively larger black businesses involved in manufacturing, data processing, and computer work, transportation, and other activities requiring substantial investment in either new equipment or in retrofitting equipment will be affected negatively by this provision.

(3) *Lower tax rates.* Depending upon the nature and quality of legal and accounting support black businesses have access to, lower tax rates will generally assist black businesses. However, since more than 70 percent of black businesses with $500,000 annual gross receipts or more rely substantially, if not predominantly, on government contracts for revenue, GRH reductions in fiscal years 1986 through 1989 can cancel any advantage in disposable income black businesses realize under tax reform.[37]

(4) *Changes in the deductibility of business expenses.* Changes in the nature and amount of allowable expenses businesses deduct can have a significant impact on cash flow, staff and professional development, and purchase, rental, or leasing of goods and services. For example, business and other professionals are allowed to deduct business-related expenses only when they exceed two percent of the adjusted gross income. For a black business with gross receipts of $200,000 in a tax year, business expenses must reach at least $2,000 in the same year to be deductible fully. However, most black busi-

nesses incur high business expenses and should have little difficulty meeting this criterion.

A second key category of black institutions affected both by GRH and Tax Reform is black-managed municipalities and other local governments. As Table 7 indicates, black local officials — those in cities, counties, local school districts, and special districts — constitute more than 90 percent of all black elected officials. They are often expected by blacks to exhibit a special advocacy of black civic and community interests and by whites to manage beyond public reproach.[38]

Table 7. Black Elected Officials in the United States, 1970–1984

Year			Office			
	Total	% Growth over Previous Period	U.S. and State Legisla-tures	City and County Offices	Law Enforce-ment	Educa-tion
1970	1,472	—	182	715	213	362
1972	2,264	53.8	224	1,108	263	669
1973	2,621	15.8	256	1,264	334	767
1974	2,991	14.2	256	1,602	340	793
1975	3,503	17.2	299	1,878	387	939
1976	3,979	13.6	299	2,274	412	994
1977	4,311	8.3	316	2,497	447	1,051
1978	4,503	4.5	316	2,595	454	1,138
1979	4,584	1.8	315	2,647	486	1,136
1980	4,890	6.7	326	2,832	526	1,206
1981	5,014	2.5	343	2,863	549	1,259
1982	5,115	2.0	342	2,951	563	1,259
1983	5,559	8.7	386	3,197	607	1,369
1984	5,654	1.7	396	3,259	636	1,363
Overall growth 1970–1984	4,182	284.1%	117.6%	355.8%	198.6%	276.5%

Source: Joint Center for Political Studies. Black Elected Officials: A National Roster. Washington, Joint Center for Political Studies, issued annually.

However, the combination of GRH and Tax Reform puts many black officials in a double bind. The increased taxation of formerly tax-exempt municipal bonds will clearly hurt infrastructural and other development in these cities. Simultaneously, GRH block grant and other federal grant reductions will make capital financing a major challenge. Although the deductibility of state and local income and property taxes is retained, state and local sales and excise taxes are no longer deductible. The consequence is that referenda and legislative proposals that include such taxes as a financing mechanism are likely to receive less support from taxpayers, just as the demand for the kinds of services these mechanisms support increases. These negative consequences of federal spending and taxing policy influence black access to and negotiation with state government and other actors in the intergovernmental process.[39]

The negotiation of local black elected officials with state government is essential because of *the issue of state tax conformity.* State tax conformity is the extent to which states reflect federal tax law changes in their own state tax codes. According to *Washington Post* staff writer, T.R. Reid, beginning in 1987, taxpayers in 28 states and the District of Columbia will face some version of the Windfall Syndrome, in which federal tax law will drive state taxes up, yielding a fiscal windfall for state treasuries — and tough political problems for governors and legislators.[40]

A preliminary report prepared by the staff of the Washington, D.C.-based Advisory Commission on Intergovernmental Relations (ACIR) estimates that the "mirror image" effect of tax overhaul, in which a decrease in federal personal income taxes tends to cause an increase in state taxes, would raise the average tax bill by seven percent or more in 14 states and by smaller percentages in 14 others and the District of Columbia.

Black elected officials in cities, counties, school boards, and special districts will need to monitor and, where possible, mitigate any adverse impacts on their constituencies resulting from state conformity. Where not successful in mitigation efforts or where adverse impacts on blacks are minimal, these officials should demand an appropriate share of windfall revenues through subventions to local jurisdictions.

A final category of black institutional impacts affected by both GRH and Tax Reform is charitable, educational, and community organizations. Black institutions relying substantially on charitable contributions for their financial resources will be adversely impacted by Tax Reform's prohibition on these deductions for non-itemizers. This is a significant income source for such institutions and comes from both blacks and other benefactors. Table 8 provides some insight into the proportion of blacks and whites who itemized income tax returns. Because of the reduction in tax brackets in the new tax provisions, more taxpayers are less likely to itemize than under current law.

It is too early to forecast real dollar declines in revenues that may result from this crucial change in the tax code, although it has been clear for almost five years that the level and kind of grants, contracts, loans, and other support made available to black churches, community organizations, educational institutions, and other human service institutions have been steadily declining. GRH and the current philosophy of the Reagan Administration towards federal support of these institutions will continue the pattern of retrenchment among these key institutions.

Macroeconomic Impacts on the Black Community

The combination of GRH reductions and both progressive and regressive impacts of tax reform on black individuals/households and black institutions

Table 8. Individual Federal Income Tax Returns, Adjusted Gross Income, and Form of Deduction, 1982

Adjusted gross income category	Total returns, in 1982 (thousands)	% of returns with itemized deductions 1982	% of blacks in income category, 1982	% of whites in income category, 1984
Less than $15,000	49,299	10.4	48.9	22.2
$15,000 to $24,999	19,338	38.5	21.7	21.7
$25,000 or more	26,701	78.1	29.4	56.1
TOTAL	95,337	35.1	100.0	100.0

Source: Computations from (1) Department of the Treasury. Internal Revenue Service. Individual income tax returns, 1982. Publication 79. October, 1984, and, (2) U.S. Department of Commerce. Bureau of the Census. Money Income. CRS-67. Poverty Status of Families and Persons in the United States: 1984. Current Population Reports, Series P-60, No. 149. Washington, D.C., Government Printing Office, 1985.

constitutes a macroeconomic impact on the black community, which is largely negative. Coming back to the Ilchman-Uphoff model, marginal declines in income resulting from budget retrenchment, tax and expenditure limitations at the state and local level, and the new tax reform legislation pose serious challenges to the cultivation of social, economic, and political resources in the black political economy. Early indications are that federal budget reductions are likely to continue while the realities of tax reform are realized.

When budget and tax impacts are considered together, the minimal benefits of tax reform for some black household and institutional taxpayers are likely to be canceled both by negative impacts of tax reform and deficit reduction. However, taxpayer adjustments to both deficit reduction and tax reform are still in progress. The consequences of these short-term and longer-term adjustments are, as yet, not fully discernible.[41]

RECOMMENDED STRATEGIES

Given the combined impact of GRH, other federal budget decisions, and tax reform, the following recommendations are proposed:

(1) Tax reform legislation should be closely monitored as it is implemented to identify both anticipated and unanticipated impacts on the black community that are significant and should be addressed;

(2) Serious review and analysis of the Congressional Black Caucus' Alternative Budget should be carried out in every major black institution and among black elected officials and managers. It is the most thoughtful and systematic analysis and statement of budgetary priorities for all U.S. citizens now available.

(3) Black business needs support in both the federal budget and in tax reform legislation. Continued support for the Small Business Administration's management of the 8(a) program,[42] Small Business Development Centers, and technical assistance programs to black businesses are needed. Far from being abolished, the SBA should be strengthened to support small and minority businesses during this turbulent period of fiscal transition. Moreover, small and minority businesses should be exempted from repeal of the investment tax credit when their expenditures on such equipment equal or exceed five percent of their net worth. In this time of shrinking manufacturing activity in the U.S., no tax or budget policy should frustrate investments in capital equipment, new technology, and retrofitting of old plants and tools.

(4) A national fiscal hotline should be developed to monitor the impacts of GRH and tax legislation on charitable, education, and community institutions. This hotline would document the impact of such measures on blacks and would coordinate efforts to lobby for modification of fiscal policy when needed.

The author expresses endless appreciation to the following individuals and institutions for their help in developing this paper: Dr. William Ellis, Congressional Research Service; Dr. Lynn Burbridge, Urban Institute; the staff of Congressman Charles Rangel; the Children's Defense Fund; Dr. Linda F. Williams of the Joint Center for Political Studies; the Office of the Budget, District of Columbia; and Dean Milton Wilson, Howard University. All shortcomings and errors in the article belong to the author.

Black Families In A Changing Society

Andrew Billingsley

INTRODUCTION

The actor and philanthropist Bill Cosby, who has become the nation's leading media symbol of the black family, once complained in mock seriousness when his wife urged him to give a benefit performance for the National Council of Negro Women. He couldn't do that, he argued, because if he did a benefit for the Negro Women, then he would be requested to do one for the black women, and then finally the Afro-American Women. He did show up, of course. And he need not have worried so much about all those organizations. They were all there in the audience as he put in his masterful performance for the NCNW.

Similarly, when Dorothy Height, the heir to Mary McLeod Bethune as president of this federation of some 31 national black women's organizations, called for a national Black Family Reunion Celebration as a fitting 50th anniversary commemoration of the NCNW, not a major black women's organization or black men's organization was missing from the event.

Thus it was that on the second weekend in September 1986, more than 200,000 persons gathered on the mall in the nation's capital for a remarkable event to celebrate the black family. They came to hear speakers, participate in workshops, enjoy cultural events, and listen to specialists on all aspects of black family life. And especially, said Dr. Height, did they come to celebrate the fact of our existence, our survival, our strength, resilience, adaptability, our heritage, the values and coping skills which have enabled us to overcome the worst features of racism and oppression from the larger society and the neglect and abuse from within our own ranks as well.

It was not a protest. The media found this a most difficult demonstration to cover. Searching for a protest angle, they found it difficult to write about a black family celebration. Several of the prominent speakers, including Alex Haley; Lerone Bennett, Jr.; Joyce Ladner; and Dr. Height reported that the journalists who interviewed them could not quite grasp the idea of a black family celebration. The reporters kept wanting to talk about teenage pregnancy, female-headed households, and black dependence upon government aid. They had their own agenda, which they had inherited from faulty scholarship and specious policy debates about black families. Consequently the national majority media did little to inform the nation about this significant event—larger than the celebrated March on Washington. Despite this large crowd, Dr. Height has reported that not a single police incident was recorded!!

What the Black Family Reunion demonstrated more than anything else is that black family life is more complex, varied, and multifaceted than generally portrayed. Walking about the grounds of the mall, the sensitive observer could see nuclear, extended, and augmented families; underclass, working class, and middle class families—the full range of black existence in contemporary America.

Many people were no doubt encouraged to attend this celebration by the August 1986 issue of *Ebony* magazine, which was devoted entirely to the black family.[1] It was the most comprehensive treatment of black families of any of the leading national publications. Most of the national publications had focused exclusively on the problems of teenage pregnancy, female-headed families, and the like, generally on patterns of irresponsible behavior. *Ebony* did not ignore these subjects; it covered them, along with other subjects. Most national publications gave a picture of the underclass—that one-third of black families at the bottom of the economic and social ladder. *Ebony* covered those, plus the one-third who are in the black blue-collar working class, and the other third who may be termed the black middle class. Other publications stressed the responsibility of black people for their own problems and for the solutions to them. *Ebony* stressed both black responsibility and national responsibility.

And beyond all this the Black Family Reunion and *Ebony* stressed optimism and hope; that if the national community and the black community both take family life seriously and do what they can do best, black families will be able to overcome the crippling consequences of their present circumstances. Already plans are being made for the 1987 Reunion for the same second weekend in September; it will be in the nation's capital *and* in several other large cities with black mayors, including Los Angeles, Detroit, and Atlanta.

The Black Family Reunion and the special issue of *Ebony* were just tips of the iceberg of concern being expressed throughout the black community, since the National Urban League and the NAACP convened the National Black Family Summit at Fisk University in May 1984.[2] It brought together representatives of 175 national black organizations along with a cadre of black scholars to examine ten major aspects of life impinging on the future of black families and to set a national agenda to deal with these matters. Shortly thereafter, at Spelman College in Atlanta, a cluster of women's and children's organizations convened a series of workshops and plenary sessions to design a national strategy to address the phenomenon of teenage parenthood. These organizations included the Children's Defense Fund, the National Council of Negro Women, the Delta Sigma Theta sorority, and the Coalition of 100 Black Women.

Other organizations which have begun to call attention to the need for both policies and local initiatives to enhance the functioning of black families and their children include: the National Black Child Development Institute, the National Association of Social Workers, Planned Parenthood, the National YWCA, the National Education Association, Family Services of America, and the Congressional Black Caucus.

Black churches are once again expressing their historic role in black family life. Two years ago in Washington, the National Congress of Black Churches focused on a nationwide series of church-sponsored programs to assist black families. In the same city, the Shiloh Baptist Church, with a history of community involvement, has built a Family Life Center, initiated by the Rev. Henry C. Gregory III.

Among the many family-related programs is the Black Male Youth Project. The men of the church have adopted a group of youth from the surrounding inner-city neighborhood to help them achieve healthy, positive, and safe passages to manhood. With the assistance of the city Health Department, the Agnes E. Meyer Foundation, and the Ford Foundation, this project is able to retain a small staff and to conduct a series of workshops on a wide range of topics including values, sexuality, and drugs; it also provides after-school study hall, recreation, and cultural activities.

If this activity in the black community represents an emphasis on self-help and positive values for black family development, it also brings to the fore a special approach to the national crisis in the nation in which black families are enmeshed.

ELEMENTS OF THE BLACK FAMILY CRISIS

What, then, are those major trends which define the crisis of black family life? Prominent among them:

1. *Poverty is once again a prominent feature of Afro-American family life, effectively undercutting the struggle for stability*

    The poverty rate declined dramatically during the decade of the 1960s, from a high of 55 percent of all Afro-American families in 1959 to a low of 32 percent by 1970; it inched down to 31 percent by 1980, then shot up dramatically to 36 percent by 1982, before easing back to 34 percent by 1984 and 31 percent in 1985. Among the black population, poverty had come to rest most heavily on black women and children in the major cities of the nation.[3]

2. *Unemployment continues to plague the black family*

    Among black men, women, and youth, unemployment has reached disastrous levels not experienced in the general community since the Great Depression of the 1930s.[4]

    Among black men, unemployment declined dramatically during the 1960s, from a high of 9.6 percent in 1960 to a low of 3.7 percent by the end of the decade. Then it soared to 11.3 percent by 1980 and to 18.9 percent in 1982, the highest in postwar history. In 1985, the third year of economic recovery after the recession, the official unemployment rate for black Americans was 15 percent. Actual unemployment, including so-called discouraged workers, was much higher.

    Among black women, unemployment declined from 8.3 percent in 1960 to 5.8 percent by the end of the decade; then it climbed to 11 percent by 1980 and 17.6 percent by 1983 before declining to 13 percent in 1985.

    Among black youth, unemployment has been even more devastating. From a high of 24.4 percent in 1960, unemployment in this group actually fluctuated upward and landed back at 24 percent by the end of the decade before soaring again to a high of 35.4 percent in 1980 and to an astronomical 40 percent by 1982, which remained steady through 1985. As a consequence, there are hundreds of thousands of black youth between 18 and 25 years of age who have never had a full-time job and are destined never to have one. When the "discouraged" workers are considered, the number out of work nearly doubles.

3. *Low family income among employed blacks continues its downward drift*

Earning about 55 percent of the median income of white families in 1960, black families witnessed a modest increase—to 60 percent in 1970 and 62 percent by 1975. That median income took a nosedive—to 58 percent by 1980, then to 55 percent by 1982 and to 56 percent by 1985.[5] Yet, black families must function in the same economic markets as white families, with half the white family income. Meanwhile, since 1980, the gap between the lowest two-fifths of the earning distribution and the highest two-fifths has widened still further in favor of upper-income families.

4. *Family structure has undergone dramatic changes in recent years*

Of all the changes in black family life during the past two decades, changes in family structure have been the most extensive and have had the most far-reaching consequences on black children. The nuclear family has continued to lose ground under the combined assault of external and internal forces. Married-couple families, which accounted for the overwhelming majority of black families in 1960—78 percent—declined dramatically to 68 percent by the end of the decade and even more dramatically to 54 percent by 1980; now, they are a bare majority of 53 percent.

During the 1960s, when the economy was growing, single, female-headed families accounted for only 22 percent of all black families; that figure climbed to 27 percent by the end of the decade, and to an astronomical 42 percent by 1980, 43 percent by 1982, and 44 percent by 1985. This dramatic increase can be attributed to the ever-increasing divorce rate, separation rate, early death of black men, and rate of unmarried parenthood.

The impact of these structural changes in family on the well-being of black children has been a major focus of scholarly research and public policy debate during the past two decades.

5. *Teenage pregnancy is a major problem in the black community*

Teenage parenthood among black families has been described as epidemic.[6] While the actual rate of births to unmarried teenagers has declined from a high of 96.9 per thousand teenagers in 1970 to 87 per thousand in 1982, the rate is still enormously high. If it continues, a majority of black women will become pregnant before their twentieth birthday. Most will be unmarried.

6. *The underclass is alive but not at all well in Black America*

The black underclass continues to grow, due in part to extensive poverty, unemployment, and family instability. An examination of the 100 cities with the largest black populations shows that the problem is pervasive. Composed of those families and individuals at the bottom of the economic and social scales—perhaps a third of all black families—this sector of the population experiences an enormous portion of suffering.

7. *Inadequate housing and the black community*

Homelessness and inadequate housing became scandals in all of the major cities of the nation in the 1980s, with black families overrepresented in this systematic deprivation.

The goal initiated by Congress in 1949 of a "decent home and suitable living environment for every American family" was as laudable as its implementation has been lamentable. While some progress has been made on housing quality and housing discrimination, both matters remain unfinished national agenda items.

More profound still, however, is the matter of housing affordability. According to economist Wilhelmena Leigh, affordability "has become the key housing issue of the seventies and eighties."[7] Even families with jobs and modest income are required to pay more than 40 percent of their earnings for housing; they are clearly in a state of severe housing deprivation.[8] By 1986, homelessness had moved from a personal and family tragedy to a national scandal, as characterized by the Catholic Bishops of Maryland.[9]

8. *Black American families suffer greater health hazards and receive less adequate health care*

The health care system has a major and unequal impact on black families. In 1983 only 44.1 percent of blacks who received health care received it from a private physician in his or her office, while 26.5 percent received health care in a hospital emergency room and 9.7 percent in the outpatient clinics. Among white patients who received health care, 57 percent received it from private physicians, 13 percent from emergency rooms, and 16 percent from outpatient clinics. Thus, "Blacks and low income people of all races rely on emergency room and outpatient clinics more and use doctors' offices and the telephone less." [10]

It is striking to note, however, that the above picture represents considerable improvement for black and low-income families after the introduction of Medicaid and Medicare in 1965. In 1964, for example, 3.6 percent of blacks and 4.7 percent of whites made visits to physicians. By 1980 the proportions were almost even at 4.6 percent of blacks and 4.8 percent of whites. The races began to diverge slightly again, however, after 1980 such that by 1983 the proportions were 4.8 percent for blacks and 5.1 percent for whites.

9. *Black students are again dropping out of school in alarming numbers*

One of the untold stories of progress during the 1960s and 1970s is the extent to which black youth and their families took advantage of the openings in educational opportunity wrought in part by a hundred years of struggle. Black youth stayed in high school in record numbers. In 1960, for example, only six percent of all high school students in the nation were black, though blacks constituted about 12 percent of the school-age population. By 1981 this had increased dramatically to 10 percent, within striking distance of closing the gap. By 1981 black adults had a median of 12.1 years of schooling or the equivalent of a high school education, which was only half a year behind the median educational level of white adults.

After 1980, however, regression set in. In many cities the black high school drop-out rate is now well over 50 percent. College enrollment has also dropped dramatically, particularly among black men who are outnumbered by black women in college by more than 100,000.[11]

10. *Prisons, a black warehouse*

More young black men are in federal, state, and local prisons than are in college, and it costs the government more than three times as much to keep them there. We must explore and solve this critical problem.

11. *The military—the black employer of last resort*

Black men enlist and re-enlist in all branches of the services in such numbers that they now constitute 20 percent of all armed services personnel. However, they are grossly underrepresented in the officer corps.

12. *The black family continues to achieve despite overwhelming odds*

Finally, despite all the odds, a majority of black families manage to avoid poverty and deprivation. A majority of blacks live within the family structure. Husband/wife families earn distinctly above the poverty level. A third of black families has reached middle-class status, and another third is in the steadily employed blue-collar working class.

Married couple families where both partners are educated and in the labor force have made substantial progress. Married couple families with two or more working adults who constitute a third of all black families had median incomes of 75 percent of similar white family income in 1969. This had increased to 80 percent by 1982.[12] Educational, occupational, and geographic mobility helped to account for these trends.

Even in the late 1980s—at the height of concern about the growing underclass and the simultaneous growth of the middle class—there is a general recognition that achieving black families are in all socio-economic groups. Even in the midst of the worst conditions in the inner city, achieving families seem to rise out of the ash heaps of history and contemporary conditions to develop high levels of family stability and capacities to meet the needs of their children for economic support, for nurturance, and for guidance.

These, then, are the major trends which help to describe black American family life in the 1980s: rising levels of poverty, declining levels of income, rising levels of unemployment, declining levels of family stability, a rising underclass, a struggling middle class, and a strong element of achieving families. These are the conditions of family life for America's largest minority—fully a century and a half after the Emancipation Proclamation; a half century after the New Deal and the Fair Deal; a quarter century after the onset of the New Frontier, the Great Society, and the most successful civil rights movement in history; a decade after "benign neglect" and "Watergate"; and six years into the Reagan Revolution.

A SEARCH FOR MEANING: A THEORETICAL PERSPECTIVE

Does the seemingly intractable poverty rates mean that poverty will always be with us? What is the most appropriate social strategy to figure out how to live with it?

Does the skyrocketing unemployment in the black community mean that black men, women, and youth have lost their will to work; and that consequently what they need is a new infusion of values; that when they return to those basic values, they will be able to solve their own unemployment problems, as a number of white and black conservative economists have suggested?

Does the astronomical rise in female-headed families mean that Moynihan was correct in his 1965 Report on Black Families,[13] and that if black leaders and scholars had not criticized his theories, the nation would have responded in ways to stem the erosion of husband/wife families, as a number of analysts have argued since 1980?

Does the persistence of the underclass mean that the black middle class has abandoned the ghetto and should not have done so?

Does the rise of the black middle class mean that racism is dead or has drastically declined in America, and that all members of the black underclass need to do is prepare themselves with values and skills, and they, too, will be able to overcome the class barriers which constrain them?

These are among the questions which fuel public debate during the 1980s.

"Tangle of Pathology" Thesis

Several analysts and media specialists have concluded that the above trends mean Moynihan was correct in his famous 1965 analysis of black families. One of the most prominent examples of this occurred in February 1986, the Bill Moyers' CBS docudrama on "The Vanishing Black Family." The program gave the impression that teenage pregnancy was only a black problem, and that the black community was largely apathetic toward solving it. The program gave no recognition to black teens and their parents who cope successfully with the awesome contradictory messages about sex in this society. And it showed no white teens who succumbed to these pressures, despite the fact that white teens in America have a higher rate of out-of-wedlock births than those of any of the other western industrialized nations.

In his 1965 report, Moynihan had observed that nine percent of white families and 22 percent of black families were female-headed families. These facts were not challenged by any of the social scientists or black leaders who criticized his report. It was his interpretation of these facts with his famous "tangle of pathology" thesis that was challenged. On observing the above facts, Moynihan concluded that the meaning was as follows: "The white family has achieved a high degree of stability and is maintaining that stability."[14] Then he observed that "by contrast, the family structure of lower-class Negroes is highly unstable, and in many urban centers, is approaching complete breakdown."[15] Moreover, Moynihan concluded that the cause of the tangle of pathology is the weakness of the family structure. "Once or twice removed, it will be found to be the principal source of most of the aberrant, inadequate, or antisocial behavior that did not establish but now serves to perpetuate the cycle of poverty and deprivation."[16]

As was pointed out at the time, one of the many problems with Moynihan's thesis was that he ignored the impact of social class, in what we have described as an overly simplistic two-way typology of white and black, stable and unstable families. It is now clear that if he had observed the social class dimension, it would have been clear as early as 1960 that among white families in the aggregate, female-headed families constituted only nine percent. If he had looked at low-income white families, he would have found the percentage of female-headed families to be 20 percent. Moreover, by 1973 this had risen to 33 percent, and among low-income white families with children under 18, the proportion of female-headed families was 48 percent.[17] And while these proportions were always higher among black families even controlling for income, it is doubtful that Moynihan could have concluded that female-headed families were a black problem, and that white female-headed families were okay.

Much to his credit, Senator Moynihan has now abandoned his "tangle of pathology" thesis, even as others try to revive it. In his new book, *Family and Nation*, based on lectures he gave in 1985, twenty years later, he observed that, "In 1965 I could state that 'the United States is approaching a new crisis in race relations because the number of nonwhite families with a female head has reached 21 percent.' " "By 1984," he continues, "the census would report that for white families with children this proportion had reached nearly 20 percent, up from nine percent in 1960 and 10 percent in 1970 . . . . This is not to dismiss the black-white disparity . . . . The gap has widened. Even so, what was a crisis for one group in 1960 is now the general condition."[18] Clearly, if he looked at low-income white families, these numbers would be higher still.

Thus, Moyers makes the same mistake in 1986 that Moynihan made in 1965 when he concluded that the black family was deteriorating while the white family remained strong and stable, and that the reason for this deterioration was to be found within the structure of the black family itself. Neither Moynihan nor Moyers seemed to recognize that the traditional American family is in disarray and that the source of that deterioration is in the structure of American society, not inside black families. The trends which cause this disarray started sometime in the middle 1950s, have intensified since then, and have yet to run their course—pushing out of their traditional mold all our social institutions, including black and white families.

The Migration Thesis

Another view on the meaning of the crisis among black families has been presented by Nicholas Lemann. Writing in the June and July 1986 issues of *The Atlantic Monthly*, Lemann has presented a penetrating analysis and graphic picture of the isolated, insulated inner-city black poor. He takes sharp issue with both of the prevailing views that poverty is caused by welfare, advanced by Charles Murray and others; and that poverty is caused by the lack of jobs—a view with which the author and increasing numbers of other social scientists have been associated. Lemann advanced his own theory about migration from the rural south in the vein of E. Franklin Frazier's earlier work with a new twist which included the migration of the black middle class from the inner city. Thus, striking an increasingly popular theme, Lemann concluded that "It is the flight of middle-class blacks from the ghettos" which has left "a disastrously isolated underclass."

Lemann joins with others in extolling the moral values and other virtues which account for the rise of the black middle class and scolds them for not sharing these values with their less fortunate brothers and sisters. "Of the millions of black Americans who have risen from poverty to the middle class since the mid-sixties, virtually all have done so by embracing bourgeois values and leaving the ghetto. So it is worth explaining why black and white leaders have fiercely resisted telling these secrets to the people left behind."[19]

While in the past it has been fashionable for some to blame the black poor for their own poverty status, a new theory is emerging which blames the black middle class for the poverty, isolation, and family instability among the black poor.

Now a number of fallacies exists with this new theory. First, it exaggerates the numbers of the black middle class who have left the inner city and moved to the white suburbs. Many never lived in the inner city. And many others still live there. Moreover, whatever their mobility pattern, the black middle class is not sufficiently large and powerful enough to make the difference ascribed.

A second fallacy is the assumption and assertion that moral values account for the ascendancy of the black middle class and the absence of these values on the part of the poor accounts for their lack of progress. A more careful reading of both social science and the black experience suggests otherwise. The poor have the same basic American values of stability, achievement, and upward mobility that other Americans have. It is their inability to attain these values which distinguishes them from the others, and this inability is a highly structured feature of the society at large.

But the most fatal flaw in this thesis of black middle class flight is that it exaggerates the resources which they took with them from the inner city and ignores completely other more powerful forces which took flight from the inner city long before the black middle class: namely, the white middle class and industry. Both of these forces left the inner city in massive numbers during the past 20 years, taking with them enormous resources including tax base, accumulated wealth, jobs, and role models. A 1986 study by the National Alliance of Business has concluded that this trend is likely to continue beyond the year 2000. "Low skill jobs associated with manufacturing will be moving to the suburbs, away from their traditional location in the central cities. Given existing transportation systems, this will leave unskilled workers in the cities unable to reach these sources of employment."[20]

While the theory of the abandonment of the inner city has merit, it would be enhanced considerably if it embraced a broader range of forces which deserted the inner city and placed less exclusive blame on the fledgling, precarious black middle class. Clearly, the black middle class, working class, and underclass have responsibility, opportunity, and resources for self-help. We have termed this the "internal system" of social reform. But just as clearly, the external system has even more responsibility, opportunity, and resources. Congresswoman Patricia Schroeder of Colorado seems to understand this better than many others. In a recent commentary, she observed that, "Yet family and marital patterns have been influenced by economic and cultural changes that have swept the western world, rather than the other way round."[21]

Problems in the Black Middle Class

Most careful observers of the black experience know that even middle class, high achieving black families are not without their problems. A study by Lawrence Gary, Lula A. Beatty, and their associates at Howard University shows that point with great clarity.[22]

These researchers studied a group of 50 strong, stable, achieving black families in the Washington, D.C., area. The families were strong in the view of the community leaders who nominated them for the study, strong in their own eyes, and strong in the assessment of the researchers. They were stable, had high salaries, high levels of education, occupational status, small numbers of children, and were highly religious. Indeed, the researchers observed that "The study families possessed all the characteristics of strong families put forth by Billingsley and Hill and as found by Scanzoni, Royce and Turner, and Christopherson and Stinnet."[23] Nevertheless, and despite their remarkable achievement, these families also discussed with the researchers a number of their problems.

The researchers observed that, "one of the most revealing aspects of the study was the extent to which these stable, strong families had experienced problems and expressed dissatisfaction with some areas of their lives . . . . Everyone complained of financial, marital, and child problems. Most were also more dissatisfied with their jobs than they were with any other aspect of their lives. Programs, therefore, need to be developed that address these areas."[24] All of which means that it is not the absence of problems which characterize strong families but the ability and resources to resolve and manage their problems which make them strong.

Moreover, few of these families found help from external agencies. They turned to their own resources for help, including their nuclear, extended, and augmented family members. Thus, before we advocate too strongly policies which will require all black middle class families to return to the inner city to help lend their values and assistance to their less fortunate brothers and sisters, we might give some further attention to public and private policies and programs to help them with their own needs in both the instrumental and expressive domains of family functioning.

PATTERNS OF SELF-SUFFICIENCY
AMONG ACHIEVING BLACK FAMILIES

While we have learned much about second and third generations of low-income, female-headed families, neither social scientists nor policy analysts have paid much attention to intergenerational processes among upwardly mobile or achieving families in the black community. Harriette McAdoo's study of 178 middle class black families in the Washington, D.C., area is a groundbreaking study which provides insight into these processes.[25]

Specifically, Dr. McAdoo found four distinct patterns of upward mobility among her subjects. One group of parents—nine percent of the total—was old-line black middle class having had middle class parents and grandparents. Another small group composed of six percent of the total achieved its status on the strength of the head start received from middle class parents who had moved up from their working class origins. A third group—23 percent of the total—represented a three-generational upward mobility pattern in which their grandparents were lower class, their parents working class, and they became middle class. Finally, the largest group of parents comprising 62 percent of the total represented the new middle class, in that both their grandparents and their parents were working class, and they became the first middle class generation. This is no doubt the most characteristic pattern of upward mobility for the contemporary black middle class.

It has been often found and asserted by social scientists that this cultural pattern of sharing basic necessities was a dysfunctional trait among black families holding down their upward strivings. It has been sometimes assumed that this widely recognized propensity, as a feature of lower-class black family life, has been a cause of poverty and that one reason for the success of the black middle class is that it had left this crippling practice of sharing behind. McAdoo's study, therefore, made an important contribution to clarifying this question.

The results from these parents indicate that this middle income group, unlike Albert McQueen's working class sample and Carol Stack's poverty sample, did not have to pull away from the reciprocal obligations of their extended kin-help network in order to realize their own mobility goals. Families in more vulnerable states would be unable to meet their own needs and those of the families and may have to separate, at least during the period of mobility. These parents continued their close interaction and help exchange pattern before, during, and after mobility. Many felt that they would have been unable to obtain their education without extensive kin-help and therefore do not feel that the reciprocal obligations are excessive. The cultural pattern is not only associated with poor economic status but is maintained after entrance into more secure status; because of the lack of wider community support, it still performs a valuable supportive function for the families. Our data support the view of Robert Hill, Andrew Billingsley, Carol Stack, and Joyce Aschenbrenner who have pointed out that the extended family pattern is not just a structural coping tactic but has evolved into a strong valuable cultural pattern.[26]

Another perspective on black achievement is provided by James P. Smith. After examining census data and data from the University of Michigan's Panel Study on Income Dynamics, he describes the existence of three socioeconomic levels among black families and the changing relationship between what he terms the poor, the middle class, and the affluent. Specifically, he shows the rise of the black middle class and the relative decline of poor black families since 1940.[27]

For poor families, Smith utilized the federal government's definition of poverty which began in 1963 and is adjusted for inflation and family size. For affluent families he arbitrarily took the annual income of the top 25 percent of white families in 1960 and adjusted annually for inflation, while assigning the middle class to the income range between these two extremes. The black economic class distribution is depicted in the table below:

Table I.

INCOME GROUP STATUS OF BLACK FAMILIES
1940-1980

	1980	1970	1960	1950	1940
Poor	30%	32%	48%	54%	71%
Middle Class	59%	59%	49%	42%	26%
Affluent	11%	9%	6%	4%	3%

While these income divisions are arbitrary, they do have the advantage of consistency and therefore show the major trends in family income over the past

40 years. While income is not exactly the same as social class, social status and social standing can be related to income. Moreover, it is clear according to recent analyses that income is far from the same as wealth, and wealth is a more reliable indicator of social standing, social position, and economic well-being, than income. With these reservations, the data compiled by Smith do provide a general indication of the changing economic situation of black families during the period 1940–1980.

INSIDE THE BLACK MIDDLE CLASS

The above data make it clear that there is, indeed, a black middle class and that the black middle class has expanded over the years and continues to grow. The data also clearly show that the black middle class is not a homogeneous grouping of families but rather a varied and complex category.

Apart from other factors, there are still other dimensions of life for black middle class families that make this what we have termed a "precarious middle class." In a number of major respects, the black middle class is more vulnerable to the threat of downward mobility than the more established white middle class.

In addition to the challenge of moving into more secure and independent occupations and accumulating family wealth, black families face a third challenge—transmitting their status and economic well-being to their children. Large numbers of middle-class black families are finding that they have not prepared their children to succeed them or to stand on their shoulders. As a consequence, many families may lose the upward mobility drive which has characterized them since before the end of American slavery.

BLACK FAMILIES AND PUBLIC POLICY

No single, complex public action would do more to strengthen families than a national commitment to a full-time, adequately paid, career-oriented job for every able-bodied man, woman, and youth. A meaningful job not only provides the means of meeting the instrumental needs of the family but also a means of instilling pride, self-reliance, and a sense of importance as well. The validity of this public policy initiative has now almost reached unanimity among the students of black families. William J. Wilson was among the first scholars in recent years to point to the significance of work, jobs, and earned income for the stability and achievement of black families.[28]

The difficulties of developing and maintaining a productive and expanding economy are enormous and only now are beginning to receive the attention they deserve at the highest levels of government and industry.[29]

Thus, as an interim measure, a government-sponsored program of national youth service to provide meaningful, if subsidized, work experience and training would provide a meaningful alternative to the military, which now serves as the employer of the last resort for black youth.[30] Affordable quality child care arrangements both within home and out-of-home day care are indispensable to low- and to moderate-income families, particularly with the new trend of mothers entering the work force.

For those families with young children, the time has come to consider children's allowances. One recommendation, patterned after the program in England, is for the government to pay allowances at the maintenance level to all families with young children and recoup the allotment from middle- and upper-income families through the income tax system. This would have the immediate effect of lifting all those children out of poverty and enabling their parents to meet their basic instrumental needs, which is not now the case.[31]

Moreover, the time has come for comprehensive welfare reform along the lines of programs in Massachusetts, California, and Ohio, which have learned from the successes and the pitfalls of previous approaches, including the "workfare" programs which have been inadequate. The new programs have developed innovative choice-oriented initiatives in education, training, work, health care, child care, and counseling which move welfare mothers toward economic independence.[32]

The program in Massachusetts is in many ways the premier such program. Titled "E.T." for Education and Training Choices, it enables welfare mothers who previously had average welfare benefits of $4,000 a year to move into jobs paying in the neighborhood of $10,000 annually. While not yet adequate, these levels of income clearly bring enormous benefits to all concerned, including the family and the state. Employers have lauded the preparation and support the program provides, which enables them to employ able, dedicated, and productive workers.[33]

There are several features of the Massachusetts program that make it so successful. First, it operates within the framework of an expanding economy. Second, it has the full commitment of the governor and the state government working in cooperation with industry. Third, it offers educational opportunity as a real option. Fourth, it provides training and counseling oriented to the realities of the current and future job markets. Fifth, it provides careful professional supervision and monitoring.

Finally, in addition to welfare reform, there is a strong need for a national policy that would provide affordable housing for low- and moderate-income families, for a national health insurance policy, and for educational reform which, for a beginning, should make Head Start universal.

These state and local experiments plus the advocacy of the Children's Defense Fund and others have encouraged Senators Daniel P. Moynihan (D-N.Y.) and Arlen Specter (R-Pa.) to introduce into Congress Senate Bill 2578, which would provide, "through greater targeting, coordination, and structuring of services, assistance to strengthen severely economically disadvantaged individuals and families by providing greater opportunities for employment preparation which can assist in promoting family economic stability."[34] Congressmen Charles Rangel (D-N.Y.) and Harold Ford (D-Tenn.) have introduced similar legislation in the House. They all recognize with Congressman Augustus Hawkins (D-Cal.) and a growing number of other members of Congress that the time for new family-oriented public policies is long overdue, and a linchpin to any such family policy is a full employment economy and—absent that—a comprehensive jobs program.

CONCLUSION

While the basic responsibility for policies and programs to enhance family life lies within the society at large, and must be resolved there, it is just as clear that a major and continuing role must be played within the black community itself.

The idea of self-help is no stranger to the black community.[35] In our own work we have specified "four levels of opportunity and responsibility for strengthening black families; namely, the individual, the family, the community, and the wider society."[36] Thus, in our view, reforms in the external community and the internal community are inextricably linked together.

Indeed, the modern civil rights movement, far from an outdated anachronism as some would suggest, might better be viewed as an example of people acting on their own behalf, then joining with the forces of the wider society. Perhaps among the many lessons of that period of successful reform is that black progress is most likely to be achieved, maintained, and enhanced when blacks themselves, through their individual and collective capacities, set the agenda and then elicit the indispensable cooperation of others who have both the responsibility and the resources for effective change.

In the years ahead, then, in view of the enormous changes in technology, the transition from industrial to post-industrial society, the changing values of the large society, and the pressures exerted on black families from all sides, extraordinary efforts at self-help within the black community must be combined in ever newer ways with structures of the larger society. Public policy reform is thus inescapably tied to internal reform within the black community.

Social Welfare Reform

Barbara Bryant Solomon

INTRODUCTION

The real American dream is to live in a society experienced by all of its citizens as equitable, just, and compassionate. Our federal system of social welfare programs and services is the primary societal mechanism created to achieve this lofty goal. However, as one author has stated: "In human terms, the program has been a disaster." (Guide to Welfare Reform 1979, p. iv.)

The widening distance between this society's "haves" and "have-nots" is a reflection of a gap between our commitment to meeting human need and our support for specific strategies by which those needs can be met. It is a matter of moving from abstract values to concrete social action which is not easy. For example, there is remarkable agreement among most Americans — black and white — regarding the principle of racial equality. Yet, at the same time, they disagree about how to achieve it. Schuman, Steeh, and Bobo (1985) recently completed a secondary analysis of data on racial attitudes in which attitudes expressed by respondents indicated large and generally consistent movement toward white acceptance of integration in most areas of American life. However, questions which elicited attitudes toward specific implementation strategies revealed a white America that is much less enthusiastic in its support of modes of implementation than in its support of abstract principles.

As a nation, we appear able to tolerate the fact that twenty percent of the population accrues over half the income while the majority of American families are constantly vulnerable to economic disaster. Public assistance payments provide income that is at times as little as 50 percent of what is required to pay for a barely sufficient level of food, shelter, clothing, and fuel while at the same time a handful of persons lives at levels of extraordinary affluence and luxury. Thus, the nation has demonstrated an unwillingness to allocate its considerable resources to increase the access of the poor to what may be termed the necessities of life.

The vulnerability of a large proportion of the population to poverty and its attendant problems may be merely a consequence of our acceptance of enormous inequalities in the ownership and distribution of economic resources as reasonable and just. If so, social welfare reform will need to focus on strategies for raising the consciousness of the public to these gross inequities and for implementing programs that will redistribute income from those with excess income into a resource pool to provide for the collective good. However, this does not take into account the fact that blacks and other minorities are disproportionately represented among the poor. Closing the gap between "haves" and "have nots" will not change the relative position of blacks and whites if racism and consequent discriminatory practices still reserve the lowest end of the socioeconomic ladder for blacks and other minorities. In that case, social welfare reform efforts will also need to continue to incorporate an affirmative action component as well.

This view is based on the perception that the ultimate goal of the social welfare system is the creation of an equitable, just, and compassionate society. Thus, these three concepts will be defined, particularly as they relate to the functioning of the economic system and its impact on family life. This will be followed by a description of the approaches which have been taken to bring about welfare reform but which have not moved us to imminent achievement of that ultimate goal. These approaches will be examined to determine their relative success in maximizing employment and assuring everyone a minimum level of subsistence while promoting and maintaining family stability. Finally, the prospects for achieving welfare reform that is perceived as beneficial by both blacks and whites will be discussed.

DEFINING EQUITY, JUSTICE, AND COMPASSION

In an equitable society, black citizens would have the same opportunities as white citizens to obtain the prerequisites for effective social functioning. At a minimum, these would include (1) the education necessary to develop skills required for effective social functioning, among them occupation skills; (2) employment commensurate with one's skills and for which one is paid a living wage; and (3) adequate support services (e.g., transportation, day care, and health care) when these services are needed to take advantage of educational or employment opportunities. Equity, in this sense, is independent of economic prosperity or recession since it requires only that whatever opportunities exist — few or many — will be available to all regardless of race.

Sowell (1984) contends that the goal of equality of opportunity should be differentiated from the goal of equality of results. The goal of equal opportunity requires that individuals be judged on their qualifications as individuals *without regard* to race, sex, age, etc. In contrast, affirmative action policies seek to achieve some equality of results; i.e., individuals are judged *with regard* to their group membership, and receive preferential or compensatory treatment in some cases in order to achieve a more proportional representation in various institutions and occupations. Sowell condemns equality of results as a goal and contends that it utilizes an all-purpose explanation — racism and discrimination — for the existing inequality of socioeconomic status among blacks and whites. However, these statistical differences may not mean discrimination at all but rather the effect of innumerable demographic, cultural, and geographic differences. From this perspective, an equitable society is only concerned with equality of opportunity rather than equality of results.

Proponents of affirmative action policies argue that the only way in which equality of opportunity is confirmed is through results; i.e., in the reduction of group differences which have resulted primarily from discrimination. Ryan (1981) is most specific:

"It is impossible to discriminate against individuals as *individuals;* it can be done only against individuals as members of a group. Racial discrimination does not consist of an unrelated series of discrete actions directed against a random group of individuals who happen to be black; it is directed against blacks in general, as a group . . . . If I don't like you for some specific reason — you're a loudmouth, you're ugly, you're hostile, or you don't laugh at my jokes — and if I treat you badly because I don't like you, that's not discrimination, unpleasant as it might be. When I decide that all women are loudmouths, all blacks are hostile, and all Jews lack a sense of humor, and when I treat members of these groups unfairly, that's discrimination. By the same token, antidiscriminatory efforts and actions must be formulated in group terms. The abandonment of discriminatory practices can be evidenced, witnessed, and measured only by the observation of changes in the distribution of members of different groups." (pp. 155-156)

From this perspective, efforts to make jobs available to all who wish to work, although commendable, would not be equitable as long as racial discrimination is permitted. Collins (1979) suggests that many if not the majority of jobs in our society can be learned through practice by almost any literate person. Yet, some job descriptions often contain vaguely defined skill requirements that are actually unnecessary for job performance. Under the circumstances, myriad reasons are available as a cloak — to justify not hiring an individual when racial discrimination is the real reason. Even full employment will not prevent such discrimination; e.g., with zero unemployment, some groups could still be disproportionately underemployed and denied access to higher paying occupations. This systematic discrimination would only be discernible in the hiring pattern of the employer, not in the analysis of specific reasons why a particular black is not hired. If such a pattern is found, the requirement that the employer implement an affirmative action program moves us in the direction of a more equitable society.

Unfortunately, our economic system is structured so as to deny a large number of persons — both black and white — the opportunity to take advantage of education and/or economic self-improvement programs; consequently, their basic needs are unmet. Massive dislocations in certain industries — e.g., oil, steel, or agriculture — may mean that a highly skilled or highly educated employee finds himself jobless after years of specialized employment in a position that no longer exists. Disparities in the quality of education in poor and predominantly minority communities have significantly contributed to the high dropout rate of youth in low-income, minority families and to their lack of skills needed to compete effectively in the job market.

A just society is one in which the victims of these types of societal dysfunction are not blamed for their resulting plight. Although whites as well as non-whites may be victims, a disproportionate number of them is black, since institutional racism frequently is a factor contributing to their vulnerability.

In response to these unmet basic needs, a complex network of social insurance, vocational training, and rehabilitation programs, as well as personal social services, has been developed to move us more closely to the definition of a just society.

There are those with unmet basic needs who cannot or will not be attached to the workplace, either through their own efforts or the efforts of a family member on whom they can depend. They include single mothers with young children, old persons ineligible for Social Security, the sick and disabled, the emotionally disturbed, the developmentally disabled, and the "street people" who have given up hope of employment (or never developed any hope).

A compassionate society can be expected to provide a minimal level of subsistence for these persons at the same time that efforts are being made to increase their motivation, competence, or ability to function independently. The public assistance programs designed for these persons however, are characteristically inadequate.

There is no way to categorize or describe all of America's social welfare programs, even when narrowly defined. For example, a recent edition of the Catalogue of Federal Domestic Assistance lists over 200 programs funded at least in part by the federal government. In addition, more than 70 different welfare programs are operated by one or more of the 50 states. Finally, several programs are initiated and developed strictly by local communities. Most important, the eligibility requirements, support levels, and other details of these programs are constantly changing. The range, the diversity, the complexity of this network of entitlements and services notwithstanding, an increasing number of individuals and families is unable to obtain the necessities of life. Moreover, this support system has itself been accused of institutional racism, frequently resulting in the perpetuation of inequities in the economic system. Some gains have been made; but the overwhelming evidence supports the conclusion that governmental programs have not moved us significantly closer to equity, justice, or compassion — for Americans in general and black Americans in particular. Thus, social welfare reform should be a priority consideration on the legislative agenda of the 100th Congress.

APPROACHES TO SOCIAL WELFARE REFORM

The current social welfare system has few advocates: it reaches only a fraction of those in genuine need; it does not provide an adequate level of subsistence for those it does reach; it fails to ensure children in poor families are exposed to the values and norms of behavior that serve to promote positive social functioning; and it fosters dependency among those who could become self-sufficient, if properly motivated and trained.

To reform this system means different things to different people. Five major approaches have been identified in the push for reform of the social welfare system (Guide to Welfare Reform, 1979). Each has been reflected in some form in governmental policy over the past decade.

Block Grants

This approach is based on the notion that social welfare needs of individuals and families vary significantly from community to community and, therefore, governmental responsibility should be defined and implemented at state and local levels. Thus, most or all of the federal budget now allocated for welfare programs should be turned over to the individual states. The only stipulation would be that the money should be spent for some program for poor people. The Reagan Administration has drastically reduced the federal role in many social welfare programs. Under the Omnibus Budget Reconciliation Act of 1981, 57 categorical health and social service programs were eliminated to make it possible to spend 7.6 billion dollars on various block grants to states. However, this was $1.2 billion less than had been allocated to the categorical programs. In 1982, the Administration sought to give states the responsibility for administering Food Stamps, Aid to Families with Dependent Children (AFDC), and 43 other programs; but that was ultimately blocked by Congress.

Those concerned with the need for resources in disproportionately black and poor inner-city populations consider block grants to be subject to the undue influence of state legislatures dominated by agricultural and suburban interests.

Program Tightening

This approach is based on a perception that current governmental social welfare programs are characterized by waste and ineffectiveness. Its major features are elimination of programs where politically feasible and slashing expenditures for those remaining. For the past five years, federal budget cuts have decimated a host of social welfare programs, most notably AFDC. In 1982, the National Urban League affiliates in 16 cities convened hearings on AFDC in which testimony confirmed that cuts had struck hardest at the working poor and ". . . worsened the lives of hundreds and thousands of people — adults and children alike." (Social Welfare Cluster, 1982.)

In December, 1985 the Gramm-Rudman-Hollings Balanced Budget and Emergency Deficit Control Act (PL 99-177) was signed into law; it establishes a complicated budget process designed to eliminate the huge federal budget deficit by fiscal year 1991. Under this law, if Congress and the President fail to agree on a budget and new laws that will reduce the federal deficit to predetermined amounts each year, then the President at the beginning of each fiscal year must make automatic, across-the-board spending cuts. Although most federal social welfare programs will be subject to the automatic cuts, a few key social welfare programs are exempted, including Medicaid, AFDC, Food Stamps, Supplemental Security Income (SSI), and the special supplemental food program for Women, Infants, and Children (WIC). However, such programs as Head Start, Compensatory Education for Disadvantaged Children, the Social Services Block Grant (Title XX), the Maternal and Child Health Block Grant, Child Welfare Services, Summer Youth Employment, and many others are vulnerable.

Incrementalism

This approach to welfare reform considers current programs to be rational in concept but restrictive and inadequate in reality. Therefore, current programs would be retained but modified in order to cover more people by changing the way the programs work; i.e., giving more benefits or making the programs easier to apply for. For example, the outreach component in the Food Stamps program was abolished in 1981. Consequently, many of the neediest families who are disproportionately black remain outside the program because they do not understand the eligibility requirements or the application procedures. Reinstating the outreach activities would be an example of an incremental approach to welfare reforms. Similarly, the federal government's major job training program, the Job Training and Partnership Act (JTPA), the Job Corps, and the Summer Youth Employment Program are operating at funding levels making them possible to serve only a fraction of those who need the services. Providing additional funding for all three of these programs supplemented by increased investment in remedial education and dropout prevention programs would also be considered incrementalism.

Expanding Social Insurance

This approach would expand the concept of social insurance to programs such as AFDC. Social insurance programs, unlike welfare programs, do not depend upon income or assets for eligibility. They work more like insurance programs since they pay money at the time of a particular event such as retirement, loss of a job, or death of the wage-earner. This approach is based on the notion that current welfare programs are stigmatizing and have been less effective in raising people out of poverty than social insurance programs. An example would be merging SSI and Social Security, dropping the SSI means test, and reducing the grants only for earnings from work or income from investments or a pension fund. The disability provisions under Social Security would be extended to cover temporary disability. Another example would be an expansion of unemployment insurance to include those persons who have exhausted regular benefits, who have never worked, or who are looking for a job after a long period of unemployment. Still another example is a program of children's allowances that are fixed monthly sums paid to parents for the benefit of their children. Ryan (1981) suggests that the simultaneous establishment of these social insurance approaches to social welfare reform would eliminate virtually all official poverty in this country, if benefit levels were high enough. Yet, such a comprehensive approach appears to have little political support.

Guaranteed Annual Income

This approach implies that the current proliferation of social welfare programs could be substantially reduced if the income required to afford basic survival needs were guaranteed to everyone. It provides that all persons with an income below a certain level would receive a government subsidy whereas persons with income above that guaranteed level would pay taxes to the government. Persons with marginal incomes — those just above the poverty line — would possibly qualify for benefits and prefer accepting the guarantee rather than work. This threat to the work ethic is perhaps the greatest obstacle to implementing such a proposal. However, even if approved, the determination of the "floor"; that is, the guaranteed income per family, may — like AFDC — be based not upon what seems to be a minimum standard of subsistence but rather on what policymakers believe the country can afford.

A variety of other models of guaranteed income programs has been described which would have the effect of increasing the amount of income provided an individual or family living below the poverty level. The most serious detraction to this approach was made in the Rand Corporation study of the New Jersey Graduated Work Incentive Experiment (Cogan, 1978). It concluded that recipients of a guaranteed annual income would work six and one-half fewer hours per week than they would work in the absence of such a program; i.e., the program generated a substantial disincentive to work.

Generally, the approaches to social welfare reform can be differentiated by their underlying perception of the amount of funds available to the government to provide some minimum level of subsistence when it is unavailable from work or other sources. It is not surprising that the current Administration has been most successful in utilizing the block grant and program-tightening approaches that require fewer rather than more social welfare expenditures. It is also not surprising that the social insurance and guaranteed income approaches that would require the greatest infusion of government financing have received little active, political support.

According to Marris and Rein (1982): "A reformer in American society faces three crucial tasks. He must recruit a coalition of power sufficient for his purpose; he must respect the democratic tradition which expects every citizen, not merely to be represented, but to play an autonomous part in the determination of his own affairs; and his policies must be demonstrably rational" (p. 7).

For black Americans, this quote translates into the principle that in order to influence the political process, reformers must garner support from both non-blacks and blacks — particularly those who would benefit most directly from reform efforts — by offering a program which makes sense to most. It is the need to make sense to most blacks and whites that creates the most difficulty for *any* social welfare effort undertaken to date. Given the heterogeneity of both black and white populations in American society, neither group has been able to agree among itself on what constitutes a rational strategy for meeting basic social needs.

All of the approaches to social welfare reform described above begin from a common assumption; that is, that the economy will be strong and will provide employment (or, in some instances, investment income) sufficient to meet the basic needs of the vast majority. Thus, each approach is concerned only with providing a minimum level of subsistence to those persons who cannot provide for themselves. Yet, social welfare reformers are equally concerned about how to achieve this goal without weakening the structure and functioning of families. Thus, three questions can be used as analytic tools in selecting that vision of social welfare reform that has the greatest potential for creating an equitable, just, and compassionate society.

How can we maximize employment?
How can we assure everyone a minimum level of subsistence?

How can we do both of these while promoting and maintaining family stability?

MAXIMIZING EMPLOYMENT

The demand for social welfare programs is in large measure a consequence of the failure of the economic system to provide employment at a living wage for all who need, want, and can work. Several voices have asserted that current social welfare programs act as a disincentive to work (Cogan, 1978; Gilder, 1981; Murray, 1984). However, considerable evidence indicates that the rise in poverty in recent years is more likely the result of multiple factors, such as increased automation eliminating unskilled and low-skilled jobs; an economy that has staggered between repetitive cycles of prosperity and recession; and the tidal wave of women and new immigrants who have entered the job market, frequently displacing younger black workers.

Almost everyone involved in the welfare reform debate agrees with the premise that welfare programs should help those who can work to work. Work is, after all, a primary source of status and positive self-concept; any provision of assistance not attached to a job is perceived as stigmatizing. Again, however, little consensus exists on how best to achieve this goal. For example, some policy analysts and politicians, including most associated with the Reagan Administration, propose a single strategy for all welfare recipients — "workfare" — a program of mandatory employment that requires all AFDC recipients to "work off" their financial assistance in public sector jobs. For the most part, a "workfare" job is temporary and part-time; the recipient must simply work the number of hours equal to the family's grant divided by the minimum wage.

Some AFDC recipients have expressed their approval of "workfare," indicating their preference for working rather than being "on welfare." Research evidence from state programs which moved recipients from the welfare to the employment rolls has shown repeatedly that recipients who are able to work prefer a payroll check to a welfare check. They not only want to work but will do so if they are provided training and the opportunity. At the same time, no evidence exists that workfare assignments represent an effective approach for improving all participants' job skills or helping them find real employment. The fact that some work experience is provided can be helpful in giving those welfare recipients who have not had a recent job experience an opportunity to obtain it. However, such programs ignore the needs for training, remedial education, and supportive services that prevent many long-term welfare recipients from becoming independent. For example, the availability of child care is a determining factor for AFDC recipients. They tend to have children under six, a large proportion with children under three. Those states developing programs to provide AFDC recipients with job training or educational opportunities recognize that, unless child care is also provided, their efforts will be ineffective.

Others advocate a more individualized and comprehensive approach than "workfare." They argue for a thorough assessment of each recipient's needs and barriers to employment, followed by a range of different job preparation options, including education and training, to help move recipients toward permanent employment. For example, the National Urban League has recently had the opportunity to address employment barriers through its participation in the development and writing of the Opportunities for Employment Preparation Act of 1986 (SB 2578) and the Aid to Families and Employment Transition Act of 1986 (SB 2579) (Glasgow, 1986). The former bill amends the Job Training Partnership Act (JTPA), and the latter amends the AFDC and Medicaid legislation (Titles IV and XIX of the Social Security Act). The intent of both bills is to strengthen single- and two-parent families that are long-term AFDC recipients or long-term unemployed.

If passed, provisions in these bills would:

a. Include vocational, adult, and post-secondary education programs as part of the employment training.
b. Create an outreach, pre-employment, and vocational education component (a feeder system) within JTPA that would target education and employment benefits to those most in need.
c. Target pre-employment services to families that have participated in AFDC for two years or more and to individuals who have been unemployed for two or more years. These services would include a structured search for an eight-week internship with a private or public agency, educational preparation and basic skills development, career counseling, family counseling, and parenting skills for teenaged parents.
d. Authorize community-based organizations, such as the Urban League, to conduct and provide pre-employment services.
e. Provide for unlimited support services, including child care and transportation.
f. Prevent participants in the proposed feeder system from losing other program benefits such as AFDC or Food Stamps as a result of employment and training benefits (for example, scholarships and educational assistance).

Although these proposals are essentially incremental in nature; i.e., they seek to expand and improve existing programs, their major provisions could also be incorporated into a more radical social insurance program. For example, the pre-employment and support services could be targeted to recipients of unemployment compensation rather than the AFDC program.

Inherent in this proposed legislation is the assumption that a tight labor market exists; that is, that more jobs are available than there are workers to fill them. Cottingham (1982) suggests that the importance of a tight labor market cannot be overstressed. This would imply that government policy should be to create a tight labor market whenever it is loose; i.e., when unemployment is unacceptably high. For example, if the private sector does not generate a sufficient number of jobs, then public employment opportunities should be developed. Properly implemented, tight labor market policies could do more than any other alternative policy to reduce sharply unemployment and aid the poor. When tight labor markets prevail, the employment situation of blacks improves.

A 1978 study assessed the feasibility of large-scale public job creation (US Department of Labor, 1979, pp. 9-11). It identified 233 potential job creation activities in 21 different program areas. An estimated seven-million jobs could be created; at least one-fourth of that total could be filled by unskilled workers. In spite of the potential benefits, black leaders have seldom devoted sustained political attention to such macroeconomic issues, with the exception of backing the Humphrey-Hawkins full-employment bill. Yet, if blacks and other allies of the poor were to exert political pressure in this area, macroeconomic policies (such as a full-employment policy) could — over the long term — reshape the incidence and distribution of poverty.

Where the significance of employment rather than welfare has been empha- sized, Piven and Cloward (1974) have argued that by providing an alternative means of subsistence, welfare programs have made unemployment a much less fearsome possibility "both for the unemployed and for those currently working" and have "altered the terms of the struggle between business and labor." The implication here, that workers have greater bargaining power if they can remain unemployed or at least threaten to do so.

The more significant implication is that fragmented, income-maintenance programs can be considered *transitional* reform. Their fragmentation points to inefficiencies and deficiencies in a real income-maintenance program, thus inadvertently providing some direction toward making substantial progress in effective welfare reform.

A MINIMUM STANDARD OF SUBSISTENCE

The American social welfare system — in its barest form — is designed to prevent those unable to provide food or the other necessities of life for them- selves from starving to death. Yet, the programs have been seriously inadequate and incapable of achieving even that minimal objective. The value of benefits has considerably retrogressed as well as differences in benefit levels in different states. Not only do decreased benefit levels mean that most AFDC families are living well below the poverty level, the nature of the bureaucracy means that many persons will not even apply for those benefits because of perceived stigma or perceived harassment.

Benefits in the AFDC program vary according to family size; that is, those benefits increase with each additional child. Almost invariably, no relationship exists between the size of the additional grant and the amount needed actually to support that child. Despite the myth that women on welfare frequently have babies to increase their grant, the birth of a child more often reduces even further the inadequate resources available to support other family members. Alabama, for example, pays about $30 monthly for an additional child, Florida, about $40, and Illinois, about $60. According to federal poverty guidelines, a family of three needs $24.25 *daily* for poverty-level subsistence. Yet, a family with a mother and children receives $4.54 per day in Tennessee, $6.48 in Kentucky, and $12.26 in Kansas (Children's Defense Fund, 1986).

Proponents of children's allowances (an automatic family allowance provided by the government for each child) point out that this provision would have the twofold effect of (1) separating the issue of reasonable compensation for a job from the issue of how many people the job can support; and (2) meeting the basic needs of all children. Ryan (1981) has pointed out that it should not be an economic catastrophe when people have children; it often is. The welfare of individual families can fluctuate drastically with the addition of a child, although the rates of birth for the country fluctuate very little and predictably. For a given number of families, the number of children is predictable within an acceptable margin of error, and a minimum level of support can be provided without the drastic consequences that the individual family might endure. Opponents of this point of view have argued that children's allowances will serve to increase drastically the birth rate, especially among the poor. This has not happened in any of the countries that currently have children's allowances, and they include all of the industrialized nations — except our own.

Welfare payments theoretically provide a minimum subsistence level; yet, many jobs do not provide this same minimal level. Therefore, a perceived disincentive to work occurs when welfare payments exceed the minimum wage. That wage could be viewed as the symbolic threshold of the level of pay that must be offered to workers to get them into the labor market. However, a female parent working at the minimum wage to support herself and three children could do at least as well in many (if not most) states on AFDC. In response to proposals to raise the minimum wage, critics suggest that it has aggravated youth employment, especially among black youth, and sped up the introduction of labor-displacing machinery (Brozen and Friedman, 1966). The arguments and counterarguments abound with little resolution of the issue (Darity, 1982).

Interestingly, economists that have been most unhappy with the minimum wage have also been unhappiest with welfare payments. It is not surprising, then, that they have generally supported the notion of a negative income tax or other guaranteed annual income proposal precisely because they are intended as work incentive types of income maintenance (Gilder, 1981). Negative income tax and guaranteed annual income plans are based on the premise that welfare policies have not worked. The current welfare system could be replaced by a negative income tax which would guarantee everyone a minimum income and encourage recipients to work by allowing them to keep a portion of their earnings without severe reductions in benefits.

PROMOTING FAMILY STABILITY

A significant portion, 39 percent, of those who leave AFDC does so because of increased earnings; yet, these earnings are generally so low that most such families are left in poverty. The welfare system further punishes these vulnerable families by rapidly phasing out their benefits and pulling out collateral support, such as Medicaid-assisted health care (Children's Defense Fund, 1986). Benefits in welfare programs are determined by earnings so that part-time or low-paying full-time jobs will lead to a cut in benefits sometimes to an extent that leaves the recipient *less* well-off than when not working. Little reward from working results. Gilder (1981) has suggested: "Any welfare system will eventually extend and perpetuate poverty if its benefits exceed prevailing wages and productivity levels in poor communities. A change in the rules can produce immediate cutbacks as Reagan proved. But in time, welfare families will readjust their lives to qualify for what is their best available economic opportunity" (p.122). This readjustment is usually destructive of family stability.

In 1986, President Reagan established three select panels to study welfare reform. One was charged with addressing the relationship between the federal and state governments. A second, with exploring specific remedies for poverty, including block grants, vouchers, and "workfare" plans. The third panel is seeking to "identify those initiatives—whether found in the public or private sector—that have helped strengthen families." More specifically, it is addressing a basic question: Will any new policy strengthen or erode the family? At a news conference on November 13, 1986, that third panel recommended that all federal agencies file statements not only showing how their welfare policies would improve economic conditions, but also how they would keep families together. The recommendation was designed to encourage policies that strengthen families morally as well as financially. Impact statements, to be called "family fairness statements," would be required for any new initiatives coming out of a federal agency.

The Children's Defense Fund has pointed out that changes in policies, programs, and practices that have already been proposed have generally been opposed by the President (Children's Defense Fund, 1986). One such proposal called for enacting legislation mandating that AFDC be made available to very poor two-parent families where both adults are unemployed (AFDC-UP). This change is strongly opposed by the Administration's Office of Management and Budget. In the half of the states that lack AFDC-UP, destitute two-parent families must split up for the mother and children to receive AFDC benefits. Unfortunately, data seem to indicate that many do so. States that have eliminated this program have found a dramatic increase in the percentage of families that later become eligible for AFDC. In Iowa, 30 percent of the former AFDC-UP families became eligible for regular AFDC benefits within nine months after the state eliminated its AFDC-UP program. The overwhelming majority of these cases was eligible because the father was no longer in the home. Concern over the impact of this type of legislation on families has led to a quick reinstatement of the AFDC-UP program in four other states since 1982.

Even in those states in which two-parent families can be eligible for AFDC-UP, serious limitations exist. For example, the program's "100-hour rule" means that a family becomes ineligible if a wage-earner works 100 or more hours per month, regardless of what is earned. Many families therefore are reluctant to take any preliminary steps toward independence.

Other eligibility regulations that required families to show relatively recent, paid employment effectively rule out many young parents, discouraging them from getting married. Youth in AFDC families who are 19 and still struggling to complete high school or a vocational training program are no longer eligible for assistance; this creates pressure for them to drop out in order to support themselves.

Finally, if a teenaged female parent with a child is living with her mother, under current law, her mother's income must be counted as available to meet the child's needs. When laws count grandparent's income against the younger parent's AFDC grant, sometimes causing the grant to be withdrawn, they may create a drain on the grandparents' limited resources. In such cases, teen parents may be forced to leave home and lose the informal social support that may have been enough to make it possible for them to remain in school. Clearly, public assistance programs currently do not promote family stability and may, in fact, be contributing to family breakdown.

WELFARE REFORM: OF MUTUAL
BENEFIT TO BLACKS AND WHITES

Current social welfare policy is inadequate and even counterproductive in ensuring the optimal development of our country's low-income children, among whom black children are overrepresented. For the first time, in 1986, more than half (52%) of black children were in households below the poverty level. Their predicament is bleak since the public appears less and less supportive of governmental expenditures for social welfare purposes.

Rather than a welfare approach, Ozawa (1986) posits a "public investment approach" based on the unique demographic imperative to be experienced in the next century. As in many other industrialized societies, the US population will continue to age so that the governmental burden for financing various types of social welfare programs to meet their needs will grow. Currently there are 19 elderly persons per 100 working-age individuals; but by the time the baby-boom generation of the '50s and '60s retires in the first part of the next century, that ratio will be 38 elderly per 100 working-age individuals. More significantly, the data imply that the degree to which the baby-boom generation will be economically secure in old age will depend largely on how productive current non-white children are when they reach adulthood.

Under the public investment approach, public spending would be justified because taxpayers consider it wise to invest in the nation's children—not only for the sake of the children, but in their own individual interest as well. Furthermore, unlike welfare benefits that would generally target benefits to low-income families, public investment programs would target benefits to all children, regardless of family income level. When spending is targeted to children, this ensures provision independent of parents' employment status or level of earnings. As a result, governmental resources would be mobilized toward promoting the physical, mental, and intellectual development of children, thereby freeing those resources now used to monitor, regulate, and control the behavior of the children's parents.

Ozawa described four major components of a public investment program aimed at achieving the stated objective:

(1) prenatal and postnatal care for all expectant mothers

(2) children's allowances in the amount necessary to support a dependent in a poverty-level household

(3) free access to basic medical care for all children; e.g., as an integral part of the public school system or in a subsidized health insurance program similar to Part B of Medicare; and

(4) quality education, promoted in part by equalization of per-pupil spending through government subsidy of poor school districts.

According to Ozawa, if policymakers decide to adopt these new programs, current welfare and related programs—including AFDC—could be either eliminated or scaled down drastically. The portion of SSI that deals with disabled children could also be eliminated. The government might altogether revamp the Food Stamp program and public housing assistance. Dependent benefits for children under Social Security could be eliminated. Personal exemptions for children could be curtailed. The net cost of this investment approach would depend on the scope of the new programs and the extent to which the old was curtailed. However, taxpayers would clearly be able to see the return on their investment. They could see the linkage between child development and the assurance of old-age income security.

Ozawa's approach is consistent with that of Gilder, the conservative policy analyst, who writes:

"The goal of welfare should be to help people out of dire but temporary problems, not to treat temporary problems as if they were permanent ones, and thus make them so . . . a sensible program would be relatively easy on applicants in emergencies but hard on clients who overstay their welcome . . . . Ideally such a system should be supplemented with child allowances given to every family of whatever income, for each child" (p.126).

CONCLUSIONS

The need for radical reform in this nation's system of social welfare may be the one issue on which both liberal and conservative politicians can agree. Some conservatives support what may be termed the most liberal of the proposals: the need to provide a subsistence level below which no child would have to fall. There is also general acceptance of the need for full employment at a living wage of all who want to work. Furthermore, the system for meeting these needs should do so in a manner that will not damage the structure or functioning of families. With so much agreement, one wonders why reform is so difficult to achieve, why our current, fragmented, inadequate, and even destructive system persists. At least three major obstacles prevent the realization of these major reform programs.

The first is the ethic which has obscured the intolerable control of wealth in this country by a few—wealth which could be shared by the public to ensure the necessities of life for everyone. There is considerable apathy about the plight of the poor because of a belief system that justifies this striking inequality. It purports that individuals who amass great wealth do so because they possess intrinsic qualities such as motivation, dedication to the work ethic, and intelligence to a greater extent than do other individuals. Thus, they fully deserve larger shares of the available resources. Ryan (1981) has gathered evidence to support his contention that the relative economic position of the family one is born into is a far better predictor of one's own economic status than is the most complex array of internal traits and abilities (p.64). From this latter perspective, the current range in incomes from minimum wage to untold millions is excessive, intolerable, and impossible to justify. The alternative is not a kind of socialism in which wealth is divided among all of us; rather, it places capital above a maximum level in the public sector and provides access to amenities shared by all—from libraries to day care, from parks to homemaker chore services for the elderly.

A second obstacle to real reform in the welfare system is the tremendous dislocation in the labor force which would be necessary in order to dismantle existing welfare programs. Thousands are employed in public social service jobs that depend upon the current social welfare system: protective service workers, eligibility workers, geriatric case managers, etc. The threat of possibly eliminating massive numbers of positions as suggested by the Ozawa proposals will be sure to create a groundswell of resistance and protest. The rationale is not likely to be fear of loss of jobs but rather criticism of the particular reform strategies on such grounds as excessive cost, potential abuse, or lack of administrative feasibility.

A third obstacle is the growing sense of threat created in many citizens by the massive wave of illegal immigrants who have entered the country in recent years. They are frequently perceived to be a drain on the taxpayer as potential competitors for jobs and potential consumers of public social services. Many would predict, therefore, that an even greater stream of "illegals" will enter the country if there are guaranteed jobs, and "free" social services. Even if these were to be provided only to citizens, the opportunity and incentives for counterfeiting documents to prove citizenship would be seen as great.

In the short run, the incremental approach to reform may be the most feasible way to meet the survival needs of the increasing numbers of poor people in this country who are disproportionately black. However, the short-term changes should be consistent with the long-range vision of more radical reform involving full employment (including vocational training and other support services for those without marketable, vocational skills) and family allowances. In order to achieve these goals, it will be necessary to change public attitudes regarding the distribution of economic resources, to provide viable alternative employment for dislocated public employees, and to reduce the threat posed by illegal immigration.

The Black Underclass In Perspective

Douglas G. Glasgow

INTRODUCTION

A generation ago, poverty in America became an urgent public issue: Seeking solutions to the problem of poverty emerged as the nation's major domestic priority.

In 1959 22.4 percent of the population, or almost 40 million persons, were poor. More than one-half of all black Americans subsisted below the poverty level, compared to 18 percent of whites.[1] The cold, alarming statistics on poverty were translated into human terms through poignant accounts of life in *The Other America,*[2] which included the black enclaves of the nation's urban centers and rural areas. Thus, in the early 1960s, the federal government, prodded by a sympathetic public, undertook the multifaceted War on Poverty, with the two-pronged objective of ensuring a decent subsistence for poverty-stricken families and individuals, and opening the doors of economic opportunity to those who were locked out of the mainstream. Indeed, poverty, especially black poverty, was not just a public issue but a national policy priority.

Twenty-five years later, poverty continues to be a massive problem, and black poverty is once again the topic of widespread commentary. In 1985 the national poverty rate stood at 14 percent, and more than 31 percent of black Americans were poor. Blacks are still almost three times more likely than whites to be below the poverty level.[3] However, the public mood is much less sympathetic than before. The tendency is for black poverty to be discussed not so much in terms of a national problem, but rather in terms of the failure of black Americans to take better advantage of perceived economic opportunities. Moreover, many observers have begun to question openly the prospect that the situation can be reversed.

The concept of the "black underclass" has gained widespread usage in the current debate, and for many has taken on highly contemptuous connotations. Members of the black underclass are less deserving than the "other Americans" who commanded society's attention in the 1960s. They are portrayed as the irresponsible fathers of illegitimate children and as uncontrollable teenage mothers who are content to live off the public dole. They are, in the popular view, the ne'er-do-well welfare recipients, the black poverty problem of the 1980s. But, contemporary black poverty is more complex than these denigrative characterizations suggest. Moreover, these characterizations leave much unsaid about the underclass concept itself and its relevance to the present situation.

In 1980 when *The Black Underclass* was written,[4] there was a need for a great understanding of this phenomenon. That need is even more urgent today.

Some analysts would have us believe that the problem is intractable, and that the nation, therefore, should not waste its fiscal resources on it. The concept of "no-waste" has been the distinguishing feature of national policy in this area recently, with federal spending on employment and training programs for the economically disadvantaged slashed by 50 percent since 1980.[5] Other human resource development programs — such as those in the education area — have also been drastically curtailed.[6] A growing legion of neoconservatives pushing the lost cause/no waste viewpoint under the guise of welfare reform has linked poverty with dependency; the salutary benefits of work with sub-minimum pay. Reactionary, narrow constructions about the black underclass are invoked as the rationale for many of these initiatives.

The purpose of this article is to lend perspective to current arguments concerning the black underclass and the broader question of black poverty.

THE UNDERCLASS CONCEPT

In the seven years since I published my initial work on this subject, other works, reports, and extensive media commentary have followed, stimulating what has become a recurring debate regarding various aspects of the underclass.

In the current national climate of moral meanness, no longer is the condition of the underclass viewed as one warranting scientific understanding and corrective policy action. Those entrapped in this condition are accused of having created it and of having developed a culture that perpetuates it. A rash of commentary and media depictions has provided the public a highly provocative view of underclass life, suggesting that this condition is endemic to, and in large measure, sustained by blacks themselves. Neoconservatives have developed the rationale for vitriolic condemnation and punitive social policy proposals.

In understanding the underclass concept, the first point to make is that it derives from social stratification theory, the arrangement of statuses in a society, the performance of social roles attendant to those statuses, and the differential rewards and privileges that accompany them.[7] The theory also encompasses the social mobility processes by which persons move from one status to another. The American stratification system is generally described in terms of different social classes, the traditional categories being "upper class," "middle class," "working class," and "lower class."[8] The underclass concept adds another dimension to this traditional class structure.

Although the American class system is considered to be open with freedom of movement from lower to higher statuses — the opportunities for mobility are greatly limited at the lower positions, and are almost nonexistent at the underclass level. In *The Black Underclass,* I emphasized the problem of dislocation or detachment from employment-related opportunities and the "disconnections with standardized institutions that act as feeder systems to the primary labor market."[9] I also emphasized that labor force dislocation is largely a structural phenomenon, a view to which I remain committed.

Factors that contribute to different class strata are classically viewed as emanating from broad structural factors in society. Hence, my conceptualization of underclasses in American society cuts across race; the phenomenon affects whites as well as blacks. But, an important qualification must be made. The black underclass not only must contend with the structural factors, but also with the continued impact of racial discrimination. As a constraint on social mobility, racial discrimination remains a limiting factor in the experiences of all black Americans. However, the interplay between race and class position effectively sets the black underclass apart from other blacks as well as from their white counterparts.

Principal among the structural factors is the changed nature of the American economy — from an industrial, goods-producing system to one based on high technology and services. This macroeconomic transformation has put the less skilled among the nation's population in a highly marginal position. The black underclass has been the chief victim of this development. While individual choices and behaviors play some role, choices and behaviors are best understood as responses to extremely limited opportunities and options.

By the conceptualization developed here, the black underclass consists of the worst-positioned persons among the black poor. The black underclass, by prevailing societal criteria, is not and has relatively little prospect of becoming self-supporting or socially mobile.

The current size of the black underclass defies precise estimates. Some sources estimate as many as five to seven million persons.[10] Even these distressing figures could be low. If we factor in the unemployed; the discouraged worker population, the almost one-million black men whose labor force status cannot be determined because they are missed in the census; blacks in prisons; the three-million blacks hidden in rural hamlets in a host of small southern towns; and the new "homeless" black poor, the size of the black underclass suggests a phenomenon of staggering magnitude. The underclass, in the urban cities, gains notoriety because of its social disruption and alleged dependency.

The contemporary public debate on the black underclass is organized around three inter-related propositions:

- That the emergence of the black underclass reflects a lack of positive values in the community;

- That the emergence of the black underclass is a consequence of the so-called feminization of poverty;

- That the emergence of the black underclass was brought on by the growth of social programs for the poor.

Each of these propositions is tremendously complex; while a single article cannot address all of the complexities, the future of black America demands that we put the argument into perspective.

THE VALUE DEFICIENCY ARGUMENT

Much of the current discussion about the black underclass stresses a weakened value system in urban black communities. It is argued that this weakness is manifested by an apparent absence of positive aspirations, behavioral norms, and social controls that promote stability. A host of writers, particularly neoconservatives, has identified this condition and concluded that it predominates over all others.[11] Despite the growing popularity of this assessment, it nonetheless begs two basic issues that must be examined separately for both analytic and policy-making purposes. First, to what extent has there actually been a deterioration of the value system, as well as a loss of viable social structure and relations in urban black communities? Second, to what extent do such socio-cultural factors explain the severity and persistence of black urban poverty?

On the first issue, the view that black urban communities are devoid of positive values and social cohesion is cogently represented in Nicholas Lemann's recent analysis.[12] However, Lemann's analysis also illustrates the limitations of some journalistic accounts of the black experience which, as one observer asserts, "are vulnerable when subjected to critical intellectual scrutiny."[13] Based on a conception that has black America bifurcated or "splitting into a middle class and an underclass that seems likely never to make it,"[14] Lemann postulates that the underclass came to prominence with the migration of members of the middle class out of urban black communities. Pronounced since the 1960s, this exodus was facilitated by the success of the civil rights movement against housing discrimination. A critical consequence of this development, in Lemann's view, was that members of the lower classes were left without the positive values, institutions, role models, and social controls that their middle class brethren had formerly provided. He writes:

> Until then the strong leaders and institutions of the ghetto had promoted an ethic of assimilation (if not into white society, at least into a black middle class) for the underclass . . . . Suddenly most of the leaders and institutions (except criminal ones) left, and the preaching of assimilation by both blacks and whites stopped. What followed was a kind of free fall into . . . social disorganization . . . . The underclass flourished when in the seventies, it was completely disengaged from the rest of society — when there were *no brakes* on it.[15] (emphasis added)

Later, the author is even more emphatic:

> Very quickly, around 1970, the ghettos went from being exclusively black to being exclusively black lower-class, and there was no countervailing force to the venerable . . . disorganized size of the ghetto culture . . . . The "losing ground" phenomenon, in which black ghettos paradoxically became worse during the time of the War on Poverty, can be explained partly by the abrupt disappearance of *all* traces of bourgeois life in the ghettos and the *complete* social breakdown that resulted.[16] (emphasis added)

In general, this "middle-class abandonment" thesis is not only plausible, but also consistent with empirical data. The data clearly show a trend toward increased suburbanization of the black population. This demographic change evidences a lowering of racial barriers in the housing market as well as increased financial ability of blacks — after protracted struggles for economic and social opportunity. To some degree, then, blacks have managed to follow the pattern of other ethnic groups in pursuit of greater social mobility.[17] The movement of more economically advantaged blacks out of the inner cities has had an adverse impact on the local economy as well as on the more social aspects of community life. But do these circumstances mean the "complete social breakdown" of urban black communities that Lemann and others suggest?

Lemann's analysis is flawed in the first place by his over-simplification of the black social class system into two strata — middle class and underclass. At the outset, it must be pointed out that the black middle-class is not nearly so large a group as this conceptualization implies. If median income is used to define middle class, about one-fourth (24%) of black families was "middle class" in 1979. Moreover, by 1983 this figure had grown to only 27 percent.[18]

While poverty is disproportionately high among blacks, the remaining three-quarters of the black population are not all "underclass," nor in poverty. There continues to be a large number of working class blacks who are not in poverty.

In any case, the black social class structure is much more elaborate than any simplified two-strata bifurcation. Billingsley, for example, has delineated an upper class, three echelons of a middle class, and three echelons of a lower class.[19] His lower class sub-stratification consists of the "working non-poor," the "working poor," and the "underclass." This paradigm is much more representative of Black America than Lemann's simplistic dichotomy.

If one assumes that the black community is divided into two class groups and that the "haves" both control the economic resources and alone maintain the community's socio-cultural viability, then one would expect that their departure would produce a complete social breakdown. The fact is that the middle class has not had an exclusive role in promoting positive values and social stability in black urban communities. This function has also been performed by the working poor. Even though they are economically unable to follow their more fortunate friends and relatives — often their own children — to "better" areas, they somehow manage to support themselves and their children, maintain positive social values, and offer beneficial socialization influences to others around them.

Another shortcoming of the middle class abandonment thesis is its failure to recognize the continued breadth and functioning of the black extended family system.[20]

Recent investigations into the extended black family and the occurrence of social interaction between ghetto dwellers and former ghetto dwellers provide impressive evidence that (1) the extended kinship network remains strong, and (2) physical disengagement often does not mean social disengagement from community life.[21] The middle class abandonment thesis disregards all of these points.

I believe that the popular discussion about the deteriorated value system in urban black communities tends to overlook some important qualifications. However, my arguments are not intended to divert attention from the pressing problem that many have rightly emphasized.[22] There is no question that the urban black community has experienced an erosion of the normative frameworks that have undergirded them in the past, and that signs indicate that the situation is worsening. Nor is there any doubt about the need to reverse the trend by providing alternatives to the negative conditions that effectively prevent many black children from realizing their potential. The working poor who have struggled to hold the line are increasingly hard pressed to do so. In developing initiatives to this end, however, we must be mindful of what is already in place. Despite the obvious problems of the inner cities, they still contain mechanisms, institutions, and people that work. Renewal efforts that overlook these resources, because of a preconception that "complete social breakdown" has occurred, will predictably not succeed.

The second issue I posed — on the relative importance of socio-cultural versus other factors — has also dominated public discussion on the black underclass. While the issue has its intellectual underpinnings in the "culture of poverty" notion that become popular in the 1960s,[23] it has gained new intensity in the contemporary debate. The difference now is that the arguments are being interpreted by neoconservatives, rather than social libertarians, as a rationale for more restrictive, even punitive, policies toward the poor. Some might even suggest that the culture of poverty phenomenon is being offered as sufficient justification to write off the black underclass altogether. Mickey Kaus is a notable proponent of the neoconservative sentiment. He writes that:

> The problem I am talking about is the culture of our largely black, largely urban ghettos. It is only part of the broader problem of poverty, although it is the most intractable part. It is only part of the problem facing black Americans, although blacks are unfairly stigmatized by the behavior of the underclass. *Today . . . the important question is no longer whether there is a culture of poverty, but what we are going to do to change it.*[24] (emphasis added)

In response, however, I want to emphasize that: *The attitude and behaviors of the black poor are, in fundamental terms, responses to limited life chances and their oppressed position in the society's racial-class structure.* Public policies that fail to recognize the importance of racial, structural, and economic variables, and the interplay among them, are either misguided or limited in their objectives. As one analyst remarks in criticizing Kaus' approach to the black underclass, "He confuses the symptoms of deprivation, concentration, isolation, abysmal education, and limited opportunity with the causes."[25]

Whatever their causes, the dysfunctional behaviors so prevalent in black urban communities must be dealt with on their own terms. Teenage pregnancy, crime and delinquency, drug abuse, and general socially dysfunctional conduct, simply cannot be excused. After all, it is the black community itself that pays the highest price. Furthermore, it is principally the responsibility of black Americans themselves to choose when and how best to confront them. The National Urban League has long recognized this need and has implemented an array of remedial programs in teenage pregnancy, crime prevention, education, and other key areas.

But even as we work to change attitudes and behaviors, the problem of black poverty and the black underclass must be kept in proper perspective. The ultimate solutions involve changing the structures of economic opportunity to accommodate those who are now locked out of the mainstream. These solutions require choices and commitments that only public policy can exercise.

THE FEMINIZATION OF POVERTY ARGUMENT

Black underclass development has often been explained within the context of the feminization of poverty thesis — a notion with particular appeal to certain sectors of American society. Liberal analysts have embraced this notion because it identifies the continuation of poverty in America as directly linked to systemic forces. Feminists find it a convenient notion as it affirms the contention that sexism functions as a major factor in the marketplace. Conservatives use the feminization concept to argue female poverty, as represented in single-parent households, undergirds the growth of black poverty. Given the current popularity of the concept, I must address two separate but related issues: (1) How applicable is the "feminization of poverty" hypothesis as a conceptual tool for understanding poverty among black females? and (2) How accurate is the notion of a feminized poor in attempting to understand black underclass development?

In my view the "feminization of poverty" framework obscures rather than clarifies the causal factors that lead to the overrepresentation of female-headed households among black Americans. The theme of the feminized poor masks the historical differences between the labor market experiences of black and white females. Historically, black females have been concentrated in a stratum of the labor market statistically contoured by class, race, and gender factors. Black females have a long history of employment and providing essential income for black families. Much work has been in low wage fields (domestic and services), and in non-unionized employment, where wages and work conditions have been uncontrolled. Black female labor force participation was for primary income and contribution to basic family needs. The feminized poverty notion implies a new or more contemporary participation and impoverishment of black women. It neglects the longstanding economic burden carried by them. The differential earning power of black females and white females is not only historical but continues currently.

For example, in 1984 the median weekly earnings of a black female were $242, in comparison with $264 for a white female; $304 for a black male; and $403 for a white male.[26] Historically, this gap was even greater. Moreover, black married females who work full-time contribute approximately one-third to the total family income and earn approximately three-fourths the level of income of their husbands. Thus, female income plays a critical role in the economic status of black families.[27]

Secondly, the feminization of poverty concept clouds the continued importance of race in general as a causal factor in the determination of poverty. Again, the data are clear. At every level of education and across all family structures, the proportion of black Americans in poverty exceeds the proportion of white Americans in poverty. The poverty rate among black families headed by both a male and female exceeds the rate of poverty among white female-headed families. The poverty rate among blacks with one or more years of college exceeds the poverty rate of whites with eight years of education. The poverty rate of blacks who worked full-time is three times higher than that of whites who worked full-time. The poverty rate of black households with only two persons is nearly equal to that of whites with seven or more persons.[30]

With respect to the formation of the black underclass, one of the most erroneous assumptions that currently shape existing conceptions is that this social stratum is the direct product of the growth in teenage pregnancies and out-of-wedlock births among black Americans. Such a notion has been used to support the assumption that the black underclass consists primarily of young, black, unwed mothers who have come to rely upon Aid to Families with Dependent Children (AFDC) as their primary source of income. It is this assumption about the demographic composition of the underclass that has been used to link the issues of poverty and dependency.

It is important to point out that — contrary to popular opinion — poverty among black female-headed households is lower today than a generation ago. In 1959, 70.6 percent of all black female-headed households existed in poverty relative to 53.2 percent of such families in 1985. However, particular attention has been focused upon the black underclass and the feminization of poverty because approximately 69.2 percent of all poor black Americans are either female unrelated persons and/or live in households which are female-headed. In 1985 there were 8.9 million poor black Americans, and 6.2 million were females and/or persons in female-headed households.[31] Such data have contributed to the belief that there is a relationship between black family structure, black poverty, and black underclass development. However, the interpretation of such data overstates the female composition of the poor.

Changes in family structure have been directly linked with the relative stability of the black poverty population that characterized the 1970s. During that decade, the rate of decrease in poverty among black Americans slowed. From 1959 to 1969 poverty decreased from 56.2 percent of the black population to 32.2 percent. From 1969 to 1979 black poverty decreased from 32 to 31 percent.[32] While black family structure did affect this rate of change, the cause of the changes in the underclass is the combined incomes of two parents. For the most part, within the black community, neither male nor female single-parent income will provide a nonpoverty standard of living. In 1984 the median income of black males was only $9,450 in comparison with $16,470 for white males. Thus, 50 percent of black families of four would have existed in poverty had black families been dependent only on the income of black males. Black females, however, had median incomes of $16,160. By combining these incomes, some black families would become able to shift themselves out of poverty.

And lastly, the central weakness of the feminized poverty notion may be that it diverts attention from the staggering dislocation and disconnection of black males from the labor market, income, and concomitantly, from the family. Current data point to a growing decline in the labor force participation rates of black males and an increasing unemployment gap between white and black males.[28] Possibly no factor of importance has received so little attention in the feminization of poverty dialogue as that which separates the plight of black males and females in poverty. Current dialogue proceeds as if the two were

136

unrelated except in respect to procreative function. Public dialogue continues to stress black male irresponsibility as the core factor for their absence from the home. This notion is reinforced by longstanding racial imagery that suggests black males as lazy, unmotivated baby-makers. It fails to recognize the important need of black males for adequate earning income to enhance responsible family participation. It further fails to recognize the destructive impact man-in-house regulations have had and continue to have in forcefully removing poor males from low-income and poor families because of their poverty. Such insensitivity has made it possible for policy-makers to currently offer stricter laws to incarcerate unemployed and idled blacks; to proffer employment for poor males in sub-minimum wage jobs, and in other forms to seek solutions to their condition outside of the family constellation.

The fact is that the interdependence of poor black females and males involves more than their sexual ties; they are bound by specific class association. As noted earlier in this paper, underclass status is affected by two important variables — dislocation from the labor force and disconnection from the institutions that act as feeders to labor force participation. In the case of black males, their labor force dislocation and resulting poverty clearly demonstrate underclass status. The same clarity with respect to impoverished females who head families and are on welfare does not exist. Such single-parent households on welfare do have an institutional connection and do receive regular cash benefits. However, while these families receive regular income, they remain poor because the income is inadequate. And while they do have an institutional attachment, welfare policy and practice has not emphasized securing employment for its recipients. Hence, single-parent families remain poor and detached from tne labor force.

The issue here is not to make a case for underclass status of single-parent families as it is to suggest that with some minor changes in welfare perspective, many poor families — marginally underclass — could begin to untangle themselves from the throes of poverty with changes in welfare that seek to assist poor persons and families secure employment and sufficient income. Large numbers of poor families could begin to see a way out of poverty. With changes in welfare regulation, which encourage the maintenance of two-parent families irrespective of employment status, then the welfare system could become a supportive and truly helpful institution for family social and economic security. Changes in policy that would have a direct impact on improving the life potential for impoverished families would assist young females to gain employment skills to access the job market. Welfare then could serve as a supportive institution during transition periods from recipient status to that of independent earner. In the second case, a policy that would emphasize keeping families together (that is, both parents and children in the same household) would reverse the practice and policy that forces families apart because of one or the other's unemployment. Most of all, it would recognize the importance of two-parent incomes as crucial to low-income family economic stability. There is needed economic interdependence if either or both are to rise out of poverty.

Over-emphasis on the feminization of poverty concept dichotomizes the status of black males and females in poverty and feeds practices that separate their plight.

Preliminary data from a study of 109 single black males and females suggest that the employment and income status of black males was the single most important factor in determining the demand and supply of husbands. The study revealed that males who were either unemployed and/or low earners were unwilling to offer themselves in the market as husbands. Indeed, the supply and demand for husbands was only equal when the male earned incomes of $25,000 and above. At income levels below $25,000, the demand for husbands exceeded the supply.[29] Such data document the importance of the economic status of black males as a determinant of family structure among black Americans.

THE SOCIAL PROGRAMS ARGUMENT

There is a widely held view that the social welfare programs that were instituted in the 1970s have done little to solve the nation's poverty problem and, in fact, have contributed to the emergence of the black underclass. This conclusion that the War on Poverty and welfare programs have not only been ineffectual but also dysfunctional was recently popularized through Charles Murray's controversial book, *Losing Ground.* [35] Unlike earlier criticisms of "welfare," which tended to concentrate on administrative efficiency, responsiveness, and cost-effectiveness issues, the conservative preoccupation presses the more fundamental questions of purpose and effects. A central argument is that social welfare programs have fostered dependency, encouraged single parenting, and otherwise contributed to the growth of a "culture of poverty," outcomes that are counterproductive and socially unacceptable.

In any event, indictments of the antipoverty strategies of the 70s have marked the public policy debate on the poor since 1980. The "lost cause/no waste" attitude must be understood in the context of the broader historical role of social programs generally, and specifically with respect to the black underclass phenomenon. The validity of the indictments, therefore, bears examination.

At the outset, expenditures on social programs, many targeted specifically for the poor, grew tremendously between 1960 and 1980.[36] Five broad expenditure categories can be delineated:

- cash transfers, including direct grants to people below a certain income level;

- in-kind transfers, to increase the consumption of specific goods by the poor (e.g., food and housing);

- direct services to increase consumption of specific services (e.g., medical care and legal aid);

- human capital programs (e.g., education and job training) to enhance the ability of individuals to function in the market economy; and

- community development programs to enhance the participation and political efficacy of the poor.[37]

How one judges the general efficacy of government spending in these areas is largely a matter of perspective.

Given the objective of reducing the absolute incidence of poverty, there is no question that expansions in the cash transfer system have been effective.[38] Thus, in 1965, for example, 21.3 percent of the population would have existed in poverty in the absence of government cash transfers (through AFDC, Supplemental Security Income, etc.). Similarly, in 1983, 24.2 percent of the population would have been (officially) poor without cash transfer programs. Taking in-kind or noncash transfers into account produces an even more dramatic effect. In 1983 cash plus in-kind transfer payments reduced the number of persons in poverty to 10 percent of the population. Measured by the extent to which they have allowed individuals and families to subsist at a higher level of well-being than they might have otherwise, transfer programs have provided significant benefits to the pre-transfer poor. Stated differently, post-transfer poverty rates have been considerably lower as a result of the growth of social programs.

On the other hand, measured against the policy goal of decreasing the rate of pre-transfer poverty, the expanded network of social programs cannot be evaluated so favorably. The pre-transfer poor are those who do not receive enough income from private sources to climb out of poverty status. To concentrate on pre-transfer poverty is to stress enabling the able-bodied poor to be or become economically self-sufficient. Targeted employment, training and education initiatives, and related support services have been key means through which the economic independence of the poor has been promoted. In any case, the pre-transfer poverty rate actually rose by three percentage points between 1965 and 1983.[39] While the pre-transfer poverty rate is influenced by a number of factors, particularly the state of the nation's economy, the fact that it increased during the period of accelerated spending on social programs has been seized by neoconservatives as evidence that these programs were ineffectual.

There is some validity to this point; however, a balanced assessment must recognize certain qualifications. In the employment and training area, some programs, such as the Job Corps,[40] have consistently shown positive results in preparing the economically disadvantaged to function in the labor market. Others could have been more effective with better implementation.[41] Such successes and potential successes are often ignored in the blanket repudiations that have recently come into vogue.

The other facet of the social programs argument — the one that stresses undesirable social consequences, such as dependency, reduced work effort, and family disorganization — is perhaps more controversial. It speaks to some fundamental concerns about the black underclass and black poverty generally. Again, the basic contention is that social programs — especially "welfare" — have not simply been nonfunctional in eliminating the black poverty problem but dysfunctional in generating conditions that aggravate it. The general sentiment is expressed succinctly by Murray: "We tried to provide more for the poor and produced more poor instead. We tried to remove the barriers to escape from poverty, and inadvertently built a trap."[42] How valid is this assessment?

Perhaps the most pernicious allegation in the indictment of social welfare programs is that they have promoted the formation and perpetuation of single-parent households. However, recent analyses that compare family structure changes with changes in the welfare system over time, and differences across states in benefit levels and family structures, strongly contradict this conclusion. Thus, Ellwood and Summers find that:

> Since 1972, the fraction of all children in a female-headed household rose from 14 percent to almost 20 percent. During that same period, the fraction of all children in homes collecting AFDC held almost constant at 12 percent. The figures are even more dramatic for blacks. Between 1972 and 1980, the number of black children in female-headed families rose nearly 20 percent; the number of black children in AFDC fell by 5 percent. If AFDC were pulling families apart and encouraging the formation of single-parent families, it is hard to understand why the number of children in the program would remain constant throughout a period in our history when family structure changed most.[43]

The investigators also challenge directly the apparent association between welfare and out-of-wedlock births among blacks. They point out that the birth rate of single black women actually declined by 13 percent between 1970 and 1980, but the rate for *married* black women decreased even more (38 percent). Consequently, the fraction of births to single women increased. During the same period, the birth rate of unmarried white women *rose* by 27 percent. The upshot: "It seems difficult to argue that AFDC was a major influence in unmarried births when there was simultaneously a rise in the birth rate to unmarried whites and a fall in the rate for blacks."[44]

In my own view, Ellwood and Summers are right on the money in their summary judgment about family structure changes among blacks: "In the black community, family structure changes may relate more to the changing fortunes of black men than to the availability of AFDC."[45]

A second troubling allegation in the indictment of the welfare system is that welfare promotes dependency. In other words, people use it to meet needs that they could meet on their own. This allegation, too, is debatable. For example, even though blacks are disproportionately represented among long-term AFDC recipients — that is, those who receive assistance for more than eight years[46] — one must consider the more limited options black females enjoy relative to white females. The two avenues to self-sufficiency for single mothers are work and marriage. Both are much less available to black single mothers than they are to whites. In particular, the relative shortage of "marriageable" black men, able to provide economic support to their families, sets severe limits on the ability of black females to leave the welfare rolls. It is all too easy to confuse this harsh reality with some notion that black women simply prefer to subsist on welfare benefits.

In short, the proposition that social welfare programs have had dysfunctional social consequences in the black poverty problem has been overstated; more powerful explanations are to be found in the changed nature of the national economy, the continued effects of racial discrimination, and the failure of policy-makers to come to grips with these forces by designing programs that provide real opportunities for economic advancement.

I am not arguing that present welfare policies should not be changed. To the contrary, there are compelling reasons for change. No able-bodied person, black or white, should have to depend on public support for subsistence; public support is too vulnerable to political whim. The political mood since 1980 has been unsympathetic toward recipients of public assistance. Restrictive changes in eligibility requirements and other budget-reducing initiatives pushed 450,000 AFDC families off the rolls in 1982. More generally, reductions in social programs have had a significant adverse impact on the incidence of poverty in recent years.[47]

POLICY DISCUSSION

Clearly, the complexities of the black underclass and the contemporary black poverty problem are a source of great frustration to the nation, as a whole, and to black Americans themselves. However, we cannot allow the complexities to cause us to resign in the fact of the challenge. American society cannot afford to "write off" large segments of its population. Nor should we adopt policy initiatives that do little more than punish and provide little hope of bringing the black underclass into the economic mainstream.

Despite wide public debate on the subject, and intense attention given to underclass behavior and social dysfunction, it is labor force disconnection and consequential economic impoverishment that distinguish this class segmentation. The black underclass condition is engendered by important macroeconomic changes that have effected the traditional workings of the lower tier of the primary sector and the secondary sector of the labor market.

Blacks traditionally highly concentrated in these areas of the economy have been most severely devastated by the changes. The formation of an underclass (dislocated labor) is the outcome of these forces (see Standback and Beverly).[48] The structurally enforced involuntary disconnection from the labor force and job market is what primarily distinguishes this stratum of the black poor from others of the black poor.

The current vogue of concentrating on underclass social disruptive impact has discouraged positive national attention to the problems of underclass formation. Public commentary continues to convey that the underclass is in large measure self-generated by a poverty culture, and that its condition is in large measure due to misdirected and limited attention by black leadership and middle-class black institutions. This message has encouraged a mean, punitive, and insensitive public posture to evolve towards blacks in general and the black poor in particular.

ROLE OF SOCIAL PROGRAMS AND
GOVERNMENT RESPONSIBILITY

No discussion of reversing underclass formation can take place without special reference to the role of social programs and government responsibility.

Public policy demands that the system of welfare be changed to be more responsive to the contemporary needs of poor families and individuals. Proposals to scrap welfare appear to be precipitous and premature, especially in lieu of more recent state experiments with the use of public welfare resources to help families and individuals find work. Experiments such as the Massachusetts Employment and Training Choices Program (E.T.)[49] and Maine's Welfare, Employment and Training Program (WEET)[50] reflect a more creative approach to use of public funds to help people find work. The voluntary adoption by some 26 states of AFDC-UP, which provides assistance to certain poor families where the principal wage earner is unemployed, also reflects a growing awareness in some states of the importance of keeping a family together. Some other initiatives are currently being put before Congress. The National Urban League has been a prime mover of legislation aimed at amending portions of the Job Training Partnership Act (Title II-A), and the Social Security Act (Title IV-A), to reduce barriers to labor market participation especially of long-term unemployed and long-term recipients of AFDC support.[51] These and other initiatives are but a few that seek to provide job market entry and labor force participation for those disconnected from the work force. Employment initiatives should be the core of "welfare reform," which is moving welfare from a "maintenance" perspective to one of active and supportive assistance to those who seek work in response to economic exigency.

As important as these innovations and initiatives are, efforts at reforming welfare practice will, nevertheless, not provide the major response to underclass formation. In the remaining years of the 1980s and into the 1990s, a new social policy must be framed to guide strategies aimed at reversing the further growth of an underclass and poverty in black America.

Again, six years of supply-side economics have also proven disastrous. Not only has this policy been ineffective to hold the line on poverty, poverty has significantly increased since 1979. Not only has supply-side policy worsened the condition of the poor, it has fostered the segmentation of America into two societies — one rich and prospering and the other becoming poorer — hence created a hardened condition in which to unfold actions that are responsive to the nation's poor.[52] It is this condition that requires that supply-side economics be repudiated as a sound approach to reverse underclass povertization. A new national policy is necessary.

Any new policy must first seek to stimulate a growth economy, as this is fundamental to assure that there are enough jobs for those who seek work. A growth economy can be stimulated by creative use of a monetary/fiscal policy that encourages business and industrial expansion.

No new actions are more critical to reversing the underclass condition than putting the idle labor force to work and providing livable incomes. The historical and continued disproportionality of black unemployment and joblessness — in periods of economic growth and in recessions — must be eliminated. Economic justice demands, at minimum, blacks equally share the benefits of prosperity and the hardships of recessions on par with all other Americans. A sensitive strategy — affirmative action — provides a tested model to undergird efforts to achieve this goal.

In the end, programs to train and update the skills capacity of the unemployed must be a part of national action. Technology and the new sciences that underpin contemporary production have significantly altered the workplace. For large portions of the underclass, absence from labor force participation has intensified work skills deficits. Training programs can do much to reverse the skills deficit capacity of those who seek work.

A primary concern for action and social intervention must be the system of poor black families. In the past two decades, no social institution has received more adverse attention than the family organization of poor blacks. It has been the object of a brutal public policy that enforced separation of parents because of their poverty; it has gained notoriety and has been studied as a system of "pathology," and its members — parents and children — and organizational patterns have been maligned daily. Most recently public commentary has pinpointed black poverty as emanating from single-parent, female-headed households, while the incorrigible young, unemployed, black males are persistently pointed to as the source of community disruption. The children of poor black families have become faceless and without personality, relegated to statistics indicating their numbers in poverty or in households afflicted by poverty. Increasingly this practice of fragmenting the poor black family and relating only to separate family components — mother, father, sister, brother, cousin — as if they were mutually exclusive entities, has compounded the problem of effective intervention. The family as a unit, as the vehicle of social and economic strength, as the protective organization of its members, and the family as a conveyor of values and strategies for effective socialization have been diminished.

The focus of social intervention by black community institutions and services can do much to generate pressures that refocus positive attention to the black family. Central to programmatic strategies must be how does this action serve to strengthen the family, to recreate its capacity to be a social instrument of power. The broad policy implications would have us examine closely proposals that seek solution for poor families in sub-minimum wage fields; that offer to reconstitute the economic viability of poor families on the single income of black families earned in a segmented workplace where class, race, and gender factors impinge on the quality of income or proposals that would put black men to work in less than minimum-wage paying jobs outside the urban cities — away from their roots and kinship ties. Black institutions and their leadership must be vigilant, to assure that no policies that threaten to have adverse impact on the black family are allowed public sanction.

I conclude by noting that while much can and must be done in the public policy arena to reverse underclass growth and restore health functioning to poor black families, nothing looms more important than mobilizing the strengths of the black community itself. Blacks as a community as never before must lead the actions necessary to counter the pattern of social disorganization concomitant with poverty, despair, and desperation.

And while not an issue of national policy, but surely one vital to the black community, a desperate need also exists for spiritual and value restoration. Those values need to be reinstilled that have been important to blacks in the past; those values need to be provided that have relevance for blacks currently: The value of dignity, respect for our elders, for our family; the disciplining of our children always tempered by blacks' love for children; the strength of our pulling together; and our commitment to go just a little farther to make it in a race controlled by unequal rules. And, too, we must recognize our victories, our strengths, and accomplishments. The capacity exists in the community of blacks that can help reverse underclass formation.

The black community's efforts must prod the public consciousness to implement the affirmative solutions to reversing underclass formation.

Drug Use: Special Implications for Black America

Beny J. Primm

INTRODUCTION

Drug abuse in the black community is, in my estimation, the most serious and perplexing problem facing Black America. Any discussion of the problem must include tobacco and alcohol, for they are more detrimental to Black America than the abuse of those substances considered by most blacks as the most common substances of abuse (heroin, cocaine, marijuana, PCP, and sedative hypnotic drugs). This contribution to the *State of Black America* focuses on the substances just mentioned, their manifestations, and the complications associated with their intravenous use, specifically infection with the human immunodeficiency virus (HIV) leading to the acquired immunodeficiency syndrome (AIDS). (See the section on AIDS, following.)

Even though tobacco contributes significantly to these complications and other disease manifestations that take a heavy toll on blacks, it will not be discussed herein because all drug users will at some time abuse it singularly or in conjunction with their substance of choice.

Alcohol use and abuse is so common in the black community that it has become accepted behavior. Its availability in large urban areas is such that there is no great distance to walk to procure it; no effort required to procure it after hours, when official places of purchase are closed; and prices are such that purchase is not prohibitive. Panhandling and pooling of funds are commonplace and tolerated, as is evidenced by the manner in which we easily dole out quarters and larger sums to alcoholics who clean our windshields, even when their services are discouraged or unwanted. This lack of an enforced collective or individual social policy against this kind of behavior results only in its encouragement.

There is little reliable statistical information concerning the number of alcoholic and other drug abusers in the United States. Even more startling is the fact that there never has been any reliable epidemiological data supporting the number of black abusers reported by the media.

This is an historical happening. Fabricated erroneous reports have often been used by racists to support policy, laws, and acts of prejudice promulgated on minorities — especially blacks in America.

While the scientific method requires as a starting point clear definitions, I would like to first note that a lack of agreement plagues those seeking suitable definitions in this field. This is especially unfortunate in an object of investigation that necessarily impinges on a wide variety of fields, since, as one Seventeenth Century author noted:

in the Solution of Question, the Maine Matter was the well-stating of them, which requires mother-witt and Logick, for let the question be but well-stated, it will work almost of itself.[1]

Nonetheless, at least two definitions of drug use have attained credence in the medical community, and they need to be recognized here. Perhaps the more widely respected definition was written by the late head of the Committee on Problems of Drug Dependence of the National Academy of Sciences, Maurice Seevers. He began by observing that the term "drug dependence" denotes predictable and reproducible individual drug interactions that can be described precisely in medical, psychological, and pharmacological terms. "Drug abuse," on the other hand, represents a value judgment by society. It may refer to any type of drug or chemical, without regard to its pharmacologic actions. The term is used to imply either individual injury or social harm, without regard to the nature of the injury or the organ systems involved. The term has only one uniform connotation — "the disapproval of society."[2]

Definitions are particularly central to our understanding of drug dependence among black Americans, since the question we all need to address is what exacerbates or makes the problem different for this population when compared to other communities. The mechanism of physiological dependence should be the same for all persons, no matter what their racial, ethnic, linguistic, national, or other category within the overall population.

For blacks, sociological factors play a predominant role; those definitions encompassing the sociological orientation are as important to the medical care of the black community as those emphasizing physical dependence, psychological predisposition, or behavioral dependence.[3] For the purpose of this article, we propose the following definition: *Drug dependence* is the state produced by repeated administration of a drug such that the drug user engages in substantive and replicable behavior patterns over an extended period of time, with such behavior leading specifically to further administrations of the drugs.[4]

HISTORICAL BACKGROUND

No report on alcohol and other forms of drug abuse among black Americans can be written without considering the history of the subject. That history cannot be confined to the recent past but must include the time of slavery and the period immediately following, in order to understand the evolution of the problem we face today.

Slavemasters gave alcohol to slaves on weekends and holidays to prevent uprisings. It was given to slaves to be consumed in a fashion that mimicked white consumption. The sale and traffic of alcohol was inextricably intertwined with the triangular slave trade among New England, Africa, and the West Indies.[5]

As the black population increased in the northeastern United States, laws were enacted to restrict blacks from using alcoholic beverages. Concern about the drinking among blacks led South Carolina in 1831 to enact a law prohibiting free blacks from owning or operating a still.

During the Civil War, it was impossible to control the use and distilling of alcohol, as well as the use of laudanum (liquid opium). Both were necessary for medicinal purposes and were used freely by Union and Confederate soldiers, as well as by blacks. Opiate use became so pervasive among ex-soldiers as to give rise to the term "Army Disease."[6]

During Reconstruction, many people perceived blacks as subhumans who drank excessively, refused to work, and were dangerous while drinking. It was felt that the major difficulty of managing the drinking problems in the South was related to the control of drinking by blacks.[7]

Many co-factors contributed to the excessive alcohol consumption of blacks: rural-to-urban migration, with the accompanying adjustment to the urban lifestyle; change of the economy from agricultural to industrial; unemployment; poor education; and the stressful living that resulted from these environmental changes. All are accepted etiological factors for substance abuse.

Nothing is more descriptive of the attitudes of the time, and *false,* than a report made in 1910 by Hamilton Wright, M.D., the State Department official responsible for U.S. drug policy, in which he stated:

> The use of cocaine by negroes of the South is one of the most elusive and troublesome questions confronting the enforcement of law in most of the Southern States. Cocaine is often the direct incentive to the crime of rape by the negroes of the South, and other sections of the Country.[8]

There was never any evidence to support Wright's thesis. A study by E.M. Green, who examined 2,119 blacks admitted to the Georgia State Sanitarium from 1909-1914, found only three cases of narcotic addiction among black patients, in contrast to 142 drug-related psychoses among whites. Of the three cases, cocaine was solely used in one instance, in combination with morphine and alcohol in another, and in combination with the opiate laudanum in the third case.[9]

Other data confirmed the low incidence of opiate use among southern blacks. Roberts (1885) reported insignificant rates in North Carolina.[10] In Tennessee, Brown (1915) found only 10 percent of the registered opiate users were black — significantly less than their proportion in the overall population.[11] Other reports revealed similar low incidence among southern blacks, leading these authors to conclude:

> The plain fact is that Dr. Wright, the chief authority of the claim of a black cocaine problem, and later the virtual author of the Harrison bill to ban it, was reporting unsubstantiated information and dishonestly misrepresenting the evidence available to him.[12]

Immediately after World War I, the demand for treatment for opioid use was so great that numerous narcotic clinics were started in urban areas such as New York City, Jacksonville, Florida, and New Orleans, Louisiana. In the New York City clinics, for the first time in the country, there was an over-representation of black narcotic users as compared to whites. Yet, this fact was almost totally ignored by public health officials.

147

Selective reporting of the excessive use of alcohol and other drugs by blacks was done in a self-serving fashion, depending on the presence of an economic recession, an excessive labor pool, too much black economic and social advancement, or too much racial integration, intermarriage, or acceptance of blacks by whites. The objective of this selective reporting was to keep the labor pool lily-white and keep mainstream society afraid of the void of blacks.

A major set of social factors relating to drug dependence behavior may be grouped under the rubric "economic." It can be clearly shown, for example, that the statistics of drug dependency vary in correlation to the availability of employment in American history. This argument has been amply set forth in a major work on drug abuse entitled *Drug Use, The Labor Market, and Class Conflict.*[13] The authors maintain that

> not only is the socioeconomic pattern of narcotics use the same as it was a century ago, but . . . the problem of widespread addiction is a recurrent one and cyclical one (and) we are forced to examine the social constants which have operated in each case or episode in the cycle.

These constants still operate in Black America today, but multiplied tenfold. Blacks constitute 12 percent of the U.S. population, but nearly twice that ratio — 22.5 percent — of inner-city dwellers are black. For many blacks, the adjustment to inner-city living, the high level of unemployment, the changing economy, and the changing labor market from manufacturing to high technology and service jobs have left them far behind the less disadvantaged. This, combined with the continued restriction of upward mobility for blacks, has placed them at high risk to become drug users and drug dependent. What was fabricated in earlier years to diminish the attractiveness of blacks to shrink the black labor pool and create fear among whites and employers has now become a reality.

Blacks are disproportionately represented among those estimated to be alcoholic and other drug abusers relative to their representation in the U.S. population. Although this estimation cannot be substantiated by actual head count, there are sources of accurate information based on treatment utilization data compiled by the National Drug and Alcoholism Treatment Utilization Survey (NDATUS). A point prevalence survey, which collects unit-identifying and some client-in-treatment data on voluntary and involuntary admissions to treatment for alcohol and other drug abuse problems, has shown:

Table I. Clients in Treatment per 100,000 Population*

Blacks	290
American Indians, Eskimos, and Aleutians	170
Others, including Whites	90

*: Persons aged 15-64

Source: NDATUS, 1982, 1980 Census, Vol. 6, Page 8051.

The table demonstrates that the rate of black, Hispanic, American Indian, and Aleutian clients in treatment in the nation is greater than it is for whites.[14]

Through 1981, treatment data were collected nationally through the Client Oriented Data Acquisition Process (CODAP). For all publicly funded programs, reporting was obligatory. The data were criticized as being biased because they did not include privately funded programs. However, few blacks are in privately funded programs. Data reported by CODAP can be legitimately used to examine distributions within race and ethnic categories. The following table shows the number and percentage of racial distributions for the 182,002 clients admitted to treatment.

Table II. Distribution of Clients by Race/Ethnicity at Admission*

Race/Ethnicity	Client Admissions Numbers	Percentage
White	98,504	54.1
Black	40,538	23.4
Hispanic	40,625	22.3
American Indian	862	0.5
Alaskan Native	12	0.1
Asian/Pacific Islander	1,461	0.8

*: Based on 23 states, Washington, D.C., and territories; California represented 46 percent of treatment admissions.[15]
Does not include clients treated for alcohol abuse.
Source: CODAP, 1983.

The CODAP study is the most comprehensive currently available. Black representation may be higher now, but not appreciably so, for the number of people in treatment changes very little over time. Many people drop out (25-40 percent yearly) and are replaced by others, but treatment numbers remain relatively static. In New York City, where the number of addicts is estimated at 250,000, only 35,000-40,000 are known to be in treatment. Over the last four years, treatment capacity has increased by only 700 slots, and that increase was only in response to the fear of the spread of acquired immune deficiency syndrome (AIDS). There is vehement community and political opposition to opening new treatment centers or increasing the population in existing ones.

PREVALENCE

The overall prevalence of drug abuse in the general household population aged 12 and older is about the same for blacks and whites. Data from the 1982 National Survey on Drug Abuse showed that about 32 percent of each group had used drugs illicitly at some time in their lives.[16] Similar levels of current use were reported by both groups: 12 percent for whites and 13 percent for blacks. These estimates must be viewed as conservative: blacks are underrepresented in the sampling, and persons without fixed residences are not included, such as prison inmates and students living in college dormitories.

Blacks were sampled proportionately to their numbers in the general population and combined with other minorities (Hispanics), with an actual sampling of only 1,093 in the survey, which is substantially smaller than that for whites — 4,520.[17] This means that the estimates for blacks are subject to larger sampling errors than those for whites; also, accurate estimates cannot be made for separate race/ethnic groups.

Much the same can be said for the National Survey of High School Seniors, which concludes that overall drug abuse in the sampled population has decreased in all categories and that blacks showed a significant decrease.[18] This conclusion is misleading for the simple reason that 40-50 percent of black students in inner-city schools drop out after the ninth grade (53 percent in New York City schools)[19], and that group is not sampled in the survey. Yet, these dropouts may have the highest incidence and prevalence of substance abuse. This survey concluded that 18-year-old high school dropouts have a higher ratio of drug use compared to high school seniors. Forty percent of those seniors, as compared with 67 percent of the dropouts, have tried illicit drugs within the last year; and 12 percent of the seniors, as compared with 33 percent of the dropouts, used marijuana in the week prior to the sampling.[20]

What is so alarming and detrimental to Black America is that federal policy and funding decisions are made on the basis of these misleading national surveys. Our communities are continually slighted because of the sampling errors and the outright omission of certain population groups. Prevention and education dollars and programs are not targeted to areas of dire need.

Drug use patterns vary according to geographical areas. The choice of drugs, the mode and extent of administration, and the use of different combinations of drugs vary from state to state, city to city, community to community. There are documented racial and age differences in the choice, use, and mode of administration of drugs. All drug use, however, depends on specific drug availability, combined with the above variables and other psycho-social and economic factors.

Blacks aged 25 and under tend to prefer marijuana by 60.5 percent; PCP by 47.4 percent; cocaine by 31.0 percent; and heroin — least of all — by 8.2 percent. In contrast, among blacks over age 25, heroin ranks number one, at 91.8 percent; cocaine, 69.0 percent; PCP, 52.6 percent; and marijuana, 31.5 percent, according to the 1983 CODAP study of drug use by race, ethnicity, and age at the admission (see Table III). This study was based on data from 23 states, Washington, D.C., and U.S. territories. Of black clients reporting a primary problem with heroin at admission to treatment, 31 percent also reported a secondary problem with cocaine. This figure was three times the figure reported by white clients with a primary problem with heroin.

Table III. Distribution of Clients by Selected Primary Drug According to Race/Ethnicity and Age at Admission

Primary Drug	White		Black	
	Under 25	25 and Over	Under 25	25 and Over
Heroin	16.1%	83.9%	8.2%	91.8%
Cocaine	45.3%	54.7%	31.0%	69.0%
Marijuana	76.4%	23.6%	68.5%	31.5%
PCP	63.3%	36.7%	47.4%	52.6%

Source: CODAP, 1983

The choice of drugs or combination of drugs and the more invasive the route of drug administration often are indicative of the severity of the addiction syndrome (duration of dependency and degree of drug tolerance).

Although cocaine inhalation ("freebasing," "crack" smoking) is not considered as invasive as intravenous use of the drug, it is considered far more detrimental because of the speed of the onset of the drug's effect, the facility of use by this route, and the increased rate of its dependency. Twenty-seven percent of black clients admitted to a drug abuse treatment program with a primary problem with cocaine reported smoking (or freebasing) as their preferred route of administration, compared to five percent of white clients. Also, black primary cocaine admissions were more likely to report intravenous use than whites. "Speedballing" (intravenously combining heroin and cocaine) is a more invasive mode of administration; it is a problem particularly predominant among black and Puerto Ricans, representing 76 percent of speedballing admissions. Perhaps this intravenous preference is partly responsible for the disproportionate representation of blacks and Hispanics among diagnosed AIDS cases, where in New York City they represent 30 and 25 percent, respectively.

ETIOLOGY

The etiology of drug abuse has been a highly controversial issue for many years. There is a laundry list of causes, each having a sound basis for its inclusion. Some recent ones are more speculative than others, particularly those based on biomolecular theory. In the past, "factors explaining why drug abuse in black communities has been so common have been cited so often that they have become cliches."[21] A partial list of such factors:

- The history of racism in the United States, and the black American's slave history and forced exile from Africa
- Poverty, unemployment, lack of job and career opportunities

- Disproportionate attention of law enforcement agencies in arresting blacks on drug charges
- Drug abuse politics and get-tough laws
- Economics of drugs as alternative careers
- Hopelessness of ghetto life
- Lifestyles that reject menial or subsistence jobs in favor of hustling and the drama of dope dealing
- Peer pressures
- Consistently high unemployment rates
- Cultural and class conflicts
- Inadequate educational preparation and the dropout syndrome
- Rising material, social, and success expectations and aspirations
- Breakdown of family life; welfare policies that encourage single-parent households
- Frustration from continuing discrimination and rejection
- Responsiveness to the dominant culture's media imperative for instant gratification
- Stress

A recent article, "Epidemiology of Drug Abuse: An Overview," by Kozel and Adams, in *Science,* Vol. 234, page 970 (November, 1986), reported a partial listing of the underlying causes of drug abuse, stating that they are as diverse as the population they affect: peer pressure, curiosity, depression, hedonism, attempts to increase or improve performance, rebellion, alienation, and a wide variety of other reasons.[22] The authors failed to mention what has been historically considered by many to be some of the most prominent causes associated with disproportionate minority representation among substance abusers: unemployment, overt racism, poor inner-city schools with high dropout rates, and the continually shrinking labor market. Furthermore, the authors failed to mention those close positive relationships between the changes in the economy, especially recession, on measures of social stress and the resultant pathological use of alcohol and other psychotropic substances in reaction to distress.

The Joint Economic Committee report (1984) highlighted the importance of economic inequality as a factor in the behavior of minority youth and the downwardly mobile. According to the document,

> Economic inequality relates to the distribution of the product of economic development. For reasons which usually depend on structural changes in the economy, specific populations may not gain — or may actually experience losses in — economic status, while the majority of the population takes part in the process of economic growth. In the United States, youth, the elderly, women, and ethnic minorities frequently experience this situation.
>
> Serious economic inequality has an even greater adverse impact, which is compounded during periods of economic growth, when the majority of society is earning at least moderate incomes and is not experiencing high unemployment. The most adverse effects are typically experienced by a

significant proportion of youth of lower socioeconomic status, especially those with minority ethnic backgrounds. Many elderly persons who are chronically impoverished and a sizable proportion of female heads of households also experience the worst effects of economic inequality.

Finally, the problems of long-term unemployment (as opposed to short-term cyclical unemployment) and low income in the last decade have been extended to former workers in the automobile, glass, steel, rubber, and other durable-goods industries which have suffered long-term declines in employment.

In periods of economic instability, the economic loss and downward mobility typically associated with recession lead to expansion of socioeconomic status differentials; thus, the effects of recession become an even greater burden, proportionally, on the downwardly mobile. Economic inequality becomes even more acute when the general population is moving out of a recession. While some individuals gain, a portion of the population never recovers. This portion, then, experiences lower socioeconomic status and exhibits higher mortality rates.[23]

Bob Englehart
Hartford Courant

While drug dependency is a response to a variety of "causative" social indicators, drug dependency may equally be viewed as a sociological phenomenon having its origin in forces outside the individual but manifested ultimately in the victim. There is a factor which I believe finds its natural position midway between the accepted causative social features noted above and drug dependency. To date, this factor has been curiously absent from much of the literature. This mediating element is *stress*. Stress is the result of a multiplicity of exogenous impulses — social, economic, or cultural in nature, but it produces clear physical responses in individuals.

For years, physicians have noted the role of stress in the health of patients. McKean and Rahe demonstrated a link between "stressful life events" and the incidence of illness.[24] George Vaillant reported, in a 40-year study, the relationship between mental health and the development of physical disease. Vaillant's and Brenner/Swank's works noted that mental health status was an accurate indicator of subsequent illness.[25] Khantizian, et al., found that addicts' failure to develop adaptive solutions to stress is a major contributor to addiction.[26]

It is possible for seemingly innocuous items to become noxious stimuli for people who have experienced patterns of failure and frustration. School buildings, nice cars, attractive couples, fine houses, prosperous businessmen, all can send some people into fits of distemper, jealousy, frustration, and depression. Beset by ubiquitous, depressing stimuli and persistent self-doubt, some victims of stress are in a state of chronic, psychic pain.

Using the Beck Depression Inventory, Inwang, et al., hypothesized that depression of this sort appears to be a primary psychological issue in narcotic addiction.[27] Zimmerman et al., put forth the same hypothesis, characterizing the main element of the "heroin behavior syndrome" as underlying depression.[28] Cowan et al., in an unpublished study, wrote:

> . . . psychoactive drugs (e.g., alcohol, opioids) may be used to relieve persistent episodic feelings of defeat.
>
> Drugs that counteract feelings of defeat need not do so by producing feelings of success; producing amnesia for defeated feelings may be sufficient.

Zimmerman cited drug use as a learned response to stress. Eric Gnepp perceived drug use as operant conditioning to cultural obstacles and frustrations.[29] From Berlin, Lurssen wrote that drugs are taken not to achieve gratification but to reduce intolerable intrapsychic tension — the user seeks an escape to nothingness.[30] From Edinburgh, Carstairs reported that U.S. heroin addicts exhibited feelings of worthlessness, anxiety, and depression.[31]

There is no community in the United States that reflects the results of stress more than Central Harlem in New York City. It has the highest numbers per 100,000 population of registered narcotic addicts by zip code number and address.[32] The latest (1980) population estimate of 121,995 is 95 percent black, making it very homogeneous. Harlem ranks number one in New York City health districts for death rates per 100,000 population in all stress-related diseases except suicide. For cirrhosis of the liver, drug dependence, and cerebro-vascular disease, the rate is two to three times that of any other New York City community.[33] Unfortunately, New York City is the only city collecting and publishing this genre of epidemiological health data. I suspect that all inner cities with large black populations would record similar statistical data, if researched.

Black Americans in Harlem live with morbidity and mortality rates far higher than those of whites in New York City, and they suffer disproportionately on every social indicator available for study. Given racial prejudice, continuing high unemployment (now at an accepted national rate of 6.9 percent), and crime in the black population districts, it is unquestionable that black Americans suffer an inordinate amount of stress. We can therefore speculate that blacks are disproportionately represented among drug-dependent cohorts because of unbearably high stress. The incapacitating effects of stress not only create a need for self-administered dependence-producing drugs, but also reduce the body's defenses to those drugs. Moreover, stress can hardly be expected to diminish for black residents in Harlem, or in the United States. Short of massive social change in America, drug dependency will no doubt continue as a result of stress, itself the creation of a host of unfavorable social conditions for black Americans. It is a small wonder that more residents of Harlem are not using drugs to alleviate the stress that is inevitably encountered in daily life there!

Obviously, the extreme social indicators present in Harlem portend a great deal for those concerned with drug dependency in Black America. There are many conclusions to be drawn from all of the aforementioned. Many age-old hypotheses, suggestions, nuances, and innuendos have been interjected so that the reader should be ever mindful that, whatever the predisposing factors, causes, and results of drug abuse in the black community, stress is the response and bottom line, common to every aspect of this perplexing phenomenon.

The word "stress," as used here, designates the aggregate of the effects of both the nonspecific factors (normal activity, environment, economy, housing, drug availability, employment, etc.) and specific factors (drug pharmacology, inter- and intracellular response, etc.).

Normally, the body responds to any stressful stimulus by secreting two powerful neuro-transmitters, adrenocortocotropin and beta endorphin. (Beta endorphin — an endogenous or internal opioid — has the same molecular configuration as morphine and heroin, and they all act at the same receptor site in the body.) The two neuro-transmitters are secreted simultaneously when stimulated by stress, and plasma levels of both rise and fall at the same time. It is well known that the use of exogenous (from the outside) cortisone often causes the adrenal gland to respond by a diminishing, and sometimes cessation, of the synthesis and secretion of the adrenocorticotropic hormone responsible for triggering the release of corticotropin. If this same principle applies to the release of beta endorphin after illicit exogenous opioid (morphine, heroin) use, and if the body's stress response system is already exhausted, opioid addiction could become a chronic relapsing problem; that illicit drug-taking may be an attempt by persons so affected to self-medicate in order to feel normal.

Avram Goldstein, M.D., had the foresight to say with great caution

> In 1973, even before the endogenous opiates were actually discovered (although their existence seemed almost certain), we suggested that a defect in a system that regulated mood, pain, and anxiety responses would almost inevitably result in behavioral disorders. We postulated such a defect could make one subject prone to addiction, to which another, whose endorphins were working normally, might prove invulnerable. I do not mean to suggest that addiction is simply a matter of genetics, which may account for some inborn predisposition. Obviously addiction is a complex social phenomenon in which, I am sure, economics and lifestyles are more significant factors than the effectiveness of endorphins in any give population. However, the endorphin system may explain why it is that, given the same drug availability, some individuals will become addicted and others will not. It may elucidate the vulnerability factor in addiction.
>
> Still another possibility is that addiction might be produced not by a constitutional defect in the endogenous system but by its suppression or severe impairment as a result of a habitual use of exogenous opiates (heroin).[34]

Several years later, Goldstein's foresight and speculation remain just that. Many eminent researchers have chosen not to pursue this logic, perhaps because scientifically documenting this hypothesis would spark a completely different approach to the problem of drug abuse by 400,000-600,000 opioid addicts in America.[35]

The ability of morphine, heroin, and methadone to relieve pain, anxiety, and stress is enhanced by the simultaneous administration of stimulant-type drugs. Addicts have been practicing this pharmacological feat by mixing cocaine and heroin, giving it the appropriate name "speedball."

The normal physiological response to stress is a release of substances (adrenalin, beta endorphin) with the same pharmacological action as the speedball, prompting speculation that this too is an act of self-medication for stress or whatever the user perceives as his or her need. The immediate gratification and euphoria realized from using cocaine has encouraged pushers and dealers to market a smokable form of the drug, costing only $10 or less, called "crack." Crack is widely available in black communities and is very popular among all age groups. Crime has escalated, and admissions to psychiatric emergency rooms are up 100 percent for the treatment of severe cocaine psychoses.[36]

The use of stimulants combined with narcotics (heroin methadone) and especially hallucinogens (PCP) is a relatively recent phenomenon among younger, beginner drug abusers. The "highs" created by crack are described as being so intense that one needs a "parachute drug" to bring himself or herself down, to slow and cushion the rapid descent of the "cocaine crash." Alcohol, marijuana, barbiturates, and valium are all becoming more popular in black communities, because they ease the crash. Bar owners report a dramatic increase in sales of cognac in black neighborhoods where cocaine and crack use is rampant.[37] The belief is that cognac (because of its ardent and body heaviness) mellows the cocaine crash. However, using cognac compounds the problems of those users by creating a dual addiction — early alcoholism.

BOARDER BABIES

In New York City hospitals, there are 140 so-called "boarder babies," ranging in age from newborns to 12 years old.[38] These children are permanent residents of their hospitals and have no access to the outside world. Their world is the pediatric ward, with multiple nurse-surrogate mothers changing every shift. The mothers of these children are intravenous drug users, alcoholics, and other substance abusers. Boarder babies have little hope of adoption because would-be foster parents and relatives fear the onset of the fetal alcohol syndrome (FAS), the fetal marijuana syndrome, cocaine (crack) and opioid protracted-abstinence effects, and — most of all — all AIDS-related complex (ARC) and full-blown AIDS leading to eventual death. This problem, one of immense proportions with few solutions, is yet another major by-product of drug abuse. One temporary solution has been Hale House, which cares for babies born to addicted mothers until the rehabilitated mother can herself care for and take the child. However, the capacity of Hale House is small. Efforts such as Hale House need expansion and support.

The continued glamourization of the use of tobacco and alcohol (via black celebrity alcohol and tobacco advertisements) and the lack of a meaningful, well-communicated, culturally oriented social policy results in the assumption that the use of chemical substances is condoned rather than disdained by black communities. With inordinately high death rates from cirrhosis of the liver and lung cancer, blacks in America and Third World countries must *condemn,* not condone, these media messages. For black women, lung cancer is now the leading cause of death from cancer for all ages — surpassing breast and uterine cancer. Black men have continuously led in the death rates for lung cancer. Both statistics are attributed to smoking by the two groups.[39] There have been anecdotal reports that Third World countries and black women are being targeted for advertising because of the impact the anti-smoking campaigns have had on profits of cigarette manufacturers.

RECOMMENDATIONS

Drug, alcohol, and tobacco addiction are without peers as detriments to the health of black Americans. We must accept that addiction is a chronic disease with remission and relapses, and we must accept and support treatment centers in our communities. A meaningful and well-defined enforceable social policy for black Americans must be established and adequately communicated to the population. It must be culturally significant and taught at pre-kindergarten levels, with home reinforcement.

National leaders and organizations must take immediate steps to reduce the stressful conditions under which black people live, emphasizing preventive health care and maintenance. They must:

- Encourage research to explore the nexus between stress and addictive behavior and the biochemical markers involved.
- Request immediate funding of adequate detoxification programs in all inner-city areas where addiction is rampant.
- Establish and maintain massive education and prevention programs, beginning in pre-kindergarten and continuing through college and even graduate school.

Adam Walinsky, in a *New York Times* commentary, summarized what could be done about "crack," the latest popular drug, with the following recommendations. They seem to be the appropriate note on which to end:

> There are useful and necessary measures we can take. One would be a real effort at law enforcement to reestablish basic order and security. Another would be welfare reform: social programs should no longer encourage single parentage, and should require work as a condition of all welfare. Still other steps would include extensive efforts to reach the more than 400,000 new children of single mothers who will have their 13th birthday this year. At the root, we must decide that we will not live with a Black illegitimacy rate in excess of 60 percent, with all that entails. We must commit ourselves to providing minority youth with a future that is not built solely on crime or the making of babies.[40]

All these things are difficult but possible. It is long past time that our leaders stop their hysterical grandstanding about new drugs and get to work on the old, persistent problems of crime, race, and poverty.

AIDS: A Special Report

Beny J. Primm

INTRODUCTION

Undoubtedly, infection with the human immunodeficiency virus (HIV) is one of the most serious problems facing members of any society. It is of particularly grave importance to the black community, for its members are disproportionately represented among those who have been found to be HIV-antibody-positive (meaning they have been exposed to and are infected by the virus, and they are infectious to others with whom they might have sexual contact or share needles). *They may not have any symptoms for years — if ever, but they remain carriers for the rest of their lives.*

The human immunodeficiency virus permanently suppresses the body's immune system, rendering it ineffective. The immune system is a conglomerate of various cells and biophysiological functions that fights against all bacteria, viruses, and other foreign bodies that may invade and infect the body. Among the cells for which the virus has an affinity are the T4 lymphocytes (also called "helper cells"), which orchestrate the body's immune response. The virus multiplies in these T4 cells and completely and permanently destroys them, thereby creating a permanent immunodeficiency.

Black Americans suffer from AIDS at an alarmingly high incidence and prevalence rate. From June 1, 1981, to September 8, 1986, U.S. physicians and health departments notified the Centers for Disease Control (CDC) of 24,576 patients meeting the AIDS case definition (positive antibody test for HIV, presence of HIV, and one opportunistic infection or malignancy). Of these 6,192 (25 percent) were blacks, whereas blacks represent only 12 percent of the U.S. population, according to the 1980 U.S. Census. The proportion of black cases has remained relatively constant (Figure 1), but the number of reported AIDS cases among persons of all racial and ethnic backgrounds continues to rise (Figure 2).

More black adults with AIDS than white adults with AIDS (62 percent and 33 percent, respectively) were likely to reside in New York, New Jersey, or Florida. Black men accounted for 23 percent of the 22,648 cases, and black women accounted for 51 percent of the 1,634 female cases (compared with whites at 28 percent of all AIDS cases).

The mode of transmission also differed among races. Homosexual or bisexual men who had AIDS and patients who acquired AIDs from blood or blood products were predominantly white. Patients with a history of intravenous drug abuse or heterosexual contact with persons of increased risk for acquiring AIDS and patients with no identified mode of transmission were predominantly black

159

Figure 1. Percentage of acquired immunodeficiency syndrome (AIDS) cases,*
by year of diagnosis and race — United States, pre-1981–1986

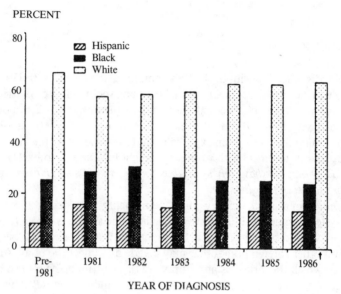

PERCENT

*Reported as of September 8, 1986, and excludes 153 AIDS patients (< 1%) of other race.
†Incomplete year.

or Hispanic. The proportion of blacks with AIDS was high in all transmission categories with the exception of hemophilia.[1]

The racial/ethnic distribution of homosexual/bisexual patients differed from that of heterosexual patients. Among homosexual/bisexual male AIDS patients, 16 percent were black, 11 percent Hispanic, and 73 percent white. Among heterosexual AIDS patients in other transmission categories, 50 percent were black, 25 percent for both Hispanic and white. In a recent *New England Journal of Medicine* article, Jackson et al., reported 35 percent of all black AIDS cases were homosexual/bisexual males.[2] Our AIDS hotline experience indicates that a significant number of these were "closet gays" who represent a silent and dangerous transmission link of the virus to the heterosexual community.

AIDS poses a definite challenge to the physical and psycho-emotional health of black women nationwide. As previously stated, black women account for 51 percent of the total diagnosed AIDS cases among women. Women make up seven percent, or 1,789 of the total number of Americans with AIDS. And of this number, 1,080 have died. The majority of these women are poor, single mothers, most of whom live in New York City.[3] A devastating by-product of this

Figure 2. Acquired immunodeficiency syndrome (AIDS) cases,* by year of diagnosis and race — United States, pre-1981–1986

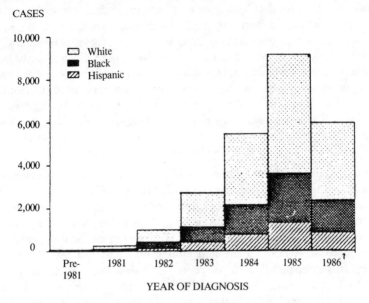

CASES

*Reported as of September 8, 1986, and excludes 153 AIDS patients (< 1%) of other race.
†Incomplete year.

Source: U.S. Census Bureaus

is that, of the total U.S. pediatric AIDS cases, 82 percent, or 204 of the 250 babies, are born to black women.[4]

To illustrate further the challenge that this disease poses for all women, and especially black women, I will use New York City as a paradigm because of its high proportion of AIDS cases. In New York, AIDS is the leading cause of death for women between 25 and 29 years of age, the second leading cause of death for women ages 30 to 34, and the third leading cause of death for women ages 15 to 19.

It is believed that, for every woman with AIDS, there may be 20 who have antibodies to the AIDS virus in their blood or who have AIDS-related sicknesses.[5] More than 50 percent of women with AIDS are intravenous drug users, who presumably have acquired AIDS through needle-sharing during drug activities or by means of sexual contact with men infected with human immunodeficiency virus. A small percentage of these women has been infected by men who have engaged in homosexual acts.

161

The question raised by this information is two-pronged. How does a woman know if the man she is sexually involved with is a "closet" intravenous drug user or has used drugs in the past, *and* how can she know if her sexual partner or potential sexual partner is a "closet" bisexual/homosexual?

Women can check for the physical signs of intravenous drug use, such as small needle marks or scarred veins or extreme behavior, but the task becomes herculean when signs of bisexuality or homosexuality are sought. Herein lies the heart of the challenge — the need to assess her risks responsibly and to the best of her ability so that her health and psycho-emotional being are not jeopardized. The art of negotiating safer sex practices must become part of her armament for healthful living. Both men and women are learning to ask about a potential partner's past health and sexual experiences, and they are reassessing their own sexual habits and practices.

* * *

Early in 1982, a significant number of AIDS cases was found among Haitians in the U.S. and Haiti. Also beginning in 1982, cases of AIDS were identified in Europe among Africans, and among Europeans of both sexes with histories of sexual contact with Africans in Europe or in Africa. Epidemiological studies conducted in central Africa by European, U.S., and African scientists revealed a high incidence of AIDS in Zaire and among west and east-central African countries. It is estimated that 50,000 people have died from the disease called "Slim" (AIDS) in central Africa since its confirmed appearances in the late 1970s. Privately some leading AIDS researchers say the death toll to date is several hundred thousand![6]

Infectivity of five percent of the general population of Zaire,[7] and a much higher percentage among the sexual contacts of symptomatic people, led many to speculate that AIDS began in Africa, possibly from mutation of a retrovirus related to the HIV found in wild (captured) green monkeys.[8] The earliest evidence of HIV was identified in blood samples of Kinshasa, Zaire, dating back to 1959. In the Rakai region of Uganda, 30 percent of the sexually active adults are estimated to be positive for the virus.

Further speculation posits that the AIDS virus reached Haiti by cultural exchange of artists, etc., between Zaire and Haiti. It is believed that male homosexuals and bisexuals who were involved with male and female prostitutes in Haiti contracted the infection and brought it back to the U.S. This theory is vehemently opposed by Haitians; it was initially opposed by Africans, who proclaim that they co-existed for millenia with the green monkeys as pets and for food and that there was never any issue of AIDS. The denials of this origin have been so adamant that the political climate subsequently created resulted in some African censorship and the boycotting of a scientific meeting on African AIDS held in Brussels November 22-23, 1985.[9]

As late as November, 1985, not a single case of AIDS had been officially reported from central Africa, although the incidence of the disease had been rising sharply, and its progenitor, HIV, was spreading at an alarming rate in some regions.[10] One very positive indication of the presence of the disease was the diagnosis of AIDS among Africans who had moved to Europe or were referred to European hospitals for treatment. The sexual distribution of these cases was of a 1:1 ratio, male to female, similar to that of Haitians. To the AIDS experts, these data signaled possible heterosexual transmission in these populations. But what is more significant is the denial of the existence of AIDS in central Africa because of political and economic reasons. Economically, it was felt the adverse publicity would discourage tourism and investment. Politically, for Haitians, it was believed that the designation unfairly stigmatized recent poor, Haitian immigrants who were already saddled with adjustment problems caused by cultural and language differences.[11] These denials very obviously retarded efforts of both communities to combat the burgeoning spread of the disease by indirectly discouraging prevention and education initiatives.

Africans and Haitians are represented significantly in the populations of New York, Washington, Miami, Delray Beach, Los Angeles, Houston, and other cities. They are street merchants, taxicab drivers, students, diplomats, lawyers, doctors, etc., and are otherwise socially interactive with all segments of American society.

When blacks are viewed by the larger society, they are often perceived as one homogeneous mass indistinguishable from one another with reference to origin or cultural differences. To the nonsophisticate, a stigma for Haitians or Africans is a stigma for all black Americans. We all suffer equally the same prejudices, racial slurs, and maltreatment by the larger society.

Another possible source of homosexual/bisexual and heterosexual transmission is the prisons. In January, 1986, the National Prison Project of the American Civil Liberties Union found that about 420 cases of AIDS had been diagnosed in state prisons across the country. Most of these inmates were intravenous drug abusers, and the majority of the cases were reported from the Middle Atlantic region: New York, New Jersey, Pennsylvania, and Washington, D.C., with all other parts of the United States contributing to much smaller percentages.

U.S. prisons have a disproportionate number of black inmates (60 percent) compared with our representation in the general population of 12 percent. In New York state, blacks constitute 70 percent of the inmate population. However, there is no available racial breakdown data of the reported 292 cases of AIDS presently in New York prisons.

At the time of the National Prison Project report, New York prisons were reported to have 245 AIDS cases and 153 deaths; 40 cases had been released and 52 cases remained incarcerated. As of this writing, New York state prisons report 292 AIDS cases, an increase of 47 cases in 10 months, for an average of about four diagnosed cases per month. If the CDC criteria were used to make the diagnosis, these new cases had to have contracted an opportunistic infection and were most likely very sick.

In the literature researched, there was no mention of AIDS related complex (ARC) or of seropositive persons who could be asymptomatic. In New York state, 13 to 15 percent of prisoners have been convicted of drug-related offenses, and 75 percent acknowledge having used illegal drugs before entering prison. Blood sera examinations of New York City patients in drug treatment programs reflect 50-60 percent seropositives. It is reasonable to extrapolate from this data and speculate that a sizable number of prisoners, if tested, would also be HIV-antibody-positive, and, therefore, infectious.

Yet prison officials naively state that the two primary means (intravenous drug use and sex) by which the disease is transmitted are prohibited behavior in all correction systems. Prisons are a definite place of viral transmission, secondary to the isolated forced and voluntary homosexual behavior, conjugal visits, and clandestine intravenous drug use.[12]

* * *

A recent report from the Department of Defense on military recruit applicants for all military branches reported examining 308,076 applicants for serologic evidence of infection with HIV. All were young adults in their late teens (54 percent) and early twenties (33 percent were 20-25 years of age). Eighty-five percent were male, and 77 percent were white. The prevalence of positive tests was higher among the 265,361 men of all ages (1.6/1000) than among the 42,715 women (0.6/1000); the ratio of male to female prevalence was 3:1. Prevalence varied by race: for the 237,586 whites, the rate was 0.9/1000; for the 55,185 blacks, the rate was 3.9/1000; and for the 15,305 applicants of other racial groups, the rate was 2.6/1000.[13]

Rates for blacks are extremely alarming: the services are universally known to not accept homosexuals/bisexuals or intravenous drug users, and such persons should not apply. If one is to assume that these young, black people were from the general population, that almost 1/250 examined was infected with HIV, and that 10-30 percent of them will eventually develop AIDS, then *Black America is in an extremely precarious position.*

* * *

Fifty-eight percent of all persons dying of AIDS in New York City are black, an obviously disproportionate rate when compared with our 30 percent representation of the total New York City AIDS cases. Researchers attribute this high death rate to: very poor health prior to contracting the disease; delayed medical consultation; lack of available, sensitive health care providers; and outright denial of the problem.

Education and prevention efforts have been very effective in reducing morbidity and mortality in the gay community, not only for AIDS, but also for other sexually transmitted diseases (gonorrhea, syphilis, herpes, and ohlamydia) as is evidenced by a reduction in reported cases from STD (sexually transmitted diseases) clinics. The adoption of safer sex practices (condom use, no body fluid exchange), monogamy, celibacy, and the reduction and cessation of drug use (particularly butyl nitrite (poppers), alcohol, tobacco and marijuana, cocaine, and heroin) have all contributed to better health and disease resistance. Gays have received a concentrated and sustained effort in AIDS prevention and education.

Black gays, jointly with whites and in their own organizations, such as the National Coalition of Black Lesbians and Gays (NCBLG), have sponsored conferences and meetings all over the country to raise awareness in black communities about the problem of AIDS, its prevention, and how to get help and counseling. Their efforts have included all minorities (Asians, Haitians, Latinos, Hispanics, Native Americans) and have been laudable despite a "brush off" from most black organizations, allegedly because of the organizations' fear of endorsing homosexual behavior.

Homophobia has been a key factor in all sectors of our society for nonsupport of the AIDS problem, particularly conservatives and "right wing" groups that say AIDS is God's way of punishing gays and drug addicts. Despite these negative responses, morbidity has been reduced and life expectancy has been prolonged among gays, with some living five to six years after diagnosis. This is alarmingly different for blacks and intravenous drug users, who reportedly live only 19 weeks to eight months after diagnosis, with the majority of that time spent in city hospitals. In some instances, these AIDS patients are abandoned by both family and friends.

Intravenous drug abusers and homosexuals/bisexuals are not well accepted by the general population. Because the problem of AIDS has been seen as one that primarily affected those groups, there has been little humanitarian interest generated in the black community. Only recently have the major national organizations and civil rights groups voiced some interest in this problem. New York Congressmen Charles Rangel and Edolphus Towns, members of the House Select Committee on Narcotics, have held two hearings focusing on the problem of AIDS in minority communities, with an update at the October 1986 meeting of the Congressional Black Caucus. Yet, little interest in this issue has been evidenced so far in those targeted communities.

What is needed is a massive and sustained prevention and education effort, culturally and ethnically focused to attract the attention of the community to those disproportionately affected by this fatal disease. Federal, state, municipal, and private funds must be allocated to support this effort. Physicians, ministers, politicians, and community leaders must be at the forefront of these efforts, in order to reduce the sensitivity that has spread in relationship to homophobia that negatively influences the degree of caring and support we give to both the afflicted and the worried well. Housing and hospices must be provided so that AIDS victims can die with dignity. Morticians must be alerted to be prepared for the 179,000 deaths predicted to occur in the U.S. by 1991. Twelve thousand of those dying will be black and from New York City where burial space is limited –– crematories are not equipped to handle these numbers. What I perceive for Black America is a major catastrophe if we do not begin effective programs immediately.

It is estimated that one to two million men and women have been infected with the human immunodeficiency virus, and not many of them are aware of their being infected and that they can be infectious. Therefore, this number is no doubt multiplying insidiously — and AIDS will continue to plague American society. Black women and men have the special task of joining all forces to prevent this disease from crippling black society.

ACKNOWLEDGEMENTS

I would like to pay tribute, and say thanks, to the Director of Executive Affairs of the Addiction Research and Treatment Corporation, Ms. Barbara Gibson; to my secretary, Ms. Maxine Dotson; to Mr. Henry Durak, my administrative assistant; to Mr. Daniel Cook, Director of Management Information Systems; and to Ms. Isolyn Richardson, secretary, who have all helped in the preparation of this document. To Ms. Gibson goes a very special thank you for her continued tolerance, support, editing, and moreover her contributing the segment on women and AIDS. Thank you all.

Blacks in State And Local Government: Progress and Constraints

Georgia A. Persons

Although there is a continuing concern nationally about the election of blacks to political office, it is of particular interest to review progress in this area in the immediate wake of the twentieth anniversary of passage of the Voting Rights Act of 1965 (VRA). The significance for blacks of passage of the VRA is not to be understated. Indeed it is with a sense of incredulity that one recalls the onerous nature of the obstacles deliberately designed to deny blacks access to the vote, including arbitrarily administered literacy tests, impromptu closings of voter registration offices when blacks appeared, physical and psychological intimidations and harassments. Such actions were particularly prevalent in the South prior to passage of the VRA, and these actions very effectively prevented blacks from participating in the most basic acts central to a democratic society: voting, and standing for elective office.

Prior to passage of the VRA, there were fewer than 200 black elected officials (BEO's) nationwide.[1] In late 1986, there were more than 6,500 BEO's nationwide, the majority of whom were elected at the municipal level.[2]

The focus of this article is on the presence of blacks in political positions at the level of state and local governments. Despite the disproportionate attention given to the election of blacks to national level offices (and a similar disproportionate attention given to the election of blacks as mayors of big cities), the election of blacks at all levels of state and local governments is at least equally significant, and perhaps even more so for various reasons.

State and local governments provide the vital public services which are basic to modern American life such as the world's largest public school system and highway network. These governments also provide most of the nation's health and welfare programs, judicial, police, correctional, and recreational services; regulate most of the activities of industry, banking, and commerce; regulate the provision of water, gas, electric, and telephone services by public utilities, the use and sale of property, and the coverage and cost of insurance; settle the greatest number of civil and criminal cases and, by far, make the majority of policy decisions and administer the majority of public programs. While these activities might not be comparatively glamorous, they are nonetheless basic to the smooth functioning of American society and to the well-being of all citizens. It is important then to raise the question of what progress blacks are making in penetrating the political arena at the state and local levels.

A second major factor accounting for the importance of directing greater attention to the presence of blacks at state and local levels is the perspective that assessments of progress at those levels provide of the very essence of the black political struggle. The civil rights movement evolved out of protest against the practices of a local bus system! While the federal government has provided much needed leverage for changing the broader framework within which states and locales must act, the struggle to define the content, structure, and specific implementation of policies and programs which most directly affect the lives of citizens is a continuing and crucial one for blacks. Much of this struggle is carried out at state and local levels.

Moreover, it is at the community level that blacks are most effectively mobilized, or, as is frequently the case, their political aspirations are dashed in a chain-reaction sequence which reaches upward to other levels of government. If blacks are not mobilized at the community level, and remain unincorporated into political networks at city and county levels, prospects for electing more blacks to state level offices or to congressional seats will remain less than sanguine. Finally, it is at the state and local levels that the most significant future gains will likely be made in increasing the number of black elected officials (BEO's) nationwide. Thus, effective mobilization and strategic planning by blacks in a range of local settings across the country in the short term are perhaps key to increasing the number of BEO's in national level offices in the long term.

How then are blacks faring in the political arenas of state and local government? While it is difficult to definitively answer this question without identifying progress and examining constraints specific to individual political settings, what is done, in the main in this analysis, is to assess aggregate trends to gain insights into overall patterns regarding the presence of BEO's. While there is discussion of the rate of increase in the number of BEO's in most categories of elective offices at state and local levels, there is no attempt here to assess the impact of black county commissioners on county government, or correspondingly, the impact of black state legislators on state government.

Alternatively, the analysis presented here focuses specifically on black mayoralties as the embodiment of the pivotal dynamics which underlies black electoral politics, and as a reflector of the benefits and constraints which accrue to black electoral successes. Thus the analysis focuses on some major activities of big-city (populations of 50,000 plus) black mayoralties in assessing the effectiveness of the black political presence at local levels in promoting the social and economic advancement of blacks. Concomitantly, the analysis focuses on the much neglected plight of small-town (population of 98 to 39,000) black mayors in highlighting the still highly tenuous nature of black political advancements in many areas. Assessment of the impact of blacks in high-level administrative positions at state and local levels is beyond the scope of this paper. However, as previous studies have shown,[3] the impact of such individuals can be significant, and we can be sure that the relative successes of black mayors depend heavily on the support of key black administrators, among others.

Developments and Constraints in Electing Blacks at State and Local Levels

The effects of the VRA on black electoral successes were both sweeping and immediate. The VRA applied to seven states in the South and set prohibitions

Table 1. Change in Number of Black Elected Officials by Category of Office, 1970–1986

Year	Total BEOs N	% Change	Federal N	% Change	State N	% Change	Substate regional N	% Change	County N	% Change	Municipal N	% Change	Judicial/law enforcement N	% Change	Education[1] N	% Change
1970	1,469	—	10	—	169	—	—	—	92	—	623	—	213	—	362	—
1971	1,860	26.6	14	40.0	202	19.5	—	—	120	30.4	785	26.0	274	28.6	465	28.5
1972	2,264	21.7	14	0.0	210	4.0	—	—	176	46.7	932	18.7	263	-4.0	669	43.9
1973	2,621	15.8	16	14.3	240	14.3	—	—	221	19.9	1,053	13.0	334	27.0	767	14.6
1974	2,991	14.1	17	6.3	239	-0.4	—	—	242	14.7	1,360	29.2	340	1.8	793	3.4
1975	3,503	17.1	18	5.9	281	17.6	—	—	305	26.0	1,573	15.7	387	13.8	939	18.4
1976	3,979	13.6	18	0.0	281	0.0	30	—	355	16.4	1,889	20.1	412	6.5	994	5.9
1977	4,311	8.3	17	-5.6	299	6.4	33	10.0	381	7.3	2,083	10.3	447	8.5	1,051	5.7
1978	4,503	4.5	17	0.0	299	0.0	26	-21.2	410	7.6	2,159	3.6	454	1.6	1,138	8.3
1979	4,607	2.3	17	0.0	313	4.7	25	-3.8	398	-2.9	2,224	3.0	486	7.0	1,144	0.5
1980	4,912	6.6	17	0.0	323	3.2	25	0.0	451	13.3	2,356	5.9	526	8.2	1,214	6.1
1981	5,038	2.6	18	5.9	341	5.6	30	20.0	449	-0.4	2,384	1.2	549	4.4	1,267	4.4
1982	5,160	2.4	18	0.0	336	-1.5	35	16.7	465	3.6	2,477	3.9	563	2.6	1,266	-0.1
1983	5,606	8.6	21	16.7	379	12.8	29	-17.1	496	6.7	2,697	10.0	607	7.8	1,377	8.8
1984*	5,700	1.7	21	0.0	389	2.6	30	3.4	518	4.4	2,735	1.4	636	4.8	1,371	-0.4
1985	6,056	6.2	20	-4.8	396	1.8	32	6.7	611	18.0	2,898	6.0	661	4.0	1,438	4.9
1986	6,424	6.1	20	0.0	400	1.0	31	-3.2	681	11.4	3,112	7.4	676	2.3	1,504	4.6

* The 1984 figures reflect blacks who took office during the seven-month period between July 1, 1983 and January 30, 1984.

[1] Figures include local school boards and some college and university boards.

Source: Joint Center for Political Studies, Washington, D.C.

against voting qualifications, practices, and procedures which might have the purpose or effect of denying or abridging the right to vote on account of race or color. The immediate results were over one million new black registered voters within the first seven years that the VRA was in effect.[4] Five years after passage of the VRA, there were 1,469 BEO's in the country.[5]

By July 1980 there were 4,912 BEO's, an increase of 234 percent during the initial ten-year period. During the period 1970-1976, there were annual increases between 13.6 percent and 26.2 percent. In 1977 the first precipitous drop occurred in the rate of increase, reflecting a low of 8.3 percent. Since 1976 the rate of increase has not exceeded 10 percent, with four years, 1979, 1981, 1982, and 1984 showing very low rates of increase. Between 1970 and 1976 the average rate of increase was 18.2 percent; since 1976 the average rate of increase has been only 4.9 percent. See Table I, *Change in Number of Black Elected Officials by Category of Office, 1979-1986.*

There are various explanations given for the substantial annual decline in the rate of increase in the number of blacks elected to office since 1975 including: relatively low rates of black voter participation, disenchantment with the political process, and the natural consequence of having realized the easy electoral victories during the years immediately following passage of the VRA;[6] that is, the election of blacks in districts with sizeable black majorities and a previous tradition of black political mobilization through the actions of local black civic and religious organizations.

To be sure, there are severe constraints on increasing the number of BEO's imposed by the refusal of a majority of white voters to vote for black candidates. Black candidates must overwhelmingly rely on a solid black vote for electoral success. The result is that, despite the presence of over 6,000 BEO's and the historical and current practice of blacks voting in very large numbers for white candidates, the voting behavior of white Americans remains disproportionately that of racial voting.[7]

The consequences of racial voting are reflected in the geographic distribution of BEO's. The South has 53 percent of the U.S. black population and 63.8 percent of all BEO's. The North Central Region has 19.8 percent of the black population and 19.6 percent of all BEO's. The Northwest has 18.5 and 10.9 percent of black population and BEO's respectively, and the West has 8.9 and 5.7 percent respectively.[8] (See *Table 2, "Distribution of Black Elected Officials by Census Region/Division and Category of Office, January 1986."*) Similarly, states states with higher percentages of blacks among the voting-age population have the greater number of BEO's. Thus, Mississippi, Louisiana, Alabama, South Carolina, and Georgia have correspondingly higher levels of blacks among the voting-age population and greater numbers of BEO's. The state of Delaware stands out as something of an anomaly with a voting-age black population of 14.7 percent and only 19 BEO's. The situation in Delaware, and in other states with similar discrepancies between the black voting-age population and the number of BEO's, may be explained as a result of low black voter registration and/or the result of a more dispersed black population and a concomitant

Table 2. Distribution of Black Elected Officials by Census Region/Division and Category of Office, January 1986

Region/ Division*	Total N	Total %+	Federal N	Federal %+	State N	State %+	Substate Regional N	Substate Regional %+	County N	County %+	Mayors N	Mayors %+	Other Municipal N	Other Municipal %+	Judicial/ Law Enforcement N	Judicial/ Law Enforcement %+	Education N	Education %+	% of U.S. Blacks in Region/ Division
NORTHEAST	696	10.9																	18.5
New England	114	1.8	0	0.0	21	5.4	0	0.0	1	0.2	1	0.3	61	2.2	3	0.4	27	1.8	2.0
Middle Atlantic	582	9.1	4	20.0	45	11.5	0	0.0	19	2.8	18	6.2	174	6.2	92	13.6	230	15.3	16.5
NORTH CENTRAL	1,255	19.6																	19.8
East North Central	1,041	16.3	6	30.0	63	16.1	2	28.6	79	11.6	43	14.9	463	16.4	115	17.0	270	18.0	16.9
West North Central	214	3.3	2	10.0	22	5.6	0	0.0	7	1.0	16	5.5	115	4.0	18	2.7	34	2.3	2.9
SOUTH	4,070	63.8																	52.8
South Atlantic	1,758	27.6	2	10.0	113	29.0	1	14.3	234	34.3	76	26.3	974	34.5	80	11.9	278	18.6	29.1
East South Central	1,112	17.4	1	5.0	59	15.1	0	0.0	194	28.5	56	19.4	476	16.9	146	21.6	180	12.0	10.4
West South Central	1,200	18.8	1	5.0	42	10.8	0	0.0	134	19.7	67	23.2	487	17.2	132	19.5	337	22.5	13.3
WEST	363	5.7																	8.9
Mountain	44	0.7	0	0.0	10	2.6	0	0.0	3	0.4	0	0.0	13	0.5	9	1.3	9	0.6	1.0
Pacific	319	5.0	4	20.0	15	3.9	4	57.1	10	1.5	12	4.2	60	2.1	81	12.0	133	8.9	7.9
TOTAL	6,384	100	20	100	390	100	7	100	681	100	289	100	2,823	100	676	100	1,498	100	100

* The 40 BEOs in the Virgin Islands are not included in this table, because that territory is not included in the census divisions

+ Percentage of all BEOs in category.

Source: Joint Center for Political Studies, Washington, D.C.

diffusion of the clout of the black vote across election districts. (See *Table 3, Black Elected Officials as a Percentage of all Elected Officials by State, January 1986*.)

Table 3. **Black Elected Officials as a Percentage all Elected Officials, by State January 1986**

State	Blacks as a Percentage of Voting-age Population	Elected Officials		
		Total	Black	% Black
Alabama	22.9	4,160	403	9.7
Alaska	3.3	1,365	4	*
Arizona	3.1	2,412	12	0.5
Arkansas	13.6	10,692	315	3.0
California	7.5	18,135	287	1.6
Colorado	3.4	7,801	14	*
Connecticut	6.2	7,920	67	0.8
Delaware	14.7	999	19	1.9
District of Columbia	66.6	370	251	67.8
Florida	10.8	4,902	178	3.6
Georgia	24.9	6,672	417	6.3
Hawaii	2.1	176	1	0.6
Idaho	*	4,183	0	*
Illinois	13.6	40,422	426	1.0
Indiana	7.1	11,029	70	0.6
Iowa	1.2	17,730	9	*
Kansas	4.9	17,070	28	*
Kentucky	6.7	7,013	46	0.7
Louisiana	26.6	4,720	488	10.3
Maine	*	5,885	3	*
Maryland	22.5	2,172	108	5.0
Massachusetts	3.7	11,605	35	*
Michigan	12.3	19,403	314	1.6
Minnesota	1.2	19,153	9	*
Mississippi	30.8	5,278	521	9.9
Missouri	9.5	17,802	161	0.9
Montana	*	4,335	0	*
Nebraska	2.7	15,747	4	*
Nevada	5.5	1,145	9	0.8
New Hampshire	*	5,991	0	*
New Jersey	11.7	9,431	200	2.1
New Mexico	1.7	2,052	5	*
New York	13.1	24,112	248	1.0
North Carolina	20.7	5,308	311	5.9
North Dakota	*	18,045	0	*
Ohio	9.6	19,913	209	1.0
Oklahoma	6.1	9,018	116	1.3
Oregon	1.2	7,880	10	*
Pennsylvania	8.2	28.928	134	0.5
Rhode Island	2.4	1,107	8	0.7

South Carolina	27.7	3,233	329	10.2
South Dakota	*	9.191	3	*
Tennessee	14.4	7,256	142	2.0
Texas	11.0	24,757	281	1.1
Utah	*	2,363	1	*
Vermont	*	7,323	1	*
Virginia	17.9	3,053	125	4.1
Washington	2.5	7,467	17	*
West Virginia	3.0	2,899	20	0.7
Wisconsin	3.4	18,973	22	*
Wyoming	*	2,174	3	*
TOTAL		490,770	6,384	1.3

* Less than 0.5 percent.
NOTE: The 40 BEOs in the Virgin Islands are not included in this table, because the Virgin Islands are not included in the 1977 Census of Governments.
Source: Joint Center for Political Studies, Washington, D.C.

Perhaps reflecting the geographical concentration of the black population more than any other factor, the largest group of BEO's is present at the level of municipal offices, comprising a 1986 total of 3,112. The greater number of municipal level BEO's are council members (2,396), followed by mayors (289). Also reflecting the concentration of blacks in sub-state level election districts are the number of BEO's serving on local (city and county) school boards (1,437), and the encouraging number of blacks serving on county governing boards (681), up by 70 in 1986. For the years 1985 and 1986, the greatest percentage increases in BEO's occurred at the county level, 18.0 and 11.4 percent respectively. This increase occurred overwhelmingly in the South and is largely attributable to changes in electoral systems from at-large to district-based elections.[9]

At the level of state government offices, the combined effects of the geographical distribution factor and white racial voting are most apparent. Because of the effect of these factors, the number of BEO's in state legislatures remains low both in terms of the comparative black percentage of the total U.S. population and in regard to the black population in the individual states. Blacks make up roughly 10.5 percent of the total U.S. voting age population, but comprise only 5.3 percent of all state legislators. Even in the state of Alabama, which has the largest percentage of black state legislators (17.1 percent), their numbers lag behind the black voting age population of 22.9 percent. (See *Table 4, Blacks in State Legislatures, January 1986.*)

Overall, black women have made impressive gains in their election to public offices. During the period 1976–1986, the number of black women elected to office more than doubled, from 684 to 1,483, comprising 23 percent of all BEO's. The majority (50 percent) of black women have been elected at the municipal level, and thirty-two percent serve in the educational area. As of late 1986, black women had been elected to forty (40) mayoralties. Given that only one black woman holds the mayoralty in a city with a population greater than

Table 4. Blacks in State Legislatures, January 1986

State	Total Number of State Legislators	Total Number of Black Legislators	% Black Legislators
Alabama	140	24	17.1
Alaska	60	1	1.7
Arizona	90	2	2.2
Arkansas	135	5	3.7
California	120	8	6.7
Colorado	100	3	3.0
Connecticut	187	10	5.4
Delaware	62	3	4.8
Florida	160	12	7.5
Georgia	236	27	11.4
Hawaii	76	0	—
Idaho	126	0	—
Illinois	177	20	11.3
Indiana	150	8	5.3
Iowa	150	1	0.7
Kansas	165	4	2.4
Kentucky	138	2	1.5
Louisiana	144	18	12.5
Maine	186	0	—
Maryland	188	24	12.8
Massachusetts	200	6	3.0
Michigan	148	17	11.5
Minnesota	201	1	0.5
Mississippi	174	20	11.5
Missouri	197	15	7.6
Montana	150	0	—
Nebraska	49	1	2.0
Nevada	63	3	4.8
New Hampshire	424	0	—
New Jersey	120	7	5.8
New Mexico	112	0	—
New York	210	20	9.5
North Carolina	170	16	9.4
North Dakota	150	0	—
Ohio	132	12	9.1
Oklahoma	149	5	3.4
Oregon	90	3	3.3
Pennsylvania	253	18	7.1
Rhode Island	150	4	2.7
South Carolina	170	20	11.8
South Dakota	105	0	—
Tennessee	132	13	9.9
Texas	181	14	7.7
Utah	104	1	1.0
Vermont	180	1	0.6
Virgin Islands	15	9	60.0

Virginia	140	9	6.4
Washington	147	3	2.0
West Virginia	134	1	0.8
Wisconsin	132	4	3.0
Wyoming	94	1	1.1
TOTAL	7,466	396	5.3

Source: Joint Center for Political Studies, Washington, D.C.

---

fifty thousand (Evanston Township, Illinois), it is apparently the case that black women feel that they can more readily obtain the mayoralty in small towns than in big cities.[10] Consistent with the pattern for male BEO's, female BEO's are concentrated in the South, similarly reflecting parallels with the concentration of the black community. (See *Table 5, Distribution of Female Black Elected Officials by Census Region/Division and Category of Office, January 1986.*)

Although much greater attention is given to BEO's in high-visibility positions such as big-city mayoralties and a few celebrity-status black state legislators, blacks have been elected to a wide variety of positions at state and local levels including: judgeships at all levels of state court systems, justices of the peace, treasurers (state and local), recorders, sheriffs, tax assessors, clerks (for cities, townships, and counties), county commissioners/ aldermen/supervisors, coroners, members of hospital boards, advisory neighborhood commissions, etc. Many of these individuals are literally unsung heroes, serving in communities where the level of black political mobilization is not such that black demands are easily incorporated into the political agenda.

However, election alone is not enough. The mere election of blacks satisfies only the descriptive dimension of representation. Descriptive representation is achieved when the elected officials resemble their constituents in terms of major social background characteristics such as age, religion, gender, and race. Substantive representation is achieved when the elected officials represent the interests of their constituency in terms of voting behavior and policy advocacy, when their ideology and policy preferences correspond to those held by their constituents, and when the representatives are effective in getting policy preferences enacted into law.[11]

The impetus behind the new black politics (a strategy for electing blacks to political office) has been to achieve the ideal combination of descriptive and substantive representation, wherein legislative and policymaking bodies would include proportional numbers of black representatives, who, in turn, would be effective in ensuring policies and programs responsive to the needs of blacks. This objective has been achieved at varying degrees in various settings. Overall, the results have been encouraging.

Social science research has shown that even when black representatives are in a decided minority on legislative bodies such as city councils, their mere presence results in positive benefits. The mere presence of blacks on legislative bodies

Table 5. Distribution of Female Black Elected Officials by Census Region/Division and Category of Office, January 1986

Region/ Division*	Total		Federal		State		Substate Regional		County		Mayors		Other Municipal		Judicial/ Law Enforcement		Education		% of U.S. Blacks in Region/ Division
	N	%+	N	%+	N	%+	N	%+	N	%+	N	%+	N	%+	N	%+	N	%+	%+
NORTHEAST	218	14.8																	18.5
New England	43	2.9	0	0.0	4	5.2	0	0.0	0	0.0	0	0.0	20	2.9	1	1.1	18	3.8	2.0
Middle Atlantic	175	11.9	0	0.0	11	14.3	0	0.0	6	7.1	2	5.0	33	4.7	12	13.2	111	23.4	16.5
NORTH CENTRAL	341	23.2																	19.8
East North Central	288	19.6	1	100.0	17	22.1	0	0.0	17	20.5	5	12.5	126	18.1	24	26.3	98	20.6	16.9
West North Central	53	3.6	0	0.0	2	2.6	0	0.0	2	2.4	3	7.5	32	4.6	1	1.1	13	2.7	2.9
SOUTH	802	54.6																	52.8
South Atlantic	402	27.4	0	0.0	20	26.0	1	25.0	26	31.0	9	22.5	254	36.5	12	13.2	80	16.8	29.1
East South Central	194	13.2	0	0.0	8	10.4	0	0.0	23	27.7	10	25.0	107	15.3	12	13.2	34	7.2	10.4
West South Central	206	14.0	0	0.0	6	7.8	0	0.0	7	8.4	10	25.0	109	15.6	12	13.2	62	13.1	13.3
WEST	108	7.4																	8.9
Mountain	6	0.4	0	0.0	4	5.1	0	0.0	0	0.0	0	0.0	0	0.0	0	0.0	2	0.4	1.0
Pacific	102	7.0	0	0.0	5	6.5	3	75.0	3	3.6	1	2.5	16	2.3	17	18.7	57	12.0	7.9
TOTAL	1,469	100	1	100	78	100	4	100	84	100	40	100	697	100	91	100	475	100	100

* The 13 female BEOs in the Virgin Islands are not included in this table, because that territory is not included in the census divisions.

+ Percentage of all BEOs in category

Source: Joint Center for Political Studies, Washington, D.C.

results in greater access to decision-making by blacks; a generally more receptive attitude toward black demands; and positive changes in decision-making processes.[12] When black legislative presence is buttressed by strong mobilization of the black community (including demand-protest activities) resulting in successful electoral coalitions with other progressive groups, blacks, in turn, get incorporated into the dominant legislative coalition and are much more effective in achieving policy and program benefits for their black constituents (than when they serve in an unenhanced minority position on legislative bodies).[13] When blacks achieve political dominance, as in the case of a black mayor *and* a black council majority, there are significant positive changes in a range of benefits accruing to black constituents.[14] This latter point is demonstrated in more detail in the discussion which follows in this paper.

The very clear evidence is that there are significant benefits to be derived from all black electoral gains, from the many individuals who may serve in relative isolation in small towns, to the high-profile, big-city black mayors. The data also shows that there are benefits to be derived from strong black political mobilization, even in the absence of specific black electoral victories, wherein the black community is organized, enjoys strong leadership, and engages in demand-protest activities[15]. In other words, black political mobilization leads to positive benefits for the black community in terms of access to decision-making, policy responsiveness, and other tangible benefits; and black political mobilization is a necessary prerequisite to black electoral gains which, in turn, add to the dividend of benefits which accrue to the black community.

BLACK MAYORALITIES: PROGRESS AND CONSTRAINTS AT LOCAL LEVELS OF GOVERNMENTS

In a significant sense, the stellar achievement of black political mobilization has been the election of black mayors in some of America's largest cities. (See *Table 6, Black Mayors of Cities With Populations Over 50,000.*)

Black mayoralties emerged out of one of the most turbulent periods in recent American history, the period of massive civil disobedience and social unrest of the late sixties. Black mayoralties, therefore, initially embodied the urgent expectations and profound hopes for providing the kind of leadership which would build a bridge across the racial divide which so glaringly separated black and white America during the period of their emergence. The following quote from the Kerner Commission Report is illustrative of the tenor of the times and reflective of the socio-political milieu which shaped expectations of emergent black mayoral leadership:

> Now as never before, the American city has need of the personal qualities of strong democratic leadership. Given the difficulties and delays involved in adminstrative reorganization or institutional change, the best hope for the city in the short run lies in this powerful instrument...
>
> It is in large part his role now to create a sense of commitment and concern for the problems of the ghetto community and to set the tone for

Table 6. Black Mayors of Cities With Populations Over 50,000

Name	Term Expires		Population	% Black
Harold Washington	4/87	Chicago, IL	3,000,000	40.0
Thomas Bradley	7/89	Los Angeles, CA	2,996,763	17.0
W. Wilson Goode	12/87	Philadelphia, PA	1,588,220	40.2
Coleman Young	12/89	Detroit, MI	1,203,339	63.1
Marion Barry	12/86	Washington, DC	637,651	66.6
Ernest Morial	3/86	New Orleans, LA	557,482	55.3
Andrew Young	12/89	Atlanta, GA	425,022	66.6
Kenneth Gibson	6/86	Newark, NJ	349,248	46.9
Lionel J. Wilson	6/89	Oakland, CA	339,288	46.9
Harvey B. Gantt	12/87	Charlotte, NC	314,447	31.0
Richard Arrington	12/87	Birmingham, AL	284,413	55.6
Roy A. West	6/86	Richmond, VA	219,214	51.3
James A. Sharp, Jr.	12/87	Flint, MI	159,611	41.4
Richard G. Hatcher	12/87	Gary, IN	151,953	70.8
Thirman L. Milner	12/87	Hartford, CT	136,392	33.9
James W. Holley, III	6/88	Portsmouth, VA	104,577	45.1
Gus Newport	12/86	Berkeley, CA	103,328	20.1
Noel Taylor	6/88	Roanoke, VA	100,247	22.0
Edward Vincent	11/86	Inglewood, CA	94,245	57.3
Melvin Primas	6/89	Camden, NJ	84,910	53.0
Walter Tucker	7/89	Compton, CA	81,286	74.8
Lawrence D. Crawford	11/87	Saginaw, MI	77,508	35.6
John Hatcher, Jr.	12/89	East Orange, NJ	77,025	83.6
Walter L. Moore	12/89	Pontiac, MI	76,715	37.2
George Livingston	5/89	Richmond, CA	74,676	47.9
Edna W. Summers	4/89	Evanston Township, IL	73,706	21.4
Ronald A. Blackwood	12/87	Mt. Vernon, NY	66,713	48.7
Carl E. Officer	5/87	East St. Louis, IL	55,200	95.6

Source: Joint Center for Political Studies, Washington, D.C.

the entire relationship between the institution of city government and all the citizenry.

...This is now the decisive role for the urban mayor. As leader and mediator, he must involve all groups—employers, newsmedia, unions, financial institutions and others—which only together can bridge the chasm now separating the racial ghetto from the community. His goal, in effect, must be to develop a new working concept of democracy within the city[16].

These were lofty ideas indeed as set forth in the Report, and it is instructive that the Report carried the explicit expectation that the new urban leadership would structure their approach to the mayoralty within the context of "interpreting the needs of the ghetto community to the citizenry at large" and to "generating channels of communication between Negro and white leadership outside of government." There was, of course, the profoundly naive (though well meaning) assumption that "interpretation" and "communication" would be actions sufficient to generate the kind and level of actions necessary to ameliorate the problems of the ghetto. There was also a reluctance to assume that elected black leaders would do anything other than attempt to use the resources of government to address the needs of the black community as other elected leaders had similarly aided their constituents throughout the history of America. It was in large part the unrealistic expectation about what black mayors would be able to achieve and what they would seek to achieve which led to the strong resistance to their emergence.

The emergence of America's first black mayors provoked intense racial conflict, and, in some instances, sustained racial polarization. The degree of racial polarization varied among cities and with regard to specific issues. For example, while the candidacy of a black in Atlanta's mayoral race in 1973 provoked an explicitly racist campaign on the part of the white opponent, the later appointment of a black chief of police, which was opposed by some blacks and most whites, led to a sustained period of intense racial polarization in a city which had historically been credited with having developed a viable bi-racial coalition.[17] Similar periods of racial polarization had followed the election of black mayors in Cleveland and Gary in 1967,[18] and had followed the mobilization of the black community in Birmingham in the mid-seventies.[19]

Sensing the significance of the reaction to black mayoralties for the long-term governance of American cities, some analysts posited conflict-based models of mayoral leadership which predicted a stalemate in leadership occurring in situations of intense racial conflict in which mayoral policies would exclusively favor members of the mayor's racial group. At least in regard to black mayoral leadership, such theories were both premature and incomplete in their explanatory and predictive powers.[20] Black mayors did not exclusively favor their own racial group,[21] nor were cities with black mayors destined to remain racially polarized despite the somewhat enduring tendency by all political elites to process issues in regard to their racial implications.[22] Racial polarization was frequently an extended, yet temporary, condition attendant to the emergence of black mayors, and as a socio-political phenomenon, was instructive for analysts and laypersons alike.

In examining the emergence of black mayors and the negative responses of whites in various locales, one might be inclined to conclude that racial conflict was associated with a particular period in time, the late sixties and early seventies, when the whole nation was characterized by significant social turmoil. However, the racial conflict which attended the emergence of a black mayor in Chicago as recently as 1983 stands out as a striking exception to that assessment. Thus, the temporal factor alone is not a valid explanation. Rather, as some analysts have suggested, the explanation lies in understanding the pattern of socio-political development specific to individual political settings, and in the extent to which the black mayoral candidate espouses an explicitly social reform agenda[23]. The differences between the reactions of the local political arenas to the candidacies of black mayoral contenders in Chicago and Philadelphia in 1983 become less striking when viewed from this perspective.

The adjustment of cities to the presence of black mayors has also been instructive, and from an historical and developmental perspective, places the emergence of black mayors within the context of broader patterns of urban political change. From an intellectual perspective, one might be intrigued by how black political empowerment induced the displacement of white political dominance in some urban settings and how this process and politics of displacement resembled previous patterns of ethnic political emergence and displacement as generic American urban processes.[24] From the practical perspective of the activist layman, one might well wonder if this, too, (i.e. black political dominance) might not pass, what it presently means for black Americans, and what will be its historical legacy.

These latter questions are particularly important, especially when one considers that black mayoralties embody the profound essence of the new black politics. The new black politics is represented in the strategic shift from protest to electoral politics as the path to black liberation.[25] William Nelson offers an eloquently stated definition of the new black politics which captures the urgency of black expectations:

> At bottom the new black politics is a politics of social and economic transformation based on the mobilization of community power....In this sense, the new black politics would become an instrument of social change, permanently eradicating obstacles to the upward mobility and continuing progress of the entire community.[26]

The early expectations of the new black politics were exaggerated, but nonetheless serve as a useful benchmark against which to measure the progress of the black struggle, however it is defined.

THE IMPACT OF BLACK MAYORS

Unlike most other BEO's who are members of larger governing bodies, black mayors are particularly positioned to impact the lives of black citizens. As chief executives of cities, mayors can more readily affect the distribution of a range of services; influence hiring, contracting, and purchasing policies; and generally affect the administration of a host of municipal programs. With the emergence of black mayors, there were charges that they had merely inherited the hollow prizes of decaying urban centers. While these charges contained a significant kernel of truth, they were premature in their suggestion of imminent doom. The important point, however, is that the factors which continue to affect urban centers are, in the main, centered within broader economic forces which operate largely independent of urban political regimes, black or white, and which also enjoy considerable independence from state or federal level controls.

Specifically, black mayoralties have had positive impacts for blacks within the context of the range of resources amenable to influence by the mayor's office. Thus, analysts have documented evidence of increases in spending for social welfare programs under black mayoralites.[27] Such increases in spending mean improvement in the quality and level of services for economically dependent constituents among whom blacks are disproportionately represented.

Black mayoralties have also resulted in increases in the number of blacks empoloyed in municipal government.[28] Again, it has not just been the mere presence of black mayors, but as importantly, the active mobilization of the black community at the local level. Thus, the decade of the seventies saw blacks achieve or approach their fair-share proportionality (in regard to their representation in the local population) in municipal employment in scores of cities.[29] However, the increases in aggregate numbers obscure some lingering inequities. For example, even in black-mayor cities, blacks remain disproportionately represented in lower-level positions, and correspondingly, underrepresented in high-level administrative posts. This discrepancy represents the lingering effects of past discrimination, lower educational levels among the black population, and in some instances, the failure and/or inability of some black mayors to effectively reform municipal personnel practices.

On the other hand, blacks in lower-level positions can be expected to advance to higher level positions overtime. More importantly, the significance of municipal employment for blacks lies in (1) the alternative it provides to a more resistant private sector as a source of employment,[30] (2) the relative stability of public sector employment over the longterm and the economic and other vital benefits to be derived from steady, longterm employment, and (3) the invaluable experience provided to many black professionals in higher level administrative positions that they would undoubtedly not be readily offered except by black mayors. Thus, overall, black mayoralties increase opportunities for blacks in municipal employment, make solid contributions to the economic stability of local black communities, and provide vital opportunities for upward mobility for black municipal workers within and external to local municipalities specifically, and the public sector generally.

BIG-CITY BLACK MAYORALTIES AND LOCAL BLACK BUSINESSES

Aside from the traditional set of municipal policies and programs which various groups compete to affect, there is the significant aspect of municipal government operations which have, until recently, been largely invisible and inaccessible to the black community; that of municipal procurement activities. Routinely, cities purchase (or procure) goods and services ranging from paper clips to fleets of motor vehicles, advice from architectural and accounting firms and other specialized professionals, building material and construction services, real estate, etc. For big cities with large budgets and sizeable needs for goods and services, municipal contracting and purchasing are big business.

One of the most controversial areas of reform for black mayors has been in the areas of municipal purchasing and contracting policies. These policies have been controversial largely because by expanding the pool of businesses with which the city contracts to include minority (and female-owned) businesses, such policies

Table 7. Minority (and women) Business Utilization in Select Black Mayor Cities

City	Population[1] (% black)	Total Budget[2] FY-86	Set-Aside[3] Policy	FY-85 MWBE[4] Business Volume
Chicago	3,000,000 (40.0)	$2,384,182,581		87,978,367
Philadelphia	1,588,220 (40.2)	$2,691,000,000	15–19%	63,000,000
Detroit	1,203,339 (63.1)	$1,651,200,000	30–40%*	79,000,000
District of Columbia	637,651 (66.6)	$3,300,000,000	35%*	158,400,000
New Orleans	557,482 (55.3)	$ 349,312,009	5–10%	No Record
Atlanta	425,022 (66.6)	$1,300,000,000	35%*	23,800,000
Newark	349,248 (46.9)	$ 271,560,339	25.0*	1,010,949[5]
Charlotte	314,447 (31.0)	$ 311,300,000	3–10%	4,208,825
Roanoke	100,247 (22.0)	$ 137,994,516	Goals	81,534
Birmingham	284,413 (55.6)	$ 157,000,000	10%	10,000,000
East St. Louis	55,200 (95.6)	$ 15,086,756	30%	3,165,000

1. Population statistics from *Roster of Black Elected Officials, 1986,* Joint Center for Political Studies, Washington, D.C.
2. Total budget includes operating and capital budgets; excludes school district funds except in case of District of Columbia.
3. Set-aside policy applies to *procurement dollars* only, not to aggregate budget of which 60-80% may be committed to salaries and benefits
4. MWBE Business Volume amounts represent actual dollars spent with minority and women vendors
5. Amount does not include construction dollars
   *Set-aside policy set by city ordinance; others represent administrative goals

have directly affected the distribution of profits to a previously overwhelmingly white business group.

By most accounts, the advent of major changes in municipal procurement policies came under the mayoralty of Maynard Jackson of Atlanta (1973–1982). Jackson's initiative was particularly beneficial to black businesses because of the multi-million dollar expansion of the Atlanta airport with which the new policy coincided. It is now almost commonplace for big-city black mayors to have a formally articulated and administered minority business utilization program.

Data from a telephone survey conducted by this author of minority business enterprise (MBE) utilization in a select set of black-mayor cities (with population of 50,000 or more) is presented in *Table 7 (Minority Business Enterprise Programs in selected big black-mayor cities).* Generally, the findings of this survey were as follows:

- all of the cities surveyed had explicit policy goals in regard to minority and female-owned businesses.

- in almost all cities surveyed, goals were set in numerical terms, as a percentage of total procurement dollars, which in effect constituted a "set-aside."
- in some cities goals were expressed as administrative requirements; in some cities goals were incorporated in city ordinances as legal requirements.
- most MBE programs extended to policies regarding the hiring requirements of sub-contractors as well as hiring practices of prime contractors.
- most MBE programs contained requirements for the hiring of city residents.
- most programs set goals for construction services separate from other procurement activities as well as separate requirements for female owned businesses.
- several cities had established offices of contract compliance and/or designated a director of MBE programs with responsibility for monitoring cities efforts.
- all cities had special provisions for notifying minority and female-owned businesses of procurement opportunities and procedures.

As can be seen in *Table 7,* in big cities, the amount of monies available for minority business utilization can be considerable. These programs are another example of how the presence of black mayoralties translates into positive benefits for segments of the black community. In most cities surveyed, the level of city purchasing with minority vendors had increased significantly (more than doubling in most cases) with the emergence of black mayors. Indeed in recent years, MBE programs have clearly emerged as the stellar achievement of big-city black mayoralties.

While there is much to be praised in regard to MBE programs, the danger is that such programs may well become the central focus of black mayoral social reform efforts to the neglect of other compelling issues. For example, one observes a decided shift in emphasis from the early days of black mayoral leadership when black mayors moved into public housing to dramatize issues and conditions of the low-income, to present times when issues of low-income housing frequently are "addressed" primarily in terms of procurement opportunities. In short, one senses a decided shift in the nature of the social reform agenda of many big-city black mayors.

In this regard the minority business programs of black mayoralties represent a dilemma for black politics. While these programs, in some instances, generate considerable wealth for a few individuals, they do very little to ameliorate the condition of the black poor. Aside from perennial charges of fraud and corruption which attend municipal contracting generally, MBE programs are roundly criticized as benefiting only a small portion of minority businesses; those with strong political and social ties to big-city black mayors. Thus, if minority business programs become the central focus of the black mayoral social reform agenda, then the obvious conclusion will be the transformation of the new black politics to "politics as usual" where the "celestial choir sings with a strong middle and upper middle-class bias," in black.

The issue of MBE programs and their attendant shortcomings is a sensitive one, but a key issue for critical discussion within the black community for it goes to the core of critical questions of how the resources created by black political mobilization (and supported by tenuous municipal tax bases) are best utilized to benefit the entire black community. Would it be unreasonable to set aside, in the form of a surcharge, a percentage of the profits of MBE beneficiaries and all other city contractors to support day-care facilities for low-income working mothers, or other worthy programs designed to assist members of the black under class who might otherwise reap very minimal benefits from the resources created by big-city black mayoralties?

SMALL-TOWN BLACK MAYORALTIES: THE CONSTRAINTS OF LOW RESOURCES

There are effectively two categories of black mayors: the small group of high profile, big-city black mayors, and the remaining two hundred plus who quietly govern in small towns. More than 90 percent of black mayors govern in small towns with populations considerably less than 50,000. In the main, the presence and plight of small-town black mayors have not been addressed by the media nor by scholars. Not surprisingly, the issues confronting small-town black mayors are very different from those confronting big-city black mayors. Populations in small towns with black mayors tend to be disproportionately low-income, and concomitantly, the tax bases in these towns are relatively low. Thus, many of the small-town black mayoralties have few if any paid professional staffers, and provide minimal levels of municipal services[31]. Issues such as municipal hiring practices and MBE programs are, in the main, not of primacy for the small-town black mayor.

The specific data presented here on small-town black mayors are based on mayoralties in the state of Alabama. Alabama has the largest number of black mayors of all the states, 32. However, only one Alabama black-mayor city, Birmingham, has a population greater than 50,000 (280,240), followed by Prichard and Tuskegee with populations of 39,729 and 12,703 respectively. The remainder 29 black-mayor cities in Alabama have populations of less than 4,500, with a low of 98 in the city of Emelle. *(See Table 8, Small Black-Mayor cities in Alabama, Population and Social Characteristics.)*

Consistent with patterns for BEO's nationwide, all of Alabama's black mayors are elected from majority black constituencies with two-exceptions, the towns of Franklin and Leighton with black populations of 26.3 and 50.2 percent respectively. Also predictably, in a majority than in the respective counties at-large. However, an encouraging trend is suggested by the greater comparability between populations of Alabama black-mayor cities and their respective county populations in average rates of income growth from 1979 to 1983.

Discussions with representatives of small-town black mayors[32] revealed deep concerns about the threat to municipal finances posed by the termination of the federally sponsored General Revenue Sharing Programs (GRS). This author thus sought to examine the probable impact of the termination of GRS on small-town

Table 8. *Small Black-Mayor Cities — Alabama*
Population and Social Characteristics
(compared with counties)

City (county)	Pop. 1984	% Change 80–84	% Black	Median Family Income 1979($)	Income Change 1979–1983
Akron (Hale)	607	12.9*	76.2 (63.0)	9,145 (10,368)	37.2 (28.3)
Beatrice (Monroe)	633	13.4	70.9 (4.3)	12,125 (14,585	32.2 (32.0)
Brighton (Jefferson)	5,274	133.1*	85.9 (33.5)	12,232 (18,880)	— (26.2)
Camp Hill (Tallapoosa)	1,447	−11.1	63.5 (27.1)	10,500 (14,905)	32.6 (33.9)
Colony (Cullman)	246	2.9	No Data[1] (8.6)	5,620[2] (7,026)[2]	38.2 (29.1)
Emelle (Sumter)	98	48.5	No Data[1] (69.5)	5,642[2] (5,642)[2]	28.7 (28.7)
Epes (Sumter)	411	3.0	81.0 (69.4)	6,290 (12,106)	31.2 (28.7)
Eutaw (Greene)	2,459	−12.9	53.2 (12.8)	16,089 (9,917)	13.7 (22.2)
Forkland (Greene)	833	−0−	771. (12.8)	10,227 (9,917)	21.8 (22.2)
Franklin (Macon)	129	−3.0	26.3 (84.8)	14,063 (11,454)	28.6 (29.3)
Geiger (Sumter)	219	9.5	75.0 (69.4)	13,393 (12,106)	27.4 (28.7)
Gordon (Houston)	301	−16.9	70.4 (22.4)	8,464 (16,327)	24.0 (30.2)
Hillsboro (Lawrence)	277	−0.4	66.5 (16.8)	11,250 (14,689)	29.9 (29.1)
Hobson City (Calhoun)	1,417	11.8	99.1 (18.0)	8,875 (16,131)	31.0 (31.0)

185

Hurtsboro (Russell)	750	–0.3	54.5 (39.5)	11,324 (13,821)	43.4 (33.1)
Leighton (Colbert)	1,305	7.1	50.1 (16.8)	12,569 (17,664)	26.5 (24.1)
Lisman (Choctaw)	638	–0–	82.6 (43.5)	12,917 (12,277)	32.5 (32.4)
McMullen (Pickens)	173	5.5	76.0 (41.9)	8,438 (12,735)	27.8 (29.4)
Memphis (Pickens)	99	4.2	100.0 (41.9)	7,045 (12,735)	29.4 (29.4)
Mosses (Lowndes)	680	4.8	99.9 (75.0)	4,018 (9,766)	30.1 (27.2)
North Cortland (Lawrence)	754	3.3	No Data[1]	3,140[2] (6,201)[2]	35.0 (29.1)
Prichard (Mobile)	39,729	0.5	74.1 (31.8)	9,923 (17,359)	24.1 (27.6)
Ridgeville (Etowah)	186	2.8*	99.9 (13.4)	6,719 (16,275)	31.1 (23.5)
Roosevelt City (Jefferson)	3,334	–0.5	99.9 (33.5)	13,750 (18,880)	29.9 (26.2)
Shorter (Macon)	457	–0.9	No Data[1] (20.0)	5,112[2] (5,230)[2]	30.2 (29.3)
Triana (Madison)	331	16.1	98.2 (84.8)	9,125 (11,454)	45.6 (29.3)
Tuskegee (Macon)	12,703	–4.7	95.4 (84.8)	13,392 (11,454)	30.8 (29.3)
Union Springs (Bullock)	4,496	1.5	68.6 (67.6)	11,368 (10,623)	25.1 (25.7)
Uniontown (Perry)	2,090	1.0	68.5	8,776 (9,983)	27.2 (26.4)

Whitehall	750	1.4	100.0	6,719	25.1
(Lowndes)			(75.0)	(9,766)	(27.2)

Yellow
Bluff[3]

Sources: U.S. Bureau of the Census, *South — 1984 Population and 1983 Per Capita Income Estimates for Counties and Incorporated Places,* Table 1, June 1986.

U.S. Bureau of the Census, *1980 Census of Population and Housing: Summary Characteristics for Governmental Units and Standard Metropolitan Statistical Areas — Alabama,* December 1982.

Alabama Department of Economic and Community Affairs, *Alabama Municipal Data Book,* 1985 and *Alabama County Data Book.*

Notes:
* percent change 1970-1980
[1] incorporated since 1980
[2] per capita income 1983
[3] There are no census data available for the recently incorporated town of Yellow Bluff.

---

black mayoralties within the constraints imposed by limited time and limited data. The profile developed in this regard is of small-town black mayoralties in the state of Alabama.

The GRS program was established by the State and Local Fiscal Assistance Act of 1972 (as part of President Nixon's "new federalism") and reauthorized in 1976, 1980, and 1983. The program died in the budget squeeze-plays of 1986. One-third of GRS funds were reserved for states, the remaining two-thirds for local governments. State governments were dropped from the GRS program in 1980. Allocations (interstate and intrastate) under GRS were made on the basis of and intricate formula inclusive of three major variables: relative income, adjusted tax collections (exclusive of educational taxes), and population. As a consequence of the allocation formula, a jurisdiction's entitlements varied directly with population and tax effort, and inversely with per capita income.

The GRS program was, in many respects, perfect for small-town governments. Governmental units did not have to make application to receive GRS funds, thus smaller governments did not have to have an administrative apparatus to receive funding. The two major administrative requirements included: (1) the chief executive officer's signature on a statement of assurance committing compliance with appropriate regulations as a precondition to receipt of funds; and (2) submission of adjusted tax and intergovernmental funds transfer data to the Census Bureau. The GRS program was thus known as the "15-minute administration program." Compliance requirements included a local public hearing on proposed use of funds, an annual audit for amounts in excess of $25,000 (changed to $100,000 in 1983), and compliance with federal civil rights laws. Following the 1976 amendments, governments could use GRS funds for any purpose legal under state and local laws. The result was that many governments used GRS funds to support vital services such as police, and to support salaries of professional employees who would otherwise not have been affordable.

As can be seen from *Table 9, (Revenue Sharing Grants and Projected Budgetary Impacts, Small Black-Mayor Cities — Alabama),* most small black-mayor cities in Alabama received some amount of GRS funds for fiscal years 1985 and 1986. FY-86 entitlements represent the final funds available under the GRS program.

Termination of the GRS program will have differential impacts on various cities. As can be seen from *Table 9,* 1986 GRS entitlements range from 2.9 to 112.0 percent of total 1986 budgets for the cities for which data are available. This means that these cities will have to make up the budget short-falls created by the loss of GRS funds from other sources, probably by raising local taxes. In the absence of local tax increases, these small towns will have to reduce staff and/or services, and in some instances, will lose vital services such as the single local policeman or paid staffer.[33]

While small-town black mayoralties may be particularly vulnerable to the impact of the loss of GRS funds, some big-city black mayoralties will also be affected. However, on the whole, black mayoralties as a group did not receive maximum benefits from the GRS program. According to a Census Bureau analysis, "Because of the tax effort factor, allocations of GRS funds to local governments are concentrated in those localities with large populations and high adjusted taxes. In 1982–83, more than 38,700 local governments were eligible to receive funds, yet *approximately 41 percent of the allocations went to 217 local governments with populations over 250,000"*[34] (emphasis added). Only 11 black mayoralties (of 289) have populations in this size category. The Census analysis further concluded that "the 18,819 local governments with below 1,000 population received less than 2 percent of all GRS allocations to local governments in 1982–83."[35]

Thus, while termination of the GRS represents a loss of much needed funds for black mayoralties, black support of efforts to restore the GRS program during the 100th Congress should emphasize the need to restructure the GRS program so as to affect a greater redistributive focus, with added benefits to smaller governments with higher levels of low-income citizens in their populations.

CONCLUSIONS: PROSPECTS FOR THE FUTURE

There are perhaps three factors of major concern when one contemplates the future of blacks in state and local governments: (1) the prospects of increasing the number of BEO's at state and local levels; (2) the prospects for enhancing the substantive representation of blacks in terms of policy advocacy, and, (3) the dilemma posed by the conjunction of the first two factors.

Considering the reliance of black candidates on the monolithic support of blacks in majority-black districts for electoral victory, one can readily see the limits to increasing the number of BEO's in state and local government. However, those limits have not yet been reached. Analysts have found that

**Table 9. General Revenue Sharing Grants and Projected Budgetary Impacts
Small Black-Mayor Cities — Alabama**

City	1984 Pop.	Revenue Sharing Funds FY–85[1]$ (per capita)	FY-86[2]$ (per capita)	FY-86[3] Budget	FY-87[4] Impact(%)
Akron	607	8,032 (13.23)	6,048 (9.96)	53,230	12.0
Beatrice	663	8,447 (13.34)	6,531 (10.32)	No Data	—
Camp Hill	1,447	44,015 (30.42)	34,350 (23.74)	350,000	9.8
Colony	246	1,287 (5.23)	5,590 (22.72)	22,000	25.4
Emelle	98	1,437 (14.66)	760 (7.76)	16,000	4.8
Epes	411	6,180 (15.04)	5,462 (13.29)	No Data	
Eutaw	2,459	29,730 (12.09)	27,887 (11.34)	25,000	112.0
Forkland	833	9,519 (11.42)	4,615 (5.54)	157,641	2.9
Franklin	129	2,598 (20.14)	3,152 (24.43)	60,400	5.2
Geiger	833	3,771 (17.22)	5,343 (24.40)	25,085	21.3
Gordon	301	9,631 (31.99)	7,344 (24.40)	100,000	7.3
Hillsboro	277	2,160 (7.80)	3,880 (14.00)	20,000	19.4
Hobson City	1,417	21,783 (15.37)	22,716 (16.03)	195,800	11.6
Hurtsboro	750	19,257 (25.68)	14,262 (19.02)	226,900	6.3
Leighton	1,305	20,192 (15.47)	24,398 (18.70)	215,350	11.3
Lisman	638	14,724 (23.08)	9,323 (14.61)	26,575	35.1
McMullen	173	2,353 (13.60)	829 (4.79)	No Data	—
Memphis	99	—	720 (7.27)	No Data	—
Mosses	680	16,332 (24.02)	16,590 (24.40)	32,218	48.1
North Courtland	754	5,803 (7.70)	6,830 (9.06)	59,843	11.4
Prichard	39,729	1,125,276 (28.32)	969,289 (24.40)	5,500,000	17.6
Ridgeville	186	908 (4.88)	1,503 (8.08)	No Data	—

Roosevelt City	3,334	12,872 (3.86)	11,219 (3.37)	339,577	33.0
Shorter	457	—	3,311 (7.25)	No Data	—
Triana	331	8,406 (25.40)	8,076 (24.40)	100,000	8.1
Tuskegee	12,703	367,826 (28.96)	306,792 (24.15)	5,371,809	5.7
Union Springs	4,496	122,582 (27.26)		1,004,000	12.2
Uniontown	2,090	57,753 (27.63)	51,210 (24.50)	682,150	7.5
Whitehall	750	10,187 (13.58)	10,048 (13.40)	No Data	—

Sources and Notes:
[1] U.S. Bureau of the Census, *Consolidated Federal Funds Report,* FY-1985, Volume II-Sub County Areas.
[2] FY-86 amounts reflect reductions in total GRS funding level. Data from: U.S. Department of the Treasury, Office of Revenue Sharing.
[3] Municipal budget data provided by Alabama Conference of Black Mayors, Tuskegee, Alabama.
[4] FY-87 budget impact (shortfall) calculated as follows: FY-86 GRS funds as percentage of FY-86 total budget.

blacks are still underrepresented in majority-black places, with the greatest level of black underrepresentation persisting in the South.[36] Those findings were substantiated in the research for this article. This author found that there was a total of 16 cities (incorporated places) in the state of Alabama with majority black populations, and white mayors. *(See Table 10, Majority-Black Cities Without Black Mayors-Alabama.)* Compounding the problem of black underrepresentation in city governments in Alabama, is a similar problem at the level of county government*(See Table 11, Majority-Black Counties and Black County Commissioners-Alabama.)*

Thus, while there is potential for increasing black representation in majority-black districts, there is also the question of what happens once that limit has been reached. Scholars have not sufficiently examined the experiences of blacks elected from majority-white districts to support definitive conclusions about the substantive dimensions of representation under such circumstances. In effect, we do not know, except intuitively, whether blacks elected by majority-white constituencies can be expected to be ardent supporters of the interests of their (minority) black constituents. This is a compelling question, particularly in relationship to efforts to elect blacks as governors. It may well be that, in the short-term, the election of a black as governor may be inconsistent with the goal of enhancing the substantive representation of blacks. One analyst has stated the issue rather bluntly: "...when black candidates can freely aspire to win election in districts where whites predominate, that's the point at which black politics, in effect, will disappear."[37]

Table 10. Majority-Black Cities Without Black Mayors
(Alabama)

Incorporated Place	Population 1984 White	Black	% Black
Bessemer	15,398	16,272	51.4
Brownville	76	2,309	96.8
Brundige	1,456	1,755	54.7
Clayton	720	869	54.7
Fairfield	6,095	6,894	53.1
Goodwater	713	1,181	62.4
Greensboro	1,253	1,986	61.3
Lafayette	1,561	2,078	57.1
Midway	110	483	97.8
Newbern	50	257	83.7
Newville	292	521	64.1
North Johns	88	155	63.8
Selma	12,392	14,047	53.1
Thomaston	315	363	53.5
Vrendenburgh	62	371	85.7
York	1,281	2,107	62.2

Source: U.S. Bureau of the Census, 1980 Census of Population and Housing: Summary Characteristics for governmental Units and Standard Metropolitan Statistical Areas in Alabama.

Table 11. Majority Black Counties and Black County Commissioners — Alabama

County	Population 1984[1] White	Black	% Black	# Black County[2] Commissioners
Bullock	3,247	7,160	68.8	3
Dallas	24.205	29,488	54.9	0
Greene	2,405	8,596	78.1	5
Hale	5,774	9,937	62.9	1
Lowndes	3,304	9,799	75.0	0
Marengo	11,663	13,346	53.4	0
Perry	5,971	9,019	60.2	3
Sumter	5,150	11,711	69.4	3
Wilcox	4,590	10,151	68.9	0

Sources and Notes:
  [1] U.S. Bureau of the Census, 1980 Census of Population and Housing: Summary Characteristics for Governmental Units and Standard Metropolitan Statistical Areas in Alabama.
  [2] Joint Center for Political Studies, *1986 Roster of Black Elected Officials.* Alabama counties are governed by commissions consisting of 3 to 7 members, elected for 4-year terms.

Scholars also have no definitive explanations for the problem of black underrepresentation in majority-black districts despite suggestions of apathy, low-income status, lower black voter turnout, the absence of an effective black majority in terms of voting-age population, etc. Nor are there definitive explanations as to why majority black districts frequently choose white representatives over black candidates when given a choice. In analyses of this phenomenon at the level of congressional elections, it has been found that, with one exception, no white (in modern times) has ever won an *open* majority black congressional seat. Rather, white incumbents have been able to *retain* seats in districts that have become majority-black subsequent to their initial election. This suggests an enormous advantage of white incumbency in congressional races (which appears to be very difficult for black challengers to overcome)[38] and may well prevail at the level of state and local races.

Of course, one might readily and validly posit that the problem of black underrepresentation in majority-black places is one of mobilization. The key ingredients of effective mobilization in black politics are posited to be (1) race consciousness, (2) racial solidarity, and (3) effective leadership and organization. The extent to which these ingredients are absent singularly, or in combination, in places of black underrepresentation is unknown.

However, unique developments in black politics such as the Jackson presidential candidacy, which presumably stimulate an enhanced level of political mobilization within the black community, are expected to have an overall positive effect on increasing the level of black representation at state and local levels. Some analyses suggest that this may well be the case, albeit in indirect and probably highly varying ways. In an analysis of the impact of the Jackson candidacy in Prince George's County Maryland, it was found that the Jackson candidacy provided an issue framework and media context for joining the issue of the "locked-out" position of blacks in the local Democratic Party machinery. The Jackson candidacy, in effect, enhanced the existing mobilization of the local black community and enabled the forging of black entry into the local Democratic Party machinery, resulting in a new level of maturation for local black politics.[39] One major result of this enhanced status of local black politics in Prince George's County was the November 1986 election of a black as State's Attorney for the county with the full support of white Democratic Party officials.

There may well be other cases of black electoral successes ensuing indirectly from the benefits of the Jackson candidacy. However, the "coattail" effects of presidential politics are not sufficient to singularly determine the outcome of local elections. Ultimately, local elections are determined by the dynamics of local politics.

As we enter the third decade of the new black politics of electoral pursuits, it may well be appropriate to critically examine the current thrusts of black politics in regard to strategies for increasing the level of black representation, as well as strategies for enhancing the impact of the new black politics on the lives of the black underclass. The level of state and local government is an essential, though not exclusive, focus for such an examination.

192

Conclusions and Recommendations

The preceding articles in *The State of Black America 1987* have drawn a clear portrait of today's Black America, one beset with economic, political, and social needs, but one with capabilities and strengths. These papers present powerful analyses which show the state of Black America as it really is and not the way it is envisioned through clouded glasses. They are arguments for removing the smokescreens, which help too many people pretend that real problems do not exist.

If the information presented makes us uncomfortable, perhaps it will also help motivate us to seek new and creative solutions to chronic problems. As we approach the end of the twentieth century, we must forge a national commitment to equality and justice — goals that were once hallmarks of our country's national policies. That national commitment must be manifested in policies and leadership that demonstrate an understanding of the link between the different facets of the complex American economy and the even more complex global economy.

This "feel-good" administration has lulled us into a false feeling of security, while it discourages any contradictory observations. It has developed a political climate that helps us be comfortable with unemployment levels that are scandalous.

Unemployment rates are at recession level for the total community and at depression level for the black community. The so-called safety net for the unemployed is in shreds. Fewer than a third of the jobless received unemployment benefits compared to about two-thirds a decade ago. The nation's overall unemployment rate has stabilized at about seven percent while black unemployment is a staggering 15 percent.

With a sluggish economy and inadequate federal policies that do not stimulate job growth, it is unlikely that the situation for black Americans will be ameliorated without a dramatic redirection in national policy.

Blacks are disproportionately concentrated in both declining industries and declining occupations, in some import-sensitive industries and government sector occupations. Black workers displaced by plant closings, relocations, and cutbacks are more likely to be worse off than their white counterparts. Only 42 percent of black workers displaced between 1979 and 1984 have found new jobs, compared to 60 percent of all workers. Those who have found new jobs, black or white, typically earn less than 80 percent of what they used to earn. In terms of purchasing power, for the first time in American history, our children can expect to earn less in real terms than their parents.

Over the past dozen years, the typical black family has lost $1,500 in income while economic needs increased. This erosion in black purchasing power has had devastating effects on black communities and on the economics of cities in which blacks are a significant portion of the population. Blacks are 12 percent of the population, but black income amounts to only 7.4 percent of all money income in the U.S.

Total personal income from property in the U.S. amounts to almost $200 billion, but blacks share only about $3 billion of it. In the area of business ownership, black income from self-employment came to only about $3 billion or 1.7 percent of total black income. In comparing the median household net worth, the Census Bureau reports that black families are at a level of $3,400 including the house and car, while white families are at a net worth of $39,100, or twelve times greater.

Income inequality is growing. The data suggest that many middle-class families are being slowly squeezed into poverty. The black community's small middle class is increasingly threatened by cuts in government jobs, corporate downsizing, and an environment that is indifferent or hostile to civil rights enforcement.

The last few years have witnessed a shift in values — from traditional ones that stressed opportunity, compassion, and equality — to today's new era of selfishness, hostility to the poor, and indifference to inequality. We hear proponents of easy solutions urging self-help and voluntary efforts. Self-help only works when society creates opportunities that help people help themselves. We must remember that America created a mass middle class after World War II — not through individual self-help, but through government programs. Those programs did not create dependency; they created opportunity. Human care agencies, individuals, and corporations have tried to support those in need through volunteer efforts — in the face of reduced government support and federal budget cuts. Tax reform may have an additional impact since reduction of the minimum tax rate lowers benefits to individuals and corporations for charitable giving.

In this climate, the National Urban League stands on four basic principles: advocacy, services to those in need, building bridges, and belief in an open, pluralistic, integrated society.

Within the Urban League, we have begun a number of new programs aimed at self-help, such as our Education Initiative and Male Responsibility Campaign. Our goals are to strengthen today's black youth and tomorrow's black families.

In spite of what we can do, the federal government must also implement a set of social and economic policies designed to expand the economy while closing the racial gap in economic performance.

In formulating the following recommendations, we have concentrated on programs and activities that are both necessary and achievable.

RECOMMENDATIONS

1. **Racism**

   Racism in any of its insidious forms, exacts a toll on those who practice it, those who tolerate it, and those who suffer from it.

   We call upon our national leadership, in both public and private domains, to repudiate racism as a tolerable element within our country's moral fiber and to condemn discriminatory acts and attitudes that serve to degrade our image as a land of freedom, justice and opportunity.

2. **Civil Rights**

   The Justice Department's failure to enforce the spirit as well as the letter of civil rights law collaborates in the perpetuation of injustices against blacks and other minorities.

   We call upon Congress to eliminate the loopholes evident in current civil rights laws and for increased civil rights enforcement by the Justice Department. We urge passing of the proposed Civil Rights Restoration Act of 1986 which would restore the broad coverage and protection embodied in Title VI of the Civil Rights Act of 1964, Title IX of the Education Amendments of 1972, Section 504 of the Rehabilitation Act of 1973 and the Age Discrimination Act of 1975.

3. **Affirmative Action**

   Affirmative action policies and practices on the part of the government and private sector are still needed as a remedy for past and present racial discrimination.

   We therefore advocate continued support of consistent,results-oriented affirmative action policies and practices with no change in Executive Order 11246 as a remedy for past and present discrimination.

4. **Full Employment**

   Joblessness has a devastating impact on unemployed people, in lowered self-esteem, higher levels of illness, mental strains, and family problems. Full employment is vital because it produces crucially important human and social benefits.

   We urge Congressional enactment of legislation establishing a full employment policy and a universal employment and training system to ensure the availability of productive work for the unemployed and the skills training necessary to obtain and hold a job.

5. **Social Welfare Reform**

   Social welfare reform must ensure a comprehensive, adequate, equitable, publicly acceptable, universal and dignified system of benefits. The welfare system should ideally be linked to both adult employment and youth training opportunities which provide a living wage. Reform of the welfare system should provide an income floor below which no child should fall.

   We encourage Congress to consider the recent legislation supported by the National Urban League, Inc. These legislative pieces, The Opportunities for Employment Preparation Act of 1986, (SB. 2578) and the Aid for Families and Employment Transition Act of 1986, (SB. 2579) were prepared to address long-term unemployed persons or AFDC recipients, thereby strengthening both one- and two-parent poor families. While incremental in nature, this legislation provides for the long-range view of full employment nationally, and other needed supportive services.

6. Education

Almost 63 percent of black students attend predominantly minority schools. In an economy that is restructuring to emphasize highly-skilled jobs and technical know-how, students must have access to the appropriate use of an educational technology.

The U.S. Department of Education and related federal agencies must reassert their roles as keepers of the flame of educational equity by ensuring that predominantly minority schools have the resources to provide quality education. Targeted, categorical supplemental academic assistance needs to be increased. With supportive federal standards for equal educational access and opportunity for success, and by organizing community-wide coalitions for reform which demand changes in the schools and changed behavior in our own families, the black community can stem the further loss of our youngsters to the dropout syndrome, to crime, and to premature parenthood.

7. Health

The nation's black community suffers from an unequal standard of health care due to a complexity of social problems: lack of financial support, resources, inadequate education, little job training or job opportunities.

We therefore call for continued governmental and community-based efforts, imperative to combating teen pregnancy through the funding of Title X of the Public Health Services Act, Medicaid, the Maternal and Child Health Block Grant, and other related services; increasing government support of male involvement in family planning programs; education for parents and teens on the importance of examining and planning life options.

8. Housing

A lack of affordable housing is the crux of the nation's housing crisis.

Congress and the administration must be committed to developing and funding a national affordable housing program with a primary emphasis on meeting the housing needs of low-income families. While shelters are effective as a temporary solution, their impact on family relationships can be damaging and far-reaching. Congress must support the Homeless Personal Survival Act as a major tool in providing comprehensive support services and permanent housing to the homeless.

The Community Development Block Grant Program has been an important component in sponsoring and stimulating housing and community development activities at the local level. The CDBG program in the current budget climate can achieve its most effective results if it is administered as a program targeted to aid the housing and community development needs of low-income families.

9. **Legislation and Advocacy**

Attacks on "big government" too often focus on the problems experienced in the implementation of programs without enough attention and creativity devoted to solving the problems that government programs were developed to address.

We strengthen our call for legislative actions to preserve and defend federal and state programs that encourage social and economic development as well as urban revitalization.

10. **The Responsibility of Black America**

While government has an obligation to care for all of its citizens, we recognize and encourage the responsibility of Black America as active participants and leaders in the struggle for equality.

We urge increased community and institutional activism, which addresses problems, offers solutions, demands accountability and commits its own resources — financial as well as moral — to make a world of difference for the black community as well as the whole of American society.

Chronology of Events
1986*

POLITICS

Jan. 11:   Douglas Wilder, the grandson of a slave, is sworn in as the first black lieutenant governor of Virginia. Wilder's victory is the culmination of a carefully orchestrated campaign in which he countered the issue of race by emphasizing his background as a Richmond lawyer, an experienced former state senator, winner of a Bronze Star in the Korean War, and richly deserving the support of the total community.

Jan. 18:   A *Washington Post*-ABC News poll shows that 56 percent of blacks regard President Reagan as a racist. When asked, "Do you consider Ronald Reagan a racist?" nearly two of every three Blacks reply in the affirmative. The poll, far more extensive than some conducted on black attitudes earlier, showed a sharp decline in Reagan's popularity among blacks.

Jan. 20:   Republican Sen. Orrin Hatch of Utah defends President Reagan as not having "a racist bone in his body." Hatch, in an appearance on ABC's "This Week With David Brinkley," said by encouraging economic growth, Reagan had done "the best things that can be done" for blacks.

Jan. 28:   The New York Times acknowledges that its December poll of black attitudes overestimated President Reagan's popularity among blacks. Adam Clymer, Assistant to the Executive Editor, says, "It now appears that our December poll has a very unrepresentative black sample, especially of black men, and the findings plainly exceeded normal sampling error." A new poll shows growth in black approval of how Reagan has handled his job, but minorities remain far more critical of Reagan than whites.

Feb. 26:   Los Angeles Mayor Tom Bradley announces he will make a second run for governor of California against incumbent Gov. George Deukmejian. Bradley, who became the first black to win the top office in a city with a white majority in 1973, lost to Deukmejian in 1982 by 1.2 percent of the total votes cast.

March 1:   For the first time in history, New Orleans voters go to the polls to choose between two black candidates in a runoff election. The

---

* *This chronology is based on news reports. In some instances the event might have occurred a day before the news item appeared.*

199

candidates are William Jefferson, a state senator, and City Council-man Sidney Barthelemy. The victor will succeed two-term Mayor Ernest "Dutch" Morial, the city's first black mayor.

April 29:   Chicago Mayor Harold Washington finally gets the chance to advance his legislative agenda by capturing a one-vote majority on the racially-polarized 50-member City Council. For three of Washington's first four years, his plans have been opposed by a white majority bloc led by Alderman Edward R. Vrdolyak.

June 2:   Retiring U.S. Congressman Parren J. Mitchell announces he is a candidate for lieutenant governor of Maryland. The ticket, headed by Maryland Attorney Gen. Stephen Sachs, must overcome a commanding lead held by popular Baltimore Mayor Donald Schaefer, the Republican nominee.

June 23:   A panel of prominent Democratic leaders, meeting in New York, asserts that the federal government must still play a role in altering the "self destructive" behavior of the urban black underclass. The forum is hosted by New York Gov. Mario M. Cuomo and led by House Budget Committee Chairman William H. Gray III, former Virginia Gov. Charles S. Robb, Sens. Daniel Patrick Moynihan and Sam Nunn.

July 22:   New Jersey Gov. Thomas Kean, speaking at the annual conference of the National Urban League in San Francisco, urges his fellow Republicans to stop writing off the black vote. "People have to go into a community and tell the community what they can do for them. That's the way groups have always advanced in this country," Kean says.

July 26:   The number of black elected officials increased at all levels last year, but blacks still hold only 1.3 percent of the nation's 490,000 elective offices, the Joint Center for Political Studies reports. The Center says there was a 6.1 percent increase in such officials between 1984 and 1985 throughout the nation.

Sept. 23:   The Democratic National Committee unveils its blueprint for overhauling the party in a report titled "New Choices in a Changing America." However, the 71-page outline for attracting disaffected voters is remarkably devoid of specifics and places emphasis on issues traditionally regarded as Republican, such as strengthening family ties and expanding the economy.

Oct. 1:   Edward J. Perkins, a black career diplomat, is nominated by President Reagan to be the new ambassador to South Africa. According to the report, the nomination is an attempt to win Senate support for his veto of legislation imposing economic sanctions on that country because of its racial separation policy known as

Apartheid. The President's veto had already been overridden in the House by a vote of 313 to 83.

Oct. 3:   The Republican-controlled Senate in a vote of 78 to 21 overrides the President's veto of legislation imposing sanctions against South Africa. The vote margin is 11 more than the 67 needed to override the veto, and Sen. Lowell P. Weicker Jr. (R-Conn.) says that the vote is "today's generation saying 'no' to the incipient holocaust of our time." The President maintains the sanctions will hurt black South Africans but pledges to implement them.

Oct. 14:   The Joint Center for Political Studies reports that blacks and whites now share similar perceptions of the country's most pressing problems — unemployment, the high cost of living and drug abuse — but hold sharply differing views about what should be done to correct them. The Center's analysis examined detailed figures compiled by the Gallup polling organization. "What is a major concern is that while civil rights ranks sixth on a list of 20 items for blacks, it is a shocking 19th for whites," said Center president Eddie Williams.

In another finding, the report notes that President Reagan's popularity among blacks has tripled from eight percent in 1984 to 25 percent this year. However, two out of every three blacks surveyed still disapprove of his performance in office.

Nov. 7:   Because of overwhelming support from black voters, four southern senators, Democrats Richard C. Shelby (Ala.), Wyche Fowler, Jr., (Ga.), John B. Breaux (La.) and Terry Sandford (N.C.), were able to defeat their Republican opponents. While these candidates were successful in winning 90 percent of the black vote which made the critical difference, Eddie N. Williams, president of the Joint Center for Political Studies states that their victories can also be attributed to the backfire of a Republican "ballot security campaign" against heavily black voting precincts.

Dec. 4:   A dispute develops between Douglas L. Wilder, the newly elected and first black lieutenant governor of Virginia and former Governor Charles S. Robb. According to the report, their relationship becomes strained because of statements made by Wilder's campaign manager shortly after his election and on other occasions that Robb tried to influence Wilder not to run and did not give him full support when he won the party's nomination.

Dec. 5:   Lt. Gov. Douglas L. Wilder of Virginia, tells reporters that the release of private letters written to him by former Gov. Charles S. Robbs "is an act of incontinence." Wilder also asserts that the Democratic Leadership Council headed by Robb is a group whose

goals are a "demeaning appeal to white southern males." Robb
says that Wilder's repeated criticism will make it difficult for him to
support a run for the governorship by Wilder in 1989.

CIVIL RIGHTS

Jan. 15:   The Rev. Jesse Jackson, speaking on the actual birthday of Dr.
Martin Luther King, Jr., warns that Dr. King's dream is being
distorted by President Reagan and others who misstate the civil
rights leader's determination to fight racial discrimination. Jackson, speaking from King's old pulpit at Ebenezer Baptist Church in
Atlanta, says "Today, President Reagan went over (to a school) and
held up little black children in his hands, rubbed his eyes to look
tearful. The same man who didn't support the boycott in Montgomery. He was old enough. Same man. Same man who didn't
support the march to Selma. Same man who implied that Dr. King
was a communist. The same man."

Jan. 20:   The Rev. Dr. Martin Luther King's birthday is observed as a federal
holiday for the first time, an honor that has never been bestowed
upon a black American. Celebrations are held around the nation.
In Montgomery, Ala., where King got his start as a civil rights
leader, a crowd of 500 heard the reading of a proclamation praising
King by former staunch segregationist Gov. George C. Wallace. In
Atlanta, Coretta Scott King celebrates the occasion by presenting
the Martin Luther King Center's Nonviolent Peace Prize to Bishop
Desmond Tutu of South Africa.

Feb. 8:   Several leaders of civil rights organizations contend that the Reagan
administration's fiscal 1987 budget reductions will have a devastating impact on those blacks and minorities eligible for social services
and welfare programs. The areas of concern cited most often by the
leaders are student loans, which would drop from $3.2 billion to
$2.5 billion; food stamps, reduced from $12.6 billion to $12.3
billion; a cut in spending on child nutrition programs of $704
million, reducing the total outlay to $5.8 billion; and Aid to
Families with Dependent Children, which would decline from $9.7
billion to $8.9 billion.

Feb. 16:   Disputing critics who claim that the National Association for the
Advancement of Colored People has lost its stature as the nation's
primary civil rights organization during his tenure, Benjamin L.
Hooks, Executive Director, declares that it is "financially solvent
and programmatically fine-tuned." Hook defends his leadership of
the NAACP in a speech before 300 members at the group's annual
board meeting.

April 6:   John H. Bunzel, a white Reagan appointee to the U.S. Commission on Civil Rights, publicly calls on commission chairman Clarence M. Pendleton, Jr., to resign. In a letter to Pendleton, Bunzel says, "By attacking the motives and integrity of your opponents, you have lost whatever opportunity you may have had to exert effective influence on the work in which we are all engaged."

April 7:   The U.S. Commission on Civil Rights, in a draft report, calls for a one-year freeze on all minority set-aside programs for women and minorities. Ralph C. Thomas III, Executive Director of the National Association of Minority Contractors, says the proposal, if adopted, will have "a devastating effect on the progress made so far" by minority business.

April 10:   The Reagan administration rejects a draft proposal by the U.S. Commission on Civil Rights urging a one-year freeze on minority set-aside programs. White House spokesman Larry Speakes says, "This administration's position is that we support the minority set-aside program."

April 11:   In the face of growing criticism, the deeply divided U.S. Commission on Civil Rights votes 5-3 to direct its staff to revise its draft report urging a one-year freeze on minority set-aside programs. Outspoken commissioner Mary Frances Berry, a frequent dissenter from the commission's conservative majority, calls the action "a tactical retreat," saying the report was "a public relations play that backfired."

April 16:   A group of prominent black Republicans, led by former Nixon administration official Robert Brown, calls for the resignation of U.S. Commission on Civil Rights chairman Clarence Pendleton. At a news conference in Washington, Brown says Pendleton has served as "a great disadvantage" to Republicans and added, "we are tired of and will no longer stand for Pendleton . . . to be looked on as a leader of black Republicans. It's him or us." Pendleton says he will not step down, despite the criticism.

April 19:   Northwestern University sociologist Charles C. Moskos reported that blacks have been more successful advancing up the ranks in the military than in corporate America. Releasing an advance copy of an article he has written for the May issue of *The Atlantic Monthly* magazine, he says blacks hold more leadership positions in proportion to their numbers in the armed forces than is reflected in civilian society. However, Julius E. Williams, director of the NAACP's Armed Services and Veterans Affairs office, says blacks are not better off because they do not hold policy-making positions in either sector.

May 25:	Five years into the Reagan presidency, civil rights lobbyists have switched tactics, and are now examining the impact of such nontraditional issues as tax revision and federal budgets to see what impact they will have on minorities and the poor, according to a report.
June 15:	An increasing number of black leaders are opening emphasizing that black Americans should rely more on their own resources than initiatives by the federal government, to deal with the economic and social conditions within the black community. In the article, John E. Jacob, President of the National Urban League, asserts: "In concentrating on the wrongs of discrimination and poverty, we may have neglected the fact that there is a lot we can do about our own problems ourselves."
July 4:	Vice President George Bush, speaking at the annual convention of the NAACP in Baltimore, says "apartheid must end" but defends the administration's policy on South Africa as the best tactic to dismantle its system of minority rule and strict racial segregation.
July 11:	The U.S. Commission on Civil Rights, votes 5-3 against a proposal request the Justice Department to stop opposing affirmative action plans. The recommendation by commissioners Mary Frances Berry, Belinda Cardenas Ramirez and Francis S. Guess, comes on the heels of a Supreme Court ruling upholding the use of race — and sex — conscious remedies to overcome employment discrimination.
July 14:	Undaunted by growing criticism of his leadership, U.S. Commission on Civil Rights chairman Clarence M. Pendleton, Jr., a black Republican, calls on both major parties to abolish their special caucuses for blacks, Hispanics, and women. Claiming that they keep these groups out of the party's political mainstream. Pendleton also alleges that the caucuses represent a form of preferential treatment for the groups.
July 21:	National Urban League President John E. Jacob says, "a new selfishness' has engulfed America and equates critics of social programs with old "snake oil salesmen" who peddled lies and distortion. Speaking at the National Urban League's annual convention in San Francisco, he cites a list of Census Bureau statistics that shows that America's economic recovery had largely bypassed black Americans.
July 22:	At the National Urban League's national convention, Secretary of Housing and Urban Development Samuel Pierce says many more blacks have prospered under President Reagan than have those under his recent predecessors. Pierce's assertion is not supported by recent Census Bureau figures showing a widening gap between the nation's rich and poor.

July 28:	On the eve of confirmation hearings for Supreme Court Chief Justice-designate William H. Rehnquist, a coalition of civil rights groups accuse the nominee of being "an extremist" and "reactionary" who is an enemy of individual rights.
Aug. 5:	Newly-appointed Supreme Court Justice Antonin Scalia says at his confirmation hearing that he supports affirmative action "for the poor and disadvantaged" even if every beneficiary "turned out to be of a particular race."
Sept. 8:	As Archbishop Desmond Tutu tours a shantytown with Coretta Scott King, the widow of slain civil rights leader, The Rev. Dr. Martin Luther King, Jr., Winnie Mandela and Rev. Alan Boesak announce they will not meet with the American civil rights figure because of her plans to meet later with South African President Pieter W. Botha. Boesak says he will decline to meet with Mrs. King because Botha's "hands are literally dripping with the blood of our children."
Sept. 9:	Coretta Scott King, on a nine-day visit to South Africa, cancels her meeting with South African President Botha just 20 minutes after it was scheduled to have begun.
Sept. 11:	Coretta Scott King meets with Winnie Mandela in her home for more than an hour. King later calls the session "one of the greatest and meaningful moments of my life."
Sept. 12:	The U.S. Commission on Civil Rights adopts a controversial draft report that asserts that racial discrimination has had a small role in the disparity earnings between black and white men. According to the report, which is based on computerized data from the Census Bureau, the dramatic decline in black men's labor-force participation rates since 1960 is the result of government assistance programs such as welfare and disability pay. The report reveals that while earning differences between black and white men shrank by 50% between the period of 1940 and 1980, in 1980, black men between the ages of 45 and 54 years still had incomes 22.1% lower than their white counterparts.
Sept. 17:	The Senate confirms William Rehnquist as Chief Justice of the United States and Antonin Scalia as an associate justice. Only two Republicans — Charles Mathias of Maryland and Lowell Weicker of Connecticut — broke rank by opposing Rehnquist, considered the most conservative member of the Supreme Court over the past 15 years.
Oct. 19:	Reaching a compromise, the House and Senate agree to cut funding for the U.S. Civil Rights Commission from $12 million to $7.5 million in fiscal 1987. The action is in response to charges by the

General Accounting Office and other sources that the commission is mismanaged and that Clarence M. Pendleton, its director, has turned the part-time job into a full-time position. Pendleton's compensation is limited to 125 days a year, just over half the 240 days of work charged to the commission at a cost of $67,344.

Oct. 20: The National Association for the Advancement of Colored People dedicates its new headquarters in Baltimore, Md., in four days of ceremonies. According to NAACP officials, the move from its headquarters in New York City, where it was founded in 1909, signals a new direction for the organization, which will include business development, in addition to its more traditional activities such as voting registration and protest demonstrations as means of achieving economic and social progress for black Americans.

Nov. 11: In a news conference, Assistant Attorney General Charles Cooper releases a 90-page study that asserts that the federal government has usurped the authority of the states in nearly all public policy matters and that Congress should examine whether standing legislation unconstitutionally hinders such authority. Attorney General Edwin Meese III applauds the report as a "milestone" in the Reagan Administration's "drive to restore federalism as a guiding principle of the nation's political life." However, Ralph Neas, Executive Director of the Leadership Conference on Civil Rights, says that if implemented, it would return the nation "to the days when the philosophies of 'states rights and separate but equal' prevailed."

Nov. 14: Following a substantial reduction in funding and staff for the U.S. Commission on Civil Rights by Congress, commission Vice Chairman Murray Friedman, in a conciliatory move, asks the other members to cooperate with each other in assessing what the future work of the commission will be. Friedman says the panel must find areas of consensus and set aside controversial issues on which they cannot agree, such as affirmative action. He calls for a summit meeting of civil rights leaders to "chart a consensus program for the remainder of the 1980s."

Dec. 3: The public release of Nixon Administration documents reveals that in a 1969 memo, Patrick J. Buchanan, the current White House Director of Communications, urged President Nixon not to visit the widow of Dr. Martin Luther King, Jr., on the first anniversary of King's death. The Buchanan memo claims "many people believe Dr. King was a fraud and a demagogue," and that the visit would pay "tribute to a figure who alienates and angers so many whites." The report says that Nixon sent a sympathy note to Mrs. King instead.

Jan. 11:   A report issued by the House Government Operations Committee concludes that mothers on welfare are not likely to benefit from job programs unless provisions are included for child care. The report states that failure to integrate quality child care in such programs "will not only be unworkable and counterproductive, but will compromise the welfare of low-income children." The congressional study notes that despite "overwhelming evidence . . . that women in poverty desire to be self-sufficient," federal welfare regulations make it harder, not easier, for recipients to become financially independent.

Jan. 16:   The Children's Defense Fund's annual report on the status of programs affecting children and the disadvantaged discloses: "The nation's progress since 1965 in improving key health indicators for poor and nonwhite mothers and babies has ground to a virtual halt." The report notes that in 1983, the latest year for which figures are available, the gap between black and white infant mortality was the greatest it has been since 1940, with black infants twice as likely as white infants to die in the first year of life. At a press conference, Marian Wright Edelman, President of the Children's Defense Fund, says: "I think it's shameful that in 1983, a black infant in Chicago, Cleveland, or Detroit was more likely to die in the first year of life than an infant born in Costa Rica."

The report also said: "The dramatic upswing in childhood poverty from 1979 to 1983 and downswing in vital public health, nutrition, and family support services from 1981 to 1983 have resulted from a market slowdown in the decline of deaths in infants up to 28 days and one year; an increase in the percentage of low birth-weight babies and in women receiving late or no prenatal care; " and the widest disparity in more than four decades between infant mortality rates of blacks and whites."

Feb. 2 :   The Republican-controlled Senate Budget Committee, acting with bipartisan support, votes 16 to 6 to reject President Reagan's proposed budget. Sen. Slade Gorton, a Republican from Washington state, says, "I don't think this budget is just wrong around the edges; it's wrong at the heart."

Feb. 3:   If the Gramm-Rudman-Hollings law takes effect in fiscal 1987, more than $10 billion will be slashed from federal programs, according to a study prepared by Fiscal Planning Services, Inc. "If Congress chooses to pull the Gramm-Rudman trigger, millions of Americans will be victimized," the report predicts. "And the most severe casualties will occur in precisely those areas of the budget that have already borne the largest share of federal funding cut-backs since 1981. "

Feb. 6:   President Reagan sends a "hard choice" $994 billion budget to Congress, cutting deeply into domestic programs but not into defense. The budget includes proposals for the elimination of the Small Business Administration, among other areas. House Minority Leader Robert H. Michel (R-Ill.) says the budget makes it clear that the President is paying for his military buildup by "taking it out of the hides of the rest of the people served by government."

Feb. 23:   Sen. Pete V. Domenici (R-N.M.), chairman of the Senate Budget Committee, tells the National Governors Association that states can expect to receive reduced funds, even if there are cuts in defense spending and an imposition of a federal tax increase.

March 19:   Openly defying President Reagan, the Senate Budget Committee approves a plan that would cut more than $25 billion from the defense proposals of the administration, increase taxes by $18.7 billion next year, and eliminate many of Reagan's deep reductions in domestic spending.

March 20:   A reluctant House of Representatives agrees to accept the Senate version of legislation that reduces the federal budget deficit by $8 billion over three years.

April 23:   The full Senate, in a vote of 83-14, overwhelmingly rejects a Reagan administration budget request that would have killed 44 domestic programs in order to cut the 1987 deficit, without touching defense spending or raising taxes.

May 2:   The Republican-controlled Senate approves a $1 trillion fiscal 1987 budget by a vote of 70-25. The measure, which must be sent to the House for action before reaching Reagan's desk, increases taxes more than the President wants and lowers his defense request by $20 billion.

May 8:   The House Budget Committee approves a fiscal 1987 budget that would increase taxes, restrain defense spending, and freeze spending for domestic programs at their current levels. Chairman William Gray, (D-Pa.) said the House budget more fairly divides cuts between domestic and defense programs than the previous version passed by the Senate. Both measures will be forwarded to a congressional committee for resolution.

May 21:   President Reagan says "a lack of knowledge" about government benefits "prevents hungry Americans from getting available help." Speaking to a group of participants in the "Close Up Foundation" program that allows high school students to study the federal government, Reagan says: "I don't think there is anyone going hungry in America simply by reason of denial or lack of ability to feed them. It is people not knowing where or how to get this help."

June 26: House-Senate conferees approve a fiscal 1987 budget of nearly $1 trillion that rejects President's Reagan's attempt to cut domestic spending, reduces his defense request, and challenges the President to raise taxes if he wants more money for the Pentagon.

The House passed the $995-million measure, 333 to 43, before forwarding it to the Senate where it was approved on voice vote.

The budget is the first worked out under the threat of Gramm-Rudman's automatic across-the-board reductions that would be triggered if certain deficit targets are not met.

July 7: The U.S. Supreme Court, overturning a key provision of the Gramm-Rudman-Hollings Act, declares that allowing the comptroller general, an officer of Congress, to dictate to the President what budget items must be cut, violates the constitutional principle of separation of powers. The court gives Congress 60 days to perfect the deficiency.

July 14: White House Budget Director James Miller concedes that the fiscal 1986 budget deficit could reach a record $220 billion. He also says that federal spending may be $10 billion to $30 billion higher than had been originally projected.

Administration officials have contended that the deficit would decrease as the economy expanded. However, economic growth is running below the four percent projected for 1986.

July 30: The Senate moves to correct the deficiency in Gramm-Rudman-Hollings balanced budget legislation by voting 63–36 to give the White House Office of Management and Budget the final say in ordering cuts, but limiting the extent of its authority by writing into law certain guidelines.

Aug. 26: The Census Bureau reports that the poverty rate fell slightly for the second consecutive year but remains higher than five years ago. The poverty rate for 1985 was 14 percent, a four-tenths drop from 1984, say Census officials. Both the number of blacks in poverty and their poverty rate have declined from 1984 to 1985, with the number of blacks dropping from 9.5 million to 8.9 million, and the black poverty rate dropping from 33.8 percent to 31.3 percent. Although there was slight improvement, the black poverty rate is still almost three times the white poverty rate of 11.4 percent.

Sept. 4: The General Accounting Office warns that there is a "strong possibility" that the fiscal 1987 deficit may exceed last month's predictions by government economists. The GAO report said the deficit may be $167.6 billion or $4.2 billion higher under the most optimistic of circumstances.

Sept. 19:   House and Senate conferees come up with a $14 billion package that would avert across-the-board spending cuts under the Gramm-Rudman-Hollings balanced budget legislation demonstrating Congress's determination to deal with the deficit problem.

Sept. 25:   The House approves a $562 billion budget by a slight 201 to 200 margin and then sends it to the Senate for action.

Oct. 3:   Following the lead of the House, the Senate approves a $556 billion spending bill. The Senate version contains provisions to fund a $1.5 billion anti-drug bill passed earlier.

Oct. 24:   According to a report, at $220 billion, the fiscal 1986 budget deficit reached its highest level in history, despite across-the-board cuts in federal programs and mid-year deficit reduction measures. The reasons cited are reduced tax revenues caused by a lagging economy and an increase in spending for military and farm programs. However, James C. Miller III, Director of the Office of Management and Budget, says that its officials are pleased that the deficit did not reach the $230 billion they predicted in August.

Nov. 9:   At a Boston news conference, Sen. Edward M. Kennedy (D-Mass.) announces that he will accept the chairmanship of the Labor and Human Resources Committee when Democrats assume control of the Senate in January to reverse "the shameful recent neglect of the needy." Kennedy says that the Democrats' reclaiming of the Senate is a repudiation of the Reagan administration's policies. He adds, however, that he recognizes the restrictions of the current budget and says that he welcomes "the challenge to do more within those constraints."

Dec. 2:   The National League of Cities adopts two resolutions "vehemently opposing any program which benefits state government at the expense of local government." The organization of city officials expresses growing concern with the increase in federal mandates and national standards being placed on municipalities without the allocation of corresponding funds to execute them. The city officials take particular issue with a welfare reform plan that they say would cost local governments $7 billion annually and would "devastate local efforts to provide low-income housing, to develop the economic base of cities, and to improve city infrastructures."

AFFIRMATIVE ACTION

Jan. 10:   Attorney General Edwin Meese III and Secretary of Labor William Brock, representing two different philosophies within the Reagan Administration on Executive Order 11246, are moving toward a compromise that would alter the standing presidential order on affirmative action for federal contractors. Reportedly, instead of the fixed requirements in current law designed to help minorities and women, the compromise substitutes "voluntary" goals.

Under the 1965 executive order and subsequent Labor Department regulations, federal contractors must attempt to hire and promote blacks and women or risk the loss of federal contracts.

Jan. 19:   In his weekly radio address, President Reagan asserts that his administration's opposition to the use of quotas is in the interest of achieving a color-blind society as espoused by the late Rev. Dr. Martin Luther King, Jr. He also claims that under his administration, blacks "have done better than ever before," which is challenged in the Democratic response by Rep. William H. Gray III of Pennsylvania, who charges that the number of black families living in poverty had increased from 32 percent in 1980 to the current level of 42 percent.

Feb. 11:   Two black Republican groups, the National Black Republican Council and the Council of 100, urge President Reagan not to alter Executive Order 11246. In a letter to President Reagan, the Council of 100 says of the 20-year old order, "We fear that the proposed change will be the trigger that aborts the development of black businesses and employment and could unleash another era of discrimination."

Feb. 25:   A controversial Rand Corp. report asserts that federal affirmative action programs have had no long-term impact on the wage gap between black and white males. The authors of the report say data "suggests that the slowly evolving historical forces (particularly improved education and migration from the rural South to the urban North) were the primary determinants of long-term economic improvement."

Feb. 25:   The U.S. Supreme Court hears oral arguments in two key affirmative action cases, originating in Cleveland and New York, involving the use of goals and timetables. Civil rights activists voice concern over whether the court will accept administration arguments that remedies for past discrimination must be limited to actual victims of racial discrimination.

March 4:   President Reagan's nominee for general counsel of the Equal Employment Opportunity Commission acknowledges in Senate testimony that he privately suggested that blacks and women can overcome discrimination by offering to work for lower wages than white employees. The nominee, Jeffrey I. Zuckerman, served as the EEOC's chief of staff for only 18 months. Prior to joining the EEOC, Zuckerman had no background in civil rights laws.

March 5:   The National Association of Counties goes on record in opposition to proposed changes in Executive Order 11246 on affirmative action. At its annual meeting, the association adopted resolutions that included a commitment to retaining affirmative action plans specifying the use of goals and timetables to increase hiring for minorities. The association represents 2,100 of the nation's 3,106 counties.

March 19:   The Supreme Court, in the first of three major affirmative action decisions, rules 5–4 that broad affirmative action plans that include hiring goals are permissible if they are carefully tailored to remedy past discrimination. Ruling on a case involving teachers laid off in Jackson, Michigan, the court sends a mixed signal by deciding that public employers cannot give affirmative action plans as a substitute for seniority when reducing their work-forces. The court seemed to be making a sharp distinction between what is permissible in hiring and promotion and steps that must be taken when people are about to lose their jobs. An examination of the written opinions shows that most of the justices are in favor of some form of affirmative action.

March 23:   The General Accounting Office reports finding numerous irregularities in the financial management, personnel practices, and travel records of the U.S. Commission on Civil Rights. Clarence M. Pendleton, chairman of the commission, calls the report "politically motivated" with the intent of discrediting him. In addition, the study finds that the commission has reduced the representation of women and minorities on its state advisory committees. The independent GAO is an investigative arm of Congress.

May 20:   The Republican-controlled Senate Labor and Human Resources committee rejects the nomination of Jeffrey I. Zuckerman to become general counsel of the EEOC. The vote is 10–5. Sen. Howard M. Metzenbaum (D-Ohio) says of the rejected nominee, "It's astounding the administration would nominate someone who has never litigated" a civil rights case. "He has never dealt with the reality of how civil rights statutes are applied."

May 22:   William Bradford Reynolds, Assistant Attorney General for Civil Rights, argues that the recent Supreme Court decision on affirmative action mandates that the presidential Executive Order 11246 on affirmative action be repealed because it has "a serious constitutional flaw, " a view that is rejected by civil rights lawyers and a spokesman for the Labor Department. According to Reynolds, the order requires federal contractors to adopt hiring goals in the absence of evidence of illegal discrimination.

June 23: John E. Jacob, President of the National Urban League, challenges the Reagan Administration on its plan to alter Executive Order 11246, on affirmative action, signed by President Johnson in 1965. "If the Administration wants to be a Rambo-like destroyer of civil rights gains, it should not pretend that its efforts are good for black citizens or that they reflect the color-blind society we have yet to become," Jacob declares during a press conference in Washington, D.C. "If there is any single message we want to send the President today, it is this: 'Hands off affirmative action.'"

July 2: In a long-awaited ruling on Cleveland printers and New York sheet metal-workers, the United States Supreme Court upholds the use of affirmative action plans designed to remedy past discrimination. It rejects the Reagan Administration's argument that only specific victims of discrimination are entitled to such relief. [According to the report,] the high court's decision reaffirms that judges should be given wide latitude in settling such disputes, as well as municipalities seeking resolution through consent decrees.

July 23: Clarence Thomas, Chairman of the Equal Employment Opportunity Commission, dissenting from the prevailing position of the Justice Department, cites recent Supreme Court rulings on affirmative action as the basis for the EEOC resumption of goals and timetables in reaching settlements in discrimination cases with offending employers. The federal agency abandoned the practice of using goals and timetables, claiming they were illegal.

Aug. 8: By a vote of 14 to 12, Clarence Thomas, EEOC Chairman, is approved for a second four-year term. According to a report, Mr. Thomas apparently won support from the Senate Labor and Human Resources Committee based on previous testimony that he would reinstitute the commission's efforts to enforce the use of hiring goals and timetables as remedies for past discrimination. The full Senate will consider the renomination.

Aug. 12: The Justice Department, after Supreme Court rulings upholding the validity of affirmative action plans, begins to drop quietly its suits against 51 localities that had dissented from its controversial view on affirmative action. In the face of defeat, Assistant Attorney General William Bradford Reynolds continued to portray the setbacks as limited defeats, although the court rejected the administration's argument that preferential treatment is unconstitutional.

Aug. 26:	Undaunted by the rejection of administration philosophy defeats on affirmative action, Assistant Attorney General William Bradford Reynolds files suit in federal court in New York to abolish a plan that uses a 50-50 quota in selecting tenants for Brooklyn's Starrett City, one of the nation's largest housing developments. The 50-50 ratio was established to assure racial integration in the sprawling development.
Sept. 15:	The Federal Communications Commission, in an abrupt shift of policy, tells a federal court in the District of Columbia that its practice of granting preferences to minorities and women seeking television and radio licenses is unconstitutional and should be eliminated. New York lawyer Alan Kaufman says the FCC has gone too far in abandoning a policy it first adopted in the 1970s.
Sept. 19:	A 121-city survey for the U.S. Conference of Mayors reveals that nearly 40 percent of the cities surveyed believe that affirmative action programs have contributed greatly to improved job efficiency and productivity. In addition, 60 percent have had fewer employee grievances and complaints, 40 percent have had less absenteeism, and 45 percent have seen declines in employee turnover rates. Mayor William H. Hudnut of Indianapolis releases the report in a news conference, and says the Reagan administration's pursuit of a color-blind society to achieve fairness in hiring and promotion is "ideal but unrealistic."
Oct. 24:	In a special news conference, a group of black foreign service officers announces the filing of a class-action suit in U.S. District Court charging systematic racial discrimination against the State Department. The suit alleges that the black officers were subjected to discriminatory evaluation, unfavorable treatment by career counselors, undesirable assignments, and lack of promotions. It seeks retroactive pay, promotions, and assignments for 257 black FSOs included as class members.
Nov. 11:	The U.S. Court of Appeals for the 11th Circuit upholds a 1985 district court ruling giving a white man, Dennis A. Walters, Jr., the job as director of a civil war exhibit in Atlanta, which he claimed the city denied him in favor of hiring less-qualified blacks and women. Walters had been rejected for the job four years earlier. Under the appeals court ruling, Walters also retained most of the $227,500 he was awarded in damages.
Nov. 13:	U.S. Solicitor General Charles Fried argues before the Supreme Court that a 1983 order requiring black and white state troopers to be promoted on a "one-for-one" basis is "profoundly illegal." Fried contends that the ruling is unfair to whites seeking promotions. However, J. Richard Cohen, the attorney for the black

troopers, maintains that the order is necessary to rectify the state's long history of discrimination.

Dec. 23: A federal district judge rules for the city of Birmingham in rejecting the reverse discrimination suit of 14 white firefighters and another municipal employee who allege they have been denied promotions in favor of less qualified blacks. The judge rules that the plaintiffs have failed to show the city to be in violation of a 1981 consent decree signed with the Justice Department to encourage the hiring and promotion of blacks and minorities. In a reversal, the Justice Department supports the white firefighters in the case claiming that the city has been misapplying the decree.

EDUCATION/DESEGREGATION

Jan. 1: Report by the House Committee on Government Operations criticizes the Reagan Administration's handling of civil rights complaints against schools and colleges. The report, issued after investigations and hearings by its Subcommittee on Intergovernmental Relations, says federal anti-discrimination agencies should not permit colleges to avoid addressing the issue of past racial discrimination simply by making good-faith efforts to correct the problem. The Education Department's Office of Civil Rights has refused to impose mandatory cutoff of federal funds after the school districts and colleges have been found to be discriminatory in their treatment of blacks, women, and the handicapped.

Jan. 15: Community colleges, even those with "open door" policies of accepting all state high school graduates, are increasingly relying on standardized testing, according to a joint report issued by the American College Testing Program and the American Association of Community and Junior Colleges. According to a report, "Few institutions employ testing admissions procedures that exclude even minimally prepared students. However, academic skills testing . . . is widely subscribed to."

Feb. 6: A panel of federal judges in Richmond, Va., upholds a lower-court decision ending court-ordered busing in Norfolk, Va. Opponents argue that the ruling will neutralize a three-decade effort to integrate the country's public school systems. The Reagan Administration had proposed that once "good-faith" efforts to comply with court orders were satisfied, that the school districts be free to choose other alternatives to busing as long as there was no intent to resegregate.

Feb. 23: Although the number of black studies courses is down from the mid-1970s, their academic status has risen as evidenced in the doctoral program in Afro-American studies offered at the University of California at Berkeley. In the mid-1970s, there were 600 Afro-American studies programs. Today, that figure is about 400.

March 25: According to a report, black parents across the nation have mixed reactions over recent federal court rulings ending busing plans devised to desegregate public schools. In cases where such plans have been terminated, the courts have ruled that the schools have succeeded in eradicating the effects of mandatory segregation. While some black parents have welcomed the rulings in the belief that the experience has not been worth the sacrifices, others say what will result is a resegregation of the public schools.

Gary Orfield, a political scientist at the University of Chicago, who conducted a study in 1983, says racial segregation has increased significantly over the past 15 years and that the movement to return to neighborhood schools will only exacerbate the problem.

April 23: Mary H. Futrell, President of the National Education Association, says financial resources, if kept at their current level, will be insufficient to bring about significant reform in the nation's public schools. The NEA issues a report that shows overall spending on education increased by 7.1 percent in the 1985–86 school year. To reform the system adequately, educational funding needs to be increased by 20 to 25 percent over the next few years, Futrell asserts.

April 24: Black college officials are faced with the dilemma of maintaining their institutions' financial stability or risking it by divesting of stock in companies that continue to operate in minority-ruled South Africa. Because the schools tend to have a fragile economic base, the consequences of divestment would hurt private black colleges much more than larger, better-financed white institutions.

June 16: The U.S. Supreme Court denies an injunction sought by black parents that would prevent the Norfolk, Va., school board from ending school busing to stem "white flight" from the city's public schools. According to the petition, the change would result in "a general resegregation of the public schools of the South. "

July 4: The 25-year-old school desegregation case requiring busing ends in Richmond, Va., when a federal judge finds no traces of state-sanctioned segregation in the school system. The case, which began with the filing of a class-action lawsuit in 1961, continued for five years at the end of which U.S. District Judge Robert Merhige, Jr., approved a "freedom of choice" desegregation plan condemned as ineffective by the local school board. In 1971, the judge approved a plan for cross-town busing to achieve racial balance among faculty members. A federal appeals court overturned an order to consolidate the Richmond Chesterfield and Henrico Counties school districts. The U.S. Supreme Court, divided 4–4, in effect, upheld the appeals court ruling.

Sept. 17: The Children's Defense Fund releases a study showing that girls who are poor and do poorly in school are almost six times more likely to become teenaged mothers than their more affluent, better educated counterparts. The report, based on Labor Department figures, shows that the teen pregnancy rates are almost identical among whites, blacks, and Hispanics of similar income.

Sept. 23: Although the U.S. has the world's highest basic literacy rate, many young adults are unable to understand a bus schedule or read a road map, a new study says. The report, by the National Assessment of Educational Progress, finds that tests given a year earlier to Americans in their early teens showed that six percent could not read as well as the average fourth-grader, 20 percent could not read as well as an eighth-grader, and 38.5 percent were unable to read at the eleventh-grade level.

Oct. 7: The 32-year old case of *Brown v. Board of Education of Topeka, Kansas* is reopened by the original plaintiff and others who maintain that the school district has failed to integrate fully its schools or to eradicate the remaining elements that permitted racial separation in the past. Richard Jones, the lawyer for the plaintiffs, says he will show that the school board approved boundaries that perpetuate racially separate schools and that have allowed white parents to avoid compliance with desegregation efforts by offering school attendance alternatives.

Nov. 4: The Supreme Court, without explanation, declines to review two school desegregation cases, one which allows the city of Norfolk to end its busing plan, and another that attempts to sanction the authority of the Oklahoma City School Board to end busing for students in grades one through four. Court observers speculate that some high court justices may want to leave the lower-courts with broad discretion in handling such cases rather than lay down a blanket rule for the nation. In the Norfolk case, black parents had claimed that the lower-court ruling ending busing would result in a general resegregation of public schools in the South.

Dec. 14: Despite a 1981 executive order issued by President Reagan urging greater private support and increased state financing for the nation's 101 historically black colleges, the schools are still being threatened by financial pressures and possible loss of accreditation. As reported, the black colleges are having trouble attracting private support to buttress public funding. While corporate contributions have increased for institutions of higher education overall, they have remained stagnant for black schools. For example, the total endowment for the 43 private colleges of the United Negro College Fund in the 1984–85 school year was $222 million compared to the $3 billion secured by Harvard University.

Dec. 14: A 26-year old desegregation case in Chattanooga, Tennessee, is dismissed by a federal district court judge who rules that the Board of Education has successfully complied with an order to racially integrate the students and faculty. However, a black real estate agent who filed the suit back in 1960, James Mapp, maintains that because there are several schools with student bodies of almost entirely one race, segregation still exists in the system. Blacks make up 51.6 percent of the school system's nearly 23,700 students.

RACE RELATIONS

Jan. 3: Federal Magistrate W. Curtis Sewell gives a Virginia couple a week to come up with a timetable for paying $11,000 to a woman and her two daughters after they were refused service in his restaurant. Roy McKoy has been jailed three times for refusing to serve blacks at his Belvoir restaurant near Marshall, Va.

Jan. 13: President Reagan, who opposed passage of the 1964 Civil Rights Act and who was a long-time opponent of a federal holiday for Dr. Martin Luther King, Jr., kicks off a week of activities in recognition of King's birthday and his work.

Feb. 6: A federal grand jury in Philadelphia indicts three white men for conspiracy to violate the civil rights of a black family that moved into a previously all-white neighborhood. On Dec. 12, the home of Charles Williams was set afire. Earlier, mobs of whites had gathered outside the dwelling shouting, "Move! Move! Move!"

Feb. 13: A black member of the Daughters of the American Revolution files a three-million dollar suit in federal court against the DAR after having been disciplined for disturbing the "harmony" of the previously all-white organization. Faith K. Tiberio of Sherborn, Mass., had been found guilty of the charge at a DAR hearing in October. The dispute grew out of an April 1984 news conference in which Tiberio and others sought to impeach the group's president and criticized a proposed amendment to the DAR bylaws that would have required applicants not only to prove a Revolutionary War connection, but to show also that their descent was "legitimate."

Feb. 27: Michele Harris, a black Brigham Young University student and prospective dancer, is the object of a campus controversy when a student director refuses to cast her in a school production of "West Side Story." The director says, "I had nobody to pair her with because the implication is that the couples were involved physically." She adds, "I had no qualms about pairing her with a white man, but . . . community members might have been upset at the implications." Mormon school officials reprimand the student director but Harris is still not given a role in the play.

March 6:   A report by a special commission studying the MOVE confrontation in Philadelphia blames Fire Commissioner William C. Richmond and Police Commissioner Gregore J. Sambor for the deaths of 11 people, including five children, last May in the back-to-nature group's clash with city officials. The commission, headed by Attorney William H. Brown III, says Mayor W. Wilson Goode was not responsible for the deaths. The one-day standoff ended when police dropped a bomb on the MOVE house, starting a fire that destroyed 61 row houses and left 250 people homeless.

March 24:   A new hearing begins on suspensions given to Dartmouth College students who attacked shanties erected on campus to protest South African apartheid. Most of the "shanty bashers," as they were dubbed, were staff members of the right-wing campus publication *The Dartmouth Review.*

June 18:   *A Washington Post*–ABC News poll finds that blacks feel racial discrimination remains a serious problem. One-half to two-thirds say blacks are discriminated against in securing decent housing and nearly 80 percent of the 1,033 blacks polled said whites do not want blacks to get ahead. Six out of 10 say at least one-tenth of America's whites share the attitudes of the Ku Klux Klan and 23 percent say more than half of all whites hold similar views. Most blacks, however, remain optimistic that chronic poverty in America can be eliminated, according to the poll.

July 14:   White House officials disclose that Robert J. Brown, a black North Carolina businessman, is the leading candidate to replace Herman W. Nickel as U.S. Ambassador to South Africa. Brown, a former executive assistant to President Richard Nixon, has been an active supporter of Reagan's "constructive engagement" policy toward South Africa.

July 21:   Key Republican leaders in Congress warn President Reagan that he must adopt tougher measures toward South Africa if he wants to avoid Congressional sanctions against the minority-ruled country. However, Reagan remains firm in his opposition to "punitive sanctions."

219

Sept. 4:   Two top-ranking Soil Conservation Service employees in Arkansas are reassigned as a result of racial discrimination complaints against the U.S. Department of Agriculture. The officials are accused of having participated in a system that excluded blacks and women from membership on 76 local conservation boards overseeing spending of federal and state funds.

Sept. 11:   Alcee Hastings, an outspoken black federal judge in Miami, goes to court seeking to avoid impeachment. Judge Hastings, who was acquitted in 1983 of conspiring to accept bribes from two convicted racketeers, faces another inquiry from Justice Department lawyers who seek to have him removed from the bench.

Sept. 14:   More than 400 demonstrators gather in front of *The Washington Post* newspaper offices to protest the depiction of blacks in the premier issue of the paper's Sunday magazine. The protesters, including D.C. Delegate Walter Fauntroy, object to a cover story about a black rap music star charged with murder and a column by Richard Cohen supporting store owners who discriminate against young black males because they suspect them of being shoplifters.

Sept. 22:   Japanese Prime Minister Yasuhiro Nakasone, boasting of Japan's highly-educated, monoracial society, asserts that blacks, Mexicans, and Puerto Ricans have brought down the literacy level in the United States. In the same speech, he adds: "In America, even today, there are many blacks who do not know how to read or write."

Sept. 26:   Prime Minister Nakasone issues a "heartfelt" apology for his characterization of blacks and other minorities as being the cause of the low literacy rate in the United States. Nakasone contends his remarks, widely criticized as racist, were misunderstood.

Sept. 30:   A Wayne County Circuit Court judge rules that a Dearborn, Michigan, law barring nonresidents from city parks is unconstitutional and has been enacted to keep blacks out of the affluent suburb. The city announces it will appeal the decision.

Oct. 15:   The U.S. Supreme Court hears arguments that a capital punishment conviction from Georgia should be thrown out because a black in that state is 11 times more likely to be sentenced to death than those convicted of killing blacks.

Nov. 11:   A fight between white student fans of the Boston Red Sox and black and Hispanic student fans of the N.Y. Mets erupts when the Mets win baseball's World Series and uncovers "racial tensions" at the University of Massachusetts in Amherst according to this report. Ten people sustain minor injuries in several battles that involve a crowd of 12,000 according to Chancellor Joseph Duffy.

Nov. 21:   Kevin Nesmith, a freshman at the Citadel, a state-supported military academy in Charleston, S.C., withdraws from the school when a group of white cadets in Ku Klux Klan garb burst into his room with a lighted paper cross uttering racial slurs. Nesmith's brother Alonzo, a graduate of the academy calls the incident an act of terrorism and charges that school officials are trying to "sweep it under the rug."

Nov. 24:   The Rev. Jesse Jackson meets with 30 cadets at the Citadel in a second visit to the state-supported military school to discuss racial problems there. The meeting is briefly interrupted by Col. George Stackhouse, chief of public safety for the school, who tells Jackson permission is required to meet with the students. Stackhouse leaves after being assured by Jackson that he will not create a disturbance but, Stackhouse declines Jackson's offer to join the group in prayer.

Dec. 9:   A second incidence of harassment at the Citadel results in the suspension of three cadets until the end of the year. According to school spokesman Lt. Col. Ben Legare, the details of the case will not be released until the outcome of an appeal by the cadets who have been allowed to remain in school until then.

Dec. 19:   The NAACP files an $800,000 federal lawsuit against the Citadel, charging that school officials have historically tolerated and sanctioned racial bigotry at the academy. The suit also charges that the school's failure to expel the five white cadets for the racial harassment of Kevin Nesmith, a black freshman, has had the effect of "condoning students and/or staff to engage in racially discriminatory conduct."

Dec. 21:   A 23-year-old black man Michael Griffith is killed while fleeing from a mob on the Shore Parkway in Howard Beach, a white community in Queens, New York. According to the report, Griffith and two companions are attacked by whites using bats and fists as they are leaving an area pizza shop. The whites shouted, "Niggers, you don't belong here!" Griffith and his companions first entered the neighborhood in search of a tow for their disabled car.

Dec. 28:   A group of 1,200 marchers, consisting largely of blacks and some whites, march through Howard Beach to protest the death of Michael Griffith who was killed by a mob of whites in what police termed a racial attack. Griffith and two other companions were chased and beaten by the reportedly drunken group of nine to 12 white men, when they entered the area in search of help for their disabled car and stopped to eat in pizza shop.

Area residents taunt the marchers with yells of "animals" and "go home" as they travel down the neighborhood's main throughfare 10 abreast and stop for a moment of silent prayer in front of the pizza shop where Griffith ate.

The NAACP's Benjamin Hooks, executive director of the organization, says that such attacks are occurring across the country and declares, "We've got to say to our white friends . . . either we stand together or we hang separately."

Dec. 30: Judge Ernest Bianchi dismisses charges of murder, manslaughter and assault against three whites allegedly involved in the racial attack that resulted in the death of Michael Griffith, a black man. The judge dismissed the charges citing insufficient evidence when the key witness for the prosecution, another black who was a victim of the attack, refuses to testify, after being advised by his attorney not to testify because of "a bad-faith investigation and prosecution." The attorney charged that the man who struck Griffith with his car was also involved in the attack. An earlier investigation by the police maintains the motorist was not involved.

A Profile of
the Black Unemployed:
A Disaggregation Analysis

Billy J. Tidwell
Director of Research
National Urban League

INTRODUCTION

Unemployment is the foremost indicator of the precarious economic status of black Americans. Considered in absolute terms or in relation to its incidence among whites, joblessness hits black Americans with devastating frequency. In 1984, for example, the reported rate of unemployment for the nation's largest racial minority exceeded 16 percent. This figure represents about two million persons and is more than double the rate of white Americans (6.4 percent). Since the official statistics exclude "discouraged workers" — i.e., persons who have stopped looking for work because they no longer believe jobs are available — and persons limited to part-time employment because they cannot find a full-time job, they understate the true magnitude of black (and white) unemployment. According to the National Urban League's Hidden Unemployment Index, which factors in both discouraged and involuntary part-time workers, the true black jobless rate in 1984 was a depression-level 28.4 percent. By comparison, the unemployment rate for whites was 12.5 percent.

Whether the official or adjusted measure is used, blacks are highly vulnerable to unemployment and its adversities. Even if they have not been unemployed themselves, most black Americans probably have shared the experience of a family member or a close friend. Black unemployment therefore is a more pervasive problem than any of the statistics convey.

The National Urban League (NUL) has consistently been in the forefront of efforts to assess and combat the black unemployment problem. Through systematic research and analysis, targeted program initiatives, and vigorous advocacy in support of remedial public policies, the NUL has sought to draw attention to the employment needs of blacks, thereby broadening the opportunities available to them. This campaign has been driven by the recognition that, in its direct and indirect effects on well-being, unemployment is the single most adverse condition black Americans face. It is, therefore, deeply disturbing that the degree of concern about black unemployment, among the general public and policy-makers alike, has declined markedly in recent years. Thus:

- Media coverage of the black unemployment problem has become much less extensive and sympathetic.

- Federal employment and training programs, of which the black jobless have been prime beneficiaries, have been drastically curtailed.

223

- Promising new legislative proposals, such as the Community Renewal Employment Act and the Youth Incentive Employment Act, have encountered unenthusiastic receptions in the Congress.

- The private sector has not been nearly so forthcoming in its preeminent role under the Job Training Partnership Act as was expected when the legislation was implemented.

- Measures to overcome race discrimination in employment have been progressively undermined; the effort to amend Executive Order 11246 is a prominent case in point.

The list could go on, but the essential point has been made: Black unemployment has been put on the back burner of the public agenda! The degree of this retrenchment is incompatible with the severity of the problem. It is true that the 16 percent black jobless rate in 1984, mirroring improvement in the economy as a whole, was a substantial improvement over the 20 percent level that ravaged Black America in 1983. That the rate dipped to about 15 percent in 1985 was also welcomed news. On the other hand, 15-16 percent unemployment is a problem of massive proportion which should be regarded as a national disgrace. The amount of misery, hardship, and wasted human resources it involves simply cannot be reconciled with any of the nation's most fundamental ideals.

How, then, can the waning interest in black unemployment be explained? Among the factors we discern is a growing tendency to believe that the problem may be intractable, centered in an expanding "underclass" segment of Black America whose members are neither receptive to nor apt to benefit from efforts to promote self-sufficiency. Indeed, if one were to conduct an association test among the American public on the topic of black unemployment, the conjured image would undoubtedly resemble the following: Male high school dropout who spends his time loitering on street corners with others like him — unskilled, unmotivated, and inexperienced in the world of work . . . in a word, "unreachable." Like most stereotypes, this one captures enough social reality to be plausible. Nonetheless, it is a dangerously incomplete and distorted conception.

In the first place, the popular stereotype greatly exaggerates the degree of homogeneity among the black unemployed. The fact is that unemployment cuts deeply across the full spectrum of black Americans — females and males, adults and youth, marrieds and singles, the more educated and the less educated, the work experienced and the inexperienced, etc. While the prevalence of the problem varies among subgroups, jobless blacks nonetheless make up a highly diverse population. In the case of whites, this observation is taken as self-evident. The extent of diversity among jobless blacks, however, is often obscured in the public debate, so dominant is the popular stereotype. The development of effective strategies to deal with black unemployment obviously requires a clear recognition of who is affected by the problem.

Secondly, the stereotype fails to take into account the fact that unemployment is systematically higher among black Americans relative to whites. Even where blacks and whites are equally matched on indicators of employability (e.g., educational attainment), blacks are unemployed at a higher rate. Moreover, blacks who are seemingly well qualified to compete in today's labor market often are more likely to be jobless than are less qualified whites. Therefore, clearly understanding this disproportionality issue — i.e., the consistently higher rates of unemployment among blacks — is crucial to understanding the contemporary black unemployment problem.

Finally, characterizations like "unreachable" or "hardcore" imply that the nation is incapable of devising ways to absorb the most needy of the black unemployed into the economic mainstream and that it is thus morally entitled to write them off. Such notions are entirely unacceptable. The League's success in training and placing severely disadvantaged blacks in productive jobs clearly demonstrates that it can be done. At the same time, we do not underestimate the difficulty and complexity of the black unemployment problem. Fundamental changes in the economy, tied to the shrinking manufacturing sector and the growing dominance of high technology, have imposed new, more stringent demands on the nation's workforce. Black Americans are experiencing the full force of these changes, and many need extensive and broad-based assistance to cope with them. Nevertheless, a nation that has overcome seemingly insurmountable obstacles and countless frustrations to reach the moon should be equally capable to "reach" and engage its unused human resources — and certainly be no less committed.

Consistent with the above concerns, this report examines the following basic questions about black unemployment:

- Who are the black unemployed?
- What is the incidence of unemployment for different groups of black Americans?
- What is the incidence of black versus white unemployment for comparable population groups?

These and similar questions have been addressed before. Nonetheless, this examination helps to clarify the nature and scope of black unemployment as it currently exists. It is essential that incomplete, misguided, or otherwise deficient popular conceptions of the problem are not allowed to persist and further constrain the public attitude and response. This report helps to set the record straight on some issues.

In addition, the examination demonstrates the importance of disaggregating black unemployment. Merely to report that blacks experience a 15 or 16 percent overall jobless rate is not very instructive. If effective remedial measures are to be developed, it is necessary to break down and analyze what this overall figure represents. Black unemployment is a multi-dimensional phenomenon that cannot be controlled by any single remedy. Of course, disaggregation exercises can be carried too far and obscure the common denominators that often must dictate public policy. Indeed, consideration of too many uniquenesses and special needs can be stifling. With respect to black unemployment, however, disaggregation analyses, such as those performed here, are sorely needed.

Finally, a principal aim of the report is to call more attention to the black unemployment problem. The well-being of millions of black Americans is vitally dependent upon moving this issue from the "back burner" to its rightful place among the nation's domestic priorities.

PROFILES OF THE BLACK UNEMPLOYED

The contemporary black unemployed comprise many different subgroups, and are therefore not nearly so homogeneous as the popular stereotype suggests. At the outset, it is useful to distinguish among them in terms of the different routes by which they joined the ranks of the unemployed. This classification generates four major subgroups: (1) *job losers,* or persons who were involuntarily terminated from their last job; (2) *job leavers,* or persons who themselves terminated their job to seek employment elsewhere; (3) *re-entrants* into the labor force, or persons who have returned following some period of absence; and (4) *new entrants* into the labor force, or those who are in pursuit of their first job.[1]

Based on data for 1984,[2] a little more than half of the black unemployed (52%) are job losers. This group can be subdivided into those who experienced a permanent termination (44%) and those who experienced a layoff (8%). In striking contrast to the high proportion of job *losers,* job *leavers* account for a mere one percent of the total black unemployed population. Re-entrants into the labor force make up about 28 percent of the total. In general, re-entrants are likely to be women, many of whom had temporarily suspended their labor force participation because of child-rearing responsibilities; others may be seeking work as a result of a divorce or separation; still others may have been attracted back to the job market by the broadened opportunities created by reduced sex discrimination. Finally, about 18 percent of the black unemployed are in search of their first job. As one might expect, new entrants into the labor force are typically teenagers and young adults.

A few additional comments about the job loser subgroup are in order. First, relative to their share of the civilian labor force, black workers tend to be greatly overrepresented among the overall population of job losers, and particularly among permanent terminees. In 1982, for example, blacks accounted for about 13 percent of the labor force but represented 24 percent of permanently terminated workers. It is also worth noting that these job losers were largely concentrated in blue collar occupations. Thus, 54 percent were blue collar workers, as opposed to 22 percent for both the white collar and service worker categories.[3]

Regardless of the manner in which they became unemployed, however, another initial and crucial differentiation among jobless blacks is length of unemployment. The 1984 data indicate that 36 percent had been job-hunting for less than five weeks and 29 percent for five–14 weeks. Defining "long-term unemployment" as 15 weeks or more, better than three out of 10 black unemployed persons are long-termers. About 23 percent may be considered "very long-term unemployed," having been without a job for more than 26 weeks. Overall, the median duration of unemployment is 8.1 weeks, with males tending to have longer jobless spells than females.[4]

The remainder of this section examines other disaggregations of the black unemployed, focusing on selected socio-demographic characteristics. In each case, the profile of the unemployed is compared with the corresponding profile of the larger black civilian labor force.

Age and Sex

About 18 percent of the black unemployed are teenagers, and another 26 percent are young adults in the 20-24 age group. A little more than 43 percent fall into what are considered the prime working years (25-44 years), during which period employment potential and career patterns tend to be established. This group is also significant because of the heavier familial and economic responsibilities (i.e., family dependents, homeownership, and various financial obligations) that are normally associated with this phase of the life cycle. The smallest proportion of the black unemployed are 45 years or older, a stage when work options typically begin to diminish (see Table 1).

Teenagers and young adults are substantially overrepresented among the black unemployed. While they represent a mere seven percent of the black civilian labor force, teenagers account for more than 18 percent of jobless blacks. Similarly, 16 percent of the black civilian labor force are young adults, compared to 26 percent of the unemployed group. These disparities document the continuing employment crisis confronting black youth, a problem that has commanded a considerable amount of attention in recent years.[5] The concern is altogether appropriate. In the words of one writer, black youth unemployment " . . . has serious social implications for the country as a whole, even though it may not appreciably affect total family income."[6] Such "social implications" were manifested dramatically in the urban riots and disturbances that convulsed the nation during the 1960s. Studies of these incidents invariably emphasized the youthfulness of the participants and the extent of unemployment among them.[7]

Table 1.
Percent Distribution of Black Unemployed by Age and Sex, 1984

Sex	16–19	20–24	Age Group 25–44	45 & older	Totals
Both Sexes	18.4 (6.9)*	26.2 (16.0)	43.3 (52.9)	11.9 (24.2)	100.0
Males					
% of group	53.3 (53.2)	54.1 (53.1)	50.7 (50.2)	53.3 (50.4)	52.4 (50.9)
% in group	18.8 (7.2)	27.1 (16.2)	42.0 (52.1)	12.1 (24.0)	100.0
Females					
% of group	46.7 (46.8)	45.9 (46.9)	49.3 (49.8)	46.7 (49.6)	47.6 (49.1)
% in group	18.1 (6.6)	25.4 (15.3)	44.9 (53.7)	11.6 (24.5)	100.0

* Figures in parentheses ( ) are corresponding percentages for the black civilian force.

Source: Prepared by National Urban League Research Department from unpublished data in the Bureau of Labor Statistics.

In contrast to the youth subgroups, prime working age adults are underrepresented among the black unemployed, as are those in the 45-and-over age category. In part, the difference reflects the fact that older blacks have simply had more time to establish themselves in the working world.

With respect to sex classification, a majority of the black unemployed (52%) are males. To varying degrees, the somewhat higher incidence of males occurs across all of the age categories, the differential being smallest in the 25-44 year-old subgroup and largest among the young adults. In any event, there is not the great preponderance of males that one might surmise from the popular stereotype. This observation is reinforced by the sex distribution of the civilian labor force, in which males constitute a comparable 51 percent of the total. Moreover, within the youth subgroups, the size of the male-female differential is virtually the same among the unemployed as among the civilian labor force. Finally, it is worth pointing out that the incidence of unemployment among black males has only recently surpassed that of black females. Up to 1980, black females were consistently unemployed at a higher rate.

Marital Status

The largest proportion of the black unemployed (53%) are single persons who have never been married. About 30 percent are currently married, including those whose spouse is temporarily absent (eight percent) — i.e., in the armed forces, institutionalized, etc. The remainder are either widowed, divorced, or separated. Some 60 percent of unemployed black males are single, compared to 47 percent of black females. The proportions of males and females who are married, with or without spouse present, are roughly comparable (see Table 2).

Although the black unemployed vary in marital status, their distribution across the marital status categories diverges considerably from the corresponding distribution of the black civilian labor force. Most notably, the proportion of unemployed singles exceeds the labor force share of this subgroup by about 20 percent. By contrast, the proportion of the unemployed who are married and with their spouse is about 19 percent lower than their percentage of the labor force. These differences, of course, are largely age-related, as many in the youth subgroups are also likely to be single.

Education

The education breakdown indicates that 44 percent of the black unemployed are high school graduates; another 13 percent attended college for one–three years; and just over four percent attended college for four years or more. At the lower end of the continuum, 29 percent show only one–three years of high school, while nine percent have no high school education at all. In terms of sex differences, unemployed black females are more likely to have attained one–

Table 2.
Percent Distribution of Black Unemployed by Marital Status and Sex, 1984

Sex	Marital Status				
	Married/w spouse	Married/wo spouse	Widowed, divorced, separated	Single never married	Totals
Both Sexes	21.2 (39.9)*	8.4 (7.5)	17.1 (20.1)	53.3 (32.5)	100.0
Males	22.7 (46.0)	6.1 (5.9)	12.0 (13.7)	59.3 (34.5)	100.0
Females	19.6 (33.8)	10.8 (7.5)	22.5 (20.1)	47.1 (32.5)	100.0

* Figures in parentheses (   ) are corresponding percentages for the black civilian labor force.
Source: Prepared by National Urban League Research Department from unpublished data in the Bureau of Labor Statistics.

three years of college and less likely to have dropped out of or failed to attend high school. The proportion of college graduates is virtually identical for males and females (see Table 3).

Relative to their share of the black civilian labor force, high school dropouts are overrepresented among the black unemployed by about 11 percent, while high school graduates are overrepresented by almost three percent. Conversely, persons who have attended or graduated from college are underrepresented by sizable margins. Thus, college graduates constitute almost 12 percent of the black civilian labor force but only four percent of the black unemployed. The data serve to reaffirm the importance of education to economic well-being.[8] Thus a higher level of educational attainment by blacks is associated with a lower probability of unemployment. As will be discussed in the next section, however, this general relationship is subject to serious qualification. The qualification surfaces as one conducts racial comparisons on the education variable.

Table 3.
Percent Distribution of Black Unemployed by Education Level and Sex, 1984

Sex	Education Level				
	No high school	High school 1–3 years	High school 4 years	College 1–3 years	College 4 years +	Totals
Both Sexes	9.5 (9.9)*	29.2 (18.4)	44.1 (41.5)	12.9 (18.4)	4.3 (11.6)	100.0
Males	11.2 (11.9)	31.7 (20.5)	43.6 (40.7)	9.3 (16.3)	4.2 (10.6)	100.0
Females	7.4 (7.9)	26.0 (16.3)	45.0 (42.4)	17.1 (20.7)	4.4 (12.6)	100.0

* Figures in parentheses (   ) are corresponding percentages for the black civilian labor force.
  Source: Prepared by National Urban League Research Department from data in *The Educational Attainment of Workers,* Bureau of Labor Statistics, March, 1984.

Occupation

Disaggregated into the major occupational categories, about 42 percent of the (experienced) black unemployed are blue collar workers, 26 percent are white collar, and 28 percent are in the service classification, including those who work in private households. Only a small fraction are farm workers. By sex, unemployed black males are mainly blue collar, while black females are concentrated in white collar and service fields (see Table 4).

Given the changes that have occurred in the nation's economy — in which the manufacturing sector has progressively given way to high technology and related occupations — it is not surprising to find that blue collar workers are overrepresented among the black unemployed, while white collar workers are substantially underrepresented. Service workers are overrepresented, but only slightly. As with educational achievement, however, the association between occupational classification and unemployment among blacks is not as straightforward as it might appear. This point, too, is discussed in some detail in the next section.

Table 4.
Percent Distribution of Experienced Black Unemployed
by Major Occupation Category and Sex, 1984

Sex	Occupation				
	White Collar	Blue Collar	Service	Farm	Totals
Both Sexes	25.7 (37.8)*	41.8 (34.2)	28.2 (25.0)	4.3 (3.0)	100.0
Males	13.4 (25.4)	58.4 (50.6)	21.7 (18.8)	6.5 (5.1)	100.0
Females	39.7 (50.8)	23.2 (17.2)	35.5 (31.3)	1.6 (0.6)	100.0

* Figures in parentheses (   ) are corresponding percentages for the black civilian labor force.
  Source: Prepared by National Urban League Research Department from unpublished data in the Bureau of Labor Statistics.

RACIAL DIFFERENCES

The profiles in the previous section underscore the importance of looking beyond the statistic on overall black unemployment. This statistic represents a very diverse population, not the homogeneous mass of "unreachables" that is often portrayed. At the same time, the examination showed that there is variation in the incidence of unemployment among different subgroups of black Americans with some subgroups being hit much harder than others.

In this section, we will examine differences between black and white unemployment levels. As was mentioned previously, the overall unemployment rate for black Americans persists at more than double the rate for whites. This overall comparison, however, conceals more discrete differences that are important in order to understand the nature of black unemployment. It is, therefore, necessary to disaggregate the black and white populations and investigate the relative incidence of unemployment among various subgroups. The examination focuses on subgroups defined by education levels and occupation. Each of these variables has been strongly emphasized in explanations of the black unemployment phenomenon.

Education Effects

There is a longstanding belief that the black/white unemployment gap is largely due to racial disparities in educational attainment. This view is embodied in the so-called "human capital" theory of the labor market, which postulates that employers base their hiring and compensation decisions on the knowledge, skills, talents, and capacities of the individual worker. These human capital attributes are believe to determine the potential or actual productivity of the worker.[9,10] Level of education is a basic measurement of human capital. Indeed, differences in education are strongly associated with differences in employment and earnings among the work force. This association is invariably cited in explanations of the contemporary black unemployment problem. For example, the following represents the prevailing view:

> Black unemployment rates exceed those of whites *ceteris paribus* because blacks in the past have typically had lower levels of educational attainment than whites, and employers have, to some degree, rationed specific training opportunities to those employees with greater amounts of general training.[11]

The general relationship between education and employment or earnings has been well documented.[12] Indeed, the earlier profile of the contemporary black unemployed is consistent with the general finding that higher levels of education result in a lower probability of unemployment. Equally well documented is the fact that black Americans continue to lag behind whites in educational attainment.[13] Just how well black/white differences in education explain the black/white unemployment gap, however, is debatable. In his review of the relevant literature, Darity concludes that, "the human capital approach simply does not stand up well against the facts it purports to explain."[14] Our disaggregation analysis lends support to this conclusion.

Table 5 presents unemployment rates by race and education level. The data show that black Americans with four or more years of college are unemployed at about 2.4 times the rate of their white counterparts, and those with one–three years of college are unemployed at about 2.3 times the rate of whites. At the other end of the spectrum, however, blacks who attended high school for one–three years show a jobless rate of 1.8 times that of their white counterparts, while those who did not attend high school at all are unemployed at 1.3 times the rate of whites. Thus, the black/white unemployment gap is wider among the highly educated than it is among persons with limited education. Stated differently, additional investment in education on the part of blacks is associated with a greater likelihood of unemployment relative to their white counterparts. This finding is not consistent with the human capital theory.

A similar pattern occurs when one considers aggregate education and unemployment statistics for the two races. In 1960, for example, the ratio of black-to-white unemployment was 1.8:1, while the median school years for whites exceeded that for blacks by only .4 years. Yet, the unemployment rate of blacks in 1984 was some 2.5 times the rate of whites. Thus, consistent with the disaggregated unemployment rates, these aggregate level data suggest that as the relative educational status of blacks has improved, the black/white disparity in unemployment has actually increased. The human capital deficiency argument, then, is a seriously inadequate explanation of the relative severity of black unemployment.

Presentation of these data here is not intended to de-emphasize the importance of education in general, or for black Americans in particular. Indeed, it is clear that improving the educational status of blacks is essential to advancing their economic well-being.[15] The data clearly show that the jobless rate for blacks (and whites) drops significantly at the higher education levels. Nonetheless, policy-makers must realize that initiatives to improve the education level of black Americans are not sufficient to close the unemployment gap with whites. The evidence suggests that factors other than deficient education sustain the disproportionate incidence of black unemployment. In this regard, one cannot avoid the conclusion that racial discrimination in the labor market remains a potent force. Thus, blacks continue to experience pervasive, race-determined problems of access to employment opportunities as well as deficiencies in educational achievement and other "human capital" variables. Discussing the perilous employment situation of black youth, one writer makes the point in asserting that ". . . the unavailability of jobs to black youth is a more important factor than their unavailability for those jobs. "[16]

Occupation Effects

In the Introduction, we referred to the fundamental change that has occurred in the nation's economy—from a predominantly industrial, goods-producing system to one based on high technology and the production of services. This process has had a profound impact on the requirements for economic well-being, as technical skills and professional expertise have become increasingly important in the job market. Thus, many American workers have found themselves displaced from occupations where technology has grown progressively more sophisticated and less labor intensive. Similarly, new entrants into the labor force face skills demands that are much more stringent than previously. They also find that job opportunities in manufacturing industries, formerly the backbone of the economy, are rapidly diminishing. These developments have evoked extensive commentary and concern, around the unemployment problem in general, and black unemployment in particular.[17]

Table 5.

Unemployment Rates by Race and Education Level, 1984*

Race	Education Level					
	No high school	High school 1–3 years	High school 4 years	College 1–3 years	College 4 years +	Totals
Black	16.0	27.3	18.3	12.0	6.3	17.2
White	12.3	15.2	7.4	5.1	2.6	7.2

* Data apply to March, 1984
  Source: Prepared by National Urban League Research Department from data in *The Educational Attainment of Workers*. Bureau of Labor Statistics.

Blacks have traditionally been concentrated in those industries and occupations that are most vulnerable to disruption and obsolescence. For example, the manufacturing industries with the highest unemployment rates in both 1981 and 1982 were the automobile, steel, apparel, and lumber industries. In each of these industries, the percentage of black and other minority workers greatly exceeded their representation in the total work-force.[18] By the same token, black Americans have been heavily concentrated in cities and areas within cities that are most prone to economic stagnation through loss of industry. The percentage of blacks living in central cities is more than double that of whites. William Wilson summarizes the situation as follows:

> The . . . minority community is disadvantaged not simply by cyclical economic stagnation but by profound structural economic changes. The shift from goods-producing to service-producing industries is polarizing the labor market . . . Technological innovations in industry are affecting the numbers and types of jobs available. Manufacturing industries are relocating out of the central city to the suburbs, to other parts of the country, and even to foreign countries. (T)hese changes . . . have been especially devastating for blacks and other minorities because these groups are concentrated in central cities and in industries that have been hardest hit by economic dislocations.[19]

Structural economic change is indeed an inescapable reality of American life. Its disproportionately adverse impact on black Americans is no less real. As an explanation of contemporary black unemployment, however, the conventional structural change arguments must be qualified.

It is true that black Americans are overrepresented in blue collar occupations and that the black unemployed are disproportionately blue collar workers. Thus, as the earlier socio-demographic data indicated, about 34 percent of the black civilian labor force and 42 percent of the black unemployed were classified as blue collar in 1984 (refer to Table 4). These data are consistent with the structural change argument. On the other hand, an examination of unemployment rates by major occupation and race discloses a curious pattern (see Table 6). While black blue collar workers were unemployed at 1.8 times the rate of their white counterparts, the black/white unemployment ratio among white collar workers was about 2.6:1. In other words, the unemployment differential is significantly larger in those occupations that have gained prominence as the economy has changed! Given that blacks are especially vulnerable to the effects of structural economic forces, one should expect the opposite result; that is, a larger black/white unemployment gap among blue collar workers.

Table 6.

Unemployment Rates by Race and Major Occupation Category, 1984*

Race					
		Occupation			
	White Collar	Blue Collar	Service	Farm	Totals
Black	9.0	16.2	14.9	19.2	13.2
White	3.5	8.8	7.7	7.2	5.7

* Data apply to experienced labor force.

Source: Prepared by National Urban League Research Department from unpublished data in Bureau of Labor Statistics.

The anomaly also occurs in data for more discrete occupational classifications. For example, among executives, administrators and managers, blacks were unemployed at 2.2 times the rate of whites; in technical fields, the ratio was even greater at 2.5:1; and in sales occupations, the jobless rate of black Americans was overwhelmingly disproportionate at 3.5 times the rate of their white counterparts. By comparison, blacks in the declining manufacturing sector were unemployed at only 1.5 times the rate of whites. Likewise, in the construction field, which tends to be acutely affected by economic downturns, black workers were also just 1.5 times more likely to experience unemployment than white workers. Without a doubt, such comparisons qualify the role of structural economic change with regard to the black unemployment problem.

In this regard, the frequent observation is made that blacks are more likely than whites to live in central cities or areas that, in Wilson's words, "have been hardest hit by economic dislocations." However, in his analysis of youth unemployment, Hill addresses this specific issue:

The movement of industries from central cities to suburban areas is . . . cited as an important determinant of minority youth unemployment. But available data reveal that *the unemployment gap between minority and white youth is about as great among those living in the suburbs as among those living in central cities.*[20] (emphasis added)

There is no questioning the fact that changes in the nation's economy have hurt the employment situation of workers in manufacturing industries—black *and* white. Given their traditional occupational and residential patterns, blacks were expected to bear the brunt of the shrinking availability of blue collar work. That the disproportionate incidence of black unemployment is more pronounced among white collar workers, however, suggests that forces other than structural factors are operating. While the structural explanation does help us understand the absolute levels of black unemployment, it clearly does not account for the observed pattern of black/white differences across occupational categories. Similarly, it does not explain the black/white unemployment gap that exists in areas which have benefited from new or relocated industries.

As we concluded in the discussion of education and human capital theory, these weaknesses in the structural explanation of black unemployment suggest the continued operation of racial discrimination in the labor market. Structural changes in the economy interact with a systematic denial of access to sustain disproportionate black unemployment rates.

The Black Community's Role

As central as government and corporate initiatives are, the black community itself has a major responsibility in reducing black unemployment. Moreover, what the black community does should not be contingent upon favorable action by the government or the private sector. Merely "blaming the system, " however justified, is not a sufficient response. There is much that black Americans can and should do on their own behalf. Fortunately, there are impressive indications of increased awareness in this regard and a commitment to act. To quote John Jacob:

On balance, we would suggest that the strongest message coming out of Black America in 1984 was that it became increasingly aware of its own strengths and increasingly willing to act independently to achieve what it considers its own best interests. This does not signal any lessening of the responsibility of government or the private sector to assist in the building of a Black America that is equal in every respect to the other sectors of our society. But it does signal that black America is not standing still waiting for others to come to its rescue. It recognizes that its salvation lies within itself.[21]

In the employment area, one of the "best interests" of black Americans is to ensure that they acquire the basic proficiencies and technical skills necessary to compete effectively in a changing labor market. Even the complete elimination of racial discrimination and greatly expanded economic opportunity will have limited benefit if blacks are unprepared to meet prevailing employer demands. Whether they are described as "hardcore, " "underclass, " or something else, the reality is that far too many blacks are not competitive. The problem is particularly serious among black youth. Under-educated and unskilled, a growing number of black youth are virtually assured a life of dependency, hardship, and degradation. The black community cannot afford to wait for the nation's formal education and training institutions to reduce the odds.

Responding to the imperative, the Urban League has resolved that improving the education of black children is an overriding priority. A multifaceted, movement-wide initiative is being undertaken to achieve this objective. It involves a coordinated mobilization of local community resources around education issues as well as the delivery of remedial and other educational services. The new initiative will be carried out alongside the many skills development and job training programs in which the League has historically been involved.

Of course, there are many other examples of black community initiatives in education and other areas having a direct bearing on the black unemployment problem. The point is that such initiatives need to be intensified. The stakes are too high to justify anything less than maximum effort.

Summary of Major Findings

- More than half of all unemployed black Americans in 1984 (52%) lost their jobs, including 44 percent who were permanently terminated. A mere one percent left their job voluntarily. The remainder of the black unemployed were either re-entrants into the labor force (28%) or first-time job seekers (18%).

- Black males are slightly more likely than females to be hit by unemployment. In 1984, 52 percent of the black unemployed were males, or about the same as the proportion of males in the black civilian labor force.

- Blue collar workers are substantially overrepresented among the black unemployed, while white collar workers are underrepresented. In 1984, about 42 percent of jobless blacks were blue collar, compared to 34 percent of the black civilian labor force. By contrast, 26 percent of the black unemployed were white collar, while 38 percent of the civilian labor force were in the white collar category.

- The incidence of unemployment among blacks declines with increased education. Although college graduates constituted 12 percent of the black civilian labor force in 1984, they accounted for only four percent of the black unemployed. Conversely, black high-school dropouts were 18 percent of the labor force but 29 percent of the unemployed.

- In terms of racial comparisons, the gap between black and white unemployment rates is greater at the higher education levels. Thus, the jobless rate of black college graduates in 1984 was 2.5 times that of their white counterparts, while the rate of black high school dropouts was only 1.8 times the rate of white dropouts. These findings evidence the continued impact of racial discrimination in the labor market.

- Further evidence of continued employment discrimination against blacks is suggested by comparisons of black and white jobless rates within different occupational categories. In particular, the unemployment rate of black blue-collar workers in 1984 was 1.8 times that of their white counterparts, while black white-collar workers were unemployed at 2.6 times the rate of their white counterparts.

NOTES AND
REFERENCES

FOOTNOTES

¹347 U.S. 483 (1954); 349 U.S. 294 (1955).

²P.L. No. 88-352, 88th Cong., 2d Sess., 78 Stat. 241 (1964).

³*See, e.g.,* text *infra* at note 14.

⁴For example, the confrontations between the United States Justice Department and Governor Ross Barnett in Mississippi, *see* Read, *School Integration Law since Brown,* 39 Law and Contemp. Prob. 1, 16 n.36 (1975) & authorities cited, and Governor George Wallace in Alabama, *see United States v. Wallace,* 222 F. Supp. 485 (M.D. Ala. 1963) *(per curiam);* or the decision of President Eisenhower to federalize the National Guard and send troops to Little Rock in 1957, *see Cooper v. Aaron,* 358 U.S. 1, 12 (1958); *Jackson v. Kuhn,* 2 Race Rel. L. Rep. 1099 (E.D. Ark. 1957).

⁵After passage of the Civil Rights Act of 1964, which included provisions both authorizing the Attorney General to bring suits to end school segregation and also making any school district which continued to practice discrimination in violation of federal regulations ineligible for federal aid, HEW issued a series of school desegregation Guidelines. These regulations required not just a theoretical system allowing black pupils to transfer, but the accomplishment of actual school integration. They were relied upon by federal courts as a basis for stiffening judicial requirements for desegregation. *E.g., Singleton v. Jackson Municipal Separate School Dist.,* 348 F.2d 729 (5th Cir. 1965); *Kemp v. Beasley,* 352 F.2d 14 (5th Cir. 1965); *United States v. Jefferson County Bd. of Educ.* 372 F.2d 836 (5th Cir.), *aff'd on rehearing en banc,* 380 F.2d 385 (1966), *cert. denied sub nom. Caddo Parish School Bd. v. United States,* 390 U.S. 840 (1967).

⁶*E.g., United States v. Montgomery County Bd. of Educ.,* 395 U.S. 225 (1969).

⁷The Solicitor General argued against black parents' attorneys in *Alexander v. Holmes County Bd. of Educ.,* 396 U.S. 19 (1969) and *Swann v. Charlotte-Mecklenburg Bd. of Educ.,* 402 U.S. 1 (1971), for instance.

⁸347 U.S. 483 (1954).

⁹S. Taylor, *The Court Sees No Evil in Ending a Busing Plan, The New York Times,* November 9, 1986, p. E7.

On the same date that it declined to review the Norfolk ruling, the Supreme Court also allowed the ruling of the United States Court of Appeals for the Tenth Circuit in *Dowell v. Board of Education of Oklahoma City,* 795 F.2d 1516 (10th Cir. 1986) to stand. In that case, the Court of Appeals indicated that even if a school system becomes "unitary," it is not automatically entitled to a dismissal of all judicial decrees unless it can demonstrate that the conditions which made entry of the decrees necessary have been eliminated. This standard, quite different from Norfolk's, would require the continuation of school desegregation in most districts. The segregated residential patterns and deliberate placement of school buildings in racially impacted areas that were the hallmarks of the dual school system in most jurisdictions are unchanged in most areas of the country.

¹⁰This argument is contrary to relevant Supreme Court decisions. In *Green v. County School Board of New Kent County,* 391 U.S. 430, 440 (1968), the Court held that if a "freedom of choice" plan "prove(s) effective, it is acceptable, but if it fails to undo segregation, other means must be used to achieve this end. The school officials have the *continuing* duty to take whatever action may be necessary to create a 'unitary, non-racial system.'" (emphasis supplied)

In *Swann v. Charlotte-Mecklenburg Board of Education,* 402 U.S. 1, 7 (1971), the Court approved an extensive pupil transportation plan ordered by the district court on plaintiffs' motion for further relief to substitute for an earlier geographic zoning plan that had been ineffective.

The Department of Justice itself, under earlier administrations, has repeatedly implemented these principles by seeking student assignment modifications when plans did not produce results in practice. *E.g., United States v. Seminole County School District,* 553 F.2d 992 (5th Cir. 1977).

¹¹*See Post-Trial Memorandum of United States as Amicus Curiae, Keyes v. School District No. 1, Denver,* Civ. No. C-1499 (D. Colo. filed July 16, 1984).

[12]*Consent Decree, United States v. Bakersfield City School District,* Civ. No. CV-F-84-39 EDP (E.D. Cal. January 25, 1984).

[13]Magnet schools may be a useful component of an acceptable desegregation plan, but we know of no instance in which magnet schools alone have successfully integrated any large school system.

[14]Quoted in *The New York Times,* November 20, 1981, p. A14.

[15]*See* Brief for United States as Amicus Curiae, *Jackson Board of Education v. Wygant,* 54 U.S.L.W. 4479 (May 19, 1986).

[16]*See Geier v. Alexander,* 593 F. Supp. 1263 (M.D. Tenn. 1984), *aff'd* 81 F.2d 799 (6th Cir. 1986).

[17]First filed in 1970 as *Adams* v. *Richardson,* the longstanding suit sought to compel the Department of Health, Education and Welfare (now the Department of Education) to comply with the provisions of Title VI of the Civil Rights Act of 1964 by withholding federal funds from state systems of higher education which retain vestiges of segregation and discriminatory practices.

[18]Originally, 19 states were covered by *Adams;* currently there are 14, six of which are "first-tier" states and eight, "second-tier" states. First-tier states are those originally ordered to desegregate in 1973. These are Arkansas, Florida, Georgia, North Carolina (community colleges only), Oklahoma and Virginia. Second-tier states are those which received notice from the Department of Education in January 1981 requiring them to submit new desegregation plans that would include all public postsecondary institutions. These are Alabama, Delaware, Kentucky, Missouri, Ohio, South Carolina, Texas, and West Virginia.

[19]One court order reinforced the time frames governing complaint investigations and compliance; the other set deadlines for OCR to secure Title VI compliance in states' higher education plans.

[20]*Bob Jones University v. United States,* 461 U.S. 574 (1983).

[21]*Thornburg* v. *Gingles,* 54 U.S.L.W. 4877 (U.S. June 30, 1986).

[22]*See Washington Post,* August 30, 1986, p. A1.

[23]The intent of Congress in amending Section 2 in 1982 is clear. The Senate Judiciary Committee report, which the Supreme Court has just emphasized is "the authoritative source for legislative intent" (*Thornburg v. Gingles,* 54 U.S.L.W. 4877, 4881 n.7 (U.S. June 30, 1986)), states:
> In light of the amendments to Section 2, it is intended that a Section 5 objection also follows if a new voting procedure itself so discriminates as to violate Section 2.

S. Rep. No. 97-417, 97th Cong., 2d Sess. 12 n.31 (1982). "Memorandum on the Applicability of Section 2 to Submissions for Preclearance Under Section 5 of the Voting Rights Act of 1965," enclosed with letter to Edwin Meese from Lawyers Committee for Civil Rights Under Law, American Civil Liberties Union, NAACP, NAACP Legal Defense and Educational Fund et al., p. 1 (Oct. 3, 1986).

[24]Until recently, the Department of Justice has adhered to the position that Section 5 of the Act incorporates Section 2 standards, and that if a voting law change violates Section 2 it should be objected to under Section 5. In its post-trial brief in a Section 5 voting rights case, *County Council of Sumter County, S.C. v. United States,* the Department told the Court:
> Thus, when the legislative history to the Voting Rights Act is examined . . ., the *inescapable conclusion* is that Congress intended that Section 5 preclearance be denied if it is determined that a voting procedure violates Section 2. (Post-Trial Brief for the United States, *County Council of Sumter County v. U.S.,* Civil No. 82-0912 (D.D.C.), p. 32.) (emphasis added)

"Memorandum on the Applicability . . .", p. 2.

[25]The Department repeatedly has expressed this position in communications with Congress. In defending the Department's position in the *Sumter County* brief, the Assistant Attorney General told Senator Hatch:
> "When, during the course of Section 5 review, the Attorney General received sufficient evidence to establish a violation of Section 2, and when the covered jurisdiction is unwilling or unable to rebut that evidence, approval of such a voting change would clearly frustrate the remedial purpose of Section 5." (Letter from William Bradford Reynolds to Senator Orrin Hatch, September 21, 1983, p. 2.)

"Memorandum on the Applicability . . .,'" p. 2.

[26]The third agency, the Department of Labor, exercises its authority through the Office of Federal Contract Compliance Programs to enforce Executive Order 11246, which bars discrimination by federal contractors.

[27]*Griggs v. Duke Power Co.,* 401 U.S. 424 (1971).

[28]*Albemarle Paper Co. v. Moody,* 422 U.S. 405 (1975).

[29]In proposing revisions to the Guidelines, Chairman Thomas expressed concern that "the theory of 'adverse impact' as applied in the Guidelines, and the statistical rule for measuring it, are conceptually unsound." Submission of Clarence Thomas to the Office of Management and Budget pursuant to Executive Order No. 12498 and OMB Bulletin No. 85-9 (Feb. 25, 1985).

[30]Consistent with the administration's opposition to statistical proof, President Reagan nominated Jeffrey I. Zuckerman to be general counsel of the EEOC. Mr. Zuckerman, who had no previous background in civil rights litigation, had been an attorney in the Anti-Trust Division of the Justice Department. He rejected the use of statistics in proving discrimination and opposed the use of hiring goals and timetables as a remedy for discrimination against minorities and women. Instead, he suggested a "free market" economic approach to employment discrimination. He indicated, for example, that blacks and women could eliminate job discrimination by offering to work for lower wages than white men, and would have allowed companies to lay off older employees as a cost-saving measure despite federal rulings holding that this practice would be illegal age discrimination. Because of Mr. Zuckerman's views, his nomination was rejected by the Senate Labor and Human Resources Committee.

[31]See July 15, 1986 letter from Clarence Thomas, Chairman, EEOC, to Rep. Augustus Hawkins, Chairman, House Committee on Education and Labor.

[32]Advances by blacks in many job categories have been significant since passage of Title VII and introduction of affirmative action programs. Public service jobs have seen the most dramatic increase. For example, in 1970, blacks were 6.34% of police officers nationwide. This translated to 23,796 black police officers out of a total of 375,494. By 1982, black police officers numbered approximately 47,000 out of a nationwide total of 505,000, or 9.3%. U.S. Bureau of Census, Census of the Population: 1970, Vol. 1, Characteristics of the Population, Part 1, United States Summary-Section 1 (1973), at Table 223: *1984 Statistical Abstract of United States* (1984), at Table 696.

[33]*Fullilove v. Klutznick,* 448 U.S. 448 (1980); *United Steelworkers v. Weber,* 443 U.S. 193 (1979); *Regents of the University of California v. Bakke,* 438 U.S. 265 (1978).

[34]*See, e.g.,* Brief for the United States as Amicus Curiae in Support of Petitioners at 22–24, *Boston Firefighters v. Boston Chapter NAACP,* 468 U.S. 1206 (1984); Brief for the United States as Intervenor-Appellee, *Williams v. City of New Orleans,* 729 F. 2d 1554, 1557 (1984) *(en banc), cert. denied,* 92 L.Ed.2d 738 (1986).

[35]*Local 28, Sheet Metal Workers v. EEOC,* 92 L.Ed.2d 344 (1986).

[36]*See* Letter Brief of the Plaintiff-Appellee EEOC, dated July 27, 1984, filed in *EEOC v. Local 28,* 753 F2d 1172 (1985).

[37]Brief for the Equal Employment Opportunity Commission at 9. The EEOC's Acting General Counsel announced in early 1986 that the Commission would no longer seek court enforcement of provisions of conciliation agreements of consent decrees that involve numerical goals and timetables. *See Supreme Court Decisions Are Expected to Resolve Lingering Bias Issues,* Chronicle of Higher Education (January 29, 1986), at 15.

[38]*Local No. 93, International Association of Firefighters v. Cleveland,* 92 L.Ed.2d 260 (1986).

[39]90 L.Ed.2d 260 (1986).

[40]*Sheet Metal Workers,* 92 L.Ed.2d at 392; *Cleveland Firefighters,* 92 L.Ed.2d at 425; *Wygant,* 90 L.Ed.2d at 268 (Powell, J., joined by Burger, C.J. & Rehnquist, J.); *ibid.* at 276 (O'Connor, J.); *id.* at 286 (Marshall, J., joined by Brennan & Blackmun, JJ.); *ibid.* at 295 (Stevens, J.).

[41]Wygant, 90 L.Ed. at 269–71 (Powell, J., joined by Burger, C.J. & Rehnquist, J.); *ibid.* at 277–80 (O'Connor, J., concurring); *Cleveland Firefighters,* 92 L.Ed. at 420 (Brennan, J., joined by Marshall, Blackmun, Powell, Stevens, & O'Connor, JJ.) (applying standards adopted in *Steelworkers v. Weber* to consent decrees).

[42]*Wygant,* 90 L.Ed. at 276–77 (O'Connor, J., concurring); *ibid.* at 289 (Marshall, J., dissenting, joined by Brennan & Blackmun, JJ.) *ibid.* at 293 (Stevens, J., dissenting).

[43]*See* Letter to Rep. Augustus Hawkins, Chairman, Committee on Education and Labor, United States House, from Clarence Thomas, Chairman, EEOC, dated July 15, 1986; Memorandum to All

District and Regional Attorneys, from Johnny Butler, General Counsel (Acting) and James H. Troy, Director, Office of Program Operations, EEOC, dated July 25, 1986.

[44]Brief for the United States, *Shimkus v. The Gersten Companies,* No. 85-2594 (9th Cir.), at 47.

[45]Supplemental Brief of the United States, *Hammon v. Barry,* Nos. 85-5669 (D.C. Cir.), at 5–6, 21.

[46]585 F. Supp. 72 (M.D. Ala. 1983), *aff'd,* 767 F.2d 1514 (11th Cir. 1985), *cert. granted,* 106 S. Ct. 3331 (1986).

[47]Brief for the United States, *United States v. Paradise* (No. 85-999), at 21.

[48]Brief for the United States at 29. The Justice Department itself notes, though, that the Patrol's "hiring discrimination for almost four years had excluded blacks from any jobs at all, including jobs in the upper ranks," *ibid.* at 21.

[49]Brief for the United States at 30–35.

[50]770 F.2d 752 (9th Cir. 1985), *cert. granted,* 106 U.S. (1986).

[51]Brief for the United States as Amicus Curiae, *Johnson v. Transportation Agency,* No. 85-1129, at 25.

[52]*See, e.g.,* Comment, *The Philadelphia Plan: A Study in the Dynamics of Executive Power,* 39 U. Chi. L. Rev., 723 (1972).

[53]*E.g., Contractors Ass'n v. Secretary of Labor,* 442 F.2d 159 (3rd Cir.), *cert. denied,* 404 U.S. 854 (1971).

[54]*See, e.g.,* Fisher, "Businessmen Like to Hire by the Numbers," *Fortune,* September 15, 1985, at 26 (hereinafter "Hire by the Numbers").

[55]*See, e.g.,* Statement by the AFL-CIO Executive Council on Civil Rights, February 20, 1986, Bal Harbour, Florida.

[56]41 C.F.R. § 60-2.12 (1984).

[57]*See, e.g.,* "Hire by the Numbers," *supra* note 54, at 26 27. Moreover, the proposed Executive Order also attempts to discourage *voluntary* affirmative action, by asserting that the Order does not "provide a legal basis" for use of goals and timetables and requiring revocation of any regulations that might be interpreted to provide such a legal basis.

[58]*See, e.g., Washington Post,* Friday, August 16, 1985, at A23; Daily Labor Report No. 162 (BNA), Wed. August 21, 1985, at A-1, A-7, A-8.

[59]*See, e.g, Washington Post,* February 12, 1986; *The New York Times,* Thursday, January 30, 1986.

[60]*Newman v. Piggie Park Enterprises, Inc.,* 390 U.S. 400 (1968).

[61]*Pennsylvania v. Delaware Valley Citizens' Council,* 478 U.S. ___, 92 L.Ed.2d 439 (1986); *North Carolina Department of Transportation v. Crest Street Community Council,* 55 U.S.L.W. 4001 (U.S. Nov. 4, 1986).

[62]*City of Riverside v. Rivera,* 477 U.S. ___, 91 L.Ed.2d 466 (1986).

[63]*Library of Congress v. Shaw,* 478 U.S. ___, 92 L.Ed.2d 250 (1986).

[64]*Blum v. Stenson,* 465 U.S. 866 (1984).

[65]*Marek v. Chesny,* 473 U.S. ___, 87 L.Ed.2d 1 (1985). *Evans v. Jeff D.,* 475 U.S. ___, 89 L.Ed.2d. 747 (1986).

[66]Not only has the Commission acquiesced in the Administration's backward progress on civil rights, it has, in the process, mismanaged appropriated funds and manipulated personnel hiring authority. Congress reacted by limiting the amounts of funds for consultants, temporary employees, external contracts and the number of billable days for Chairman Clarence Pendleton; and has directed the Commission to spend money on supporting regional offices, state advisory committees and on monitoring federal civil rights compliance. Throughout 1986, the behavior and pronouncements of the Commission undermined the integrity of the agency as an independent, nonpolitical voice.

[67]President Reagan has appointed 226 federal district court judges: 210 whites, 11 Hispanics, 4 blacks, and 1 other; of these 206 are men and 20 are women. The President's appointments to the

blacks, and 1 other; of these 206 are men and 20 are women. The President's appointments to the appellate courts total 63 (57 men and 6 women). Of these, 61 are white, 1 is black, and 1, Hispanic. Source: Sheldon Goldman, "Reorganizing the Judiciary," *Judicature* 68 (April-May 1985), pp. 312–29.

68Source: Sheldon Goldman, "Carter's Judicial Appointments: A Lasting Legacy," *Judicature* 64 (March 1981).

69*Ibid.,* p. 348.

70*McCleskey v. Kemp,* 753 F.2d 877 (11th Cir. 1985) *(en banc), cert. granted,* ___, U.S. ___, 92 L.Ed.2d 737 (1986).

71*Swain v. Alabama,* 380 U.S. 202 (1965).

72*Batson v. Kentucky,* 54 U.S.L.W. 4425 (U.S. April 30, 1986).

73*Vasquez v. Hillery,* 54 U.S.L.W. 4068 (U.S. Jan. 14, 1986).

74*Turner v. Murray,* 54 U.S.L.W. 4411 (U.S. April 30, 1986).

Taking Charge: An Approach to Making the Educational Problems of Blacks Comprehensible and Manageable, *Sharon P. Robinson*

FOOTNOTES

1*A Nation Prepared: Teachers for the 21st Century, The Report of the Task Force on Teaching as a Profession* (Washington, D.C.: Carnegie Forum on Education and the Economy, 1986); *What Next? More Leverage for Teachers?* (Denver, Colo.: Education Commission of the States, 1986); *Time of Results: The Governors' 1991 Report on Education* (Washington, D.C.: National Governors' Association, 1986); *Who Will Teach Our Children?* (Sacramento, Cal.: California Commission on the Teaching Profession, 1985).

2*State of Black America 1986* (Washington, D.C.: The National Urban League, Inc., 1986); *Barriers to Excellence: Our Children at Risk* (Boston: The National Coalition of Advocates for Students, 1985); *Saving the African American Child, A Report of the Task Force on Black Academic and Cultural Excellence* (Washington, D.C., 1984).

3*Education Week,* January 30, 1985, p. 1.

4Charles Moody, Sr., "Equity and Excellence: An Educational Imperative," in *State of Black America 1986* (Washington, D.C.: The National Urban League, 1986), pp. 23-39; Linda Darling Hammond, *Equality and Excellence: The Education Status of Black Americans* (New York: The College Board, 1985).

5Daniel C. Thompson, *Black Elite: A Profile of Graduates of UNCF Colleges* (Westport, Conn.: Greenwood Press, 1986).

6Edward L. McDill, Gary Natriello, and Aaron M. Dallas, "Raising Standards and Retaining Students: The Impact of the Reform Recommendations on Potential Dropouts," *Review of Educational Research,* Vol. 55 (Winter 1985), p. 417.

7*Education Daily,* June 3, 1986, p. 3.

8McDill et al., pp. 418-420.

9*With Consequences for All, A Report of the ASCD Task Force on Increased High School Graduation Requirements* (Alexandria, Va.: The Association for Supervision and Curriculum Development, 1986).

10Harold L. Hodgkinson, *All One System, Demographics of Education, Kindergarten through Graduate School* (Washington, D.C.: The Institute for Educational Leadership, Inc., 1985).

11*Teen Pregnancy: What is Being Done, A Report of the Select Committee on Children, Youth and Families* (Washington, D.C.: Government Printing Office, 1985), p. 4.

12"Children Having Children," *Time,* December 9, 1985.

13*The New York Times,* February 20, 1986, p. C11.

14"Native Son: Inner City Black Males America's Newest Lost Generation," *Time,* December 1, 1986, pp. 26-29.

15G. Pritchy Smith, "The Impact of Competency Tests on Teacher Education: Ethical and Legal Issues in Selecting and Certifying Teachers," ERIC Document Reproduction Service No. ED 254493, Clearinghouse on Teacher Reducation No. SP 019478. Another study focusing on this problem is Joan C. Baratz, "Black Participation in the Teacher Pool," a report prepared for the Carnegie Forum's Task Force on Teaching as a Profession, January 1986.

16Brent Staples, "The Dwindling Black Presence on Campus," *The New York Times Magazine,* April 27, 1986, pp. 46-50; Valerie Lee, *Access to Higher Education: The Experience of Blacks, Hispanics and Low Socio-Economic Status Whites* (Washington, D.C.: American Council on Education, 1985).

17Nicholas Lemann, "The Origins of the Underclass," *The Atlantic Monthly,* June 1986, pp. 31-55.

18Smith, op. cit., p. 38.

19Hodgkinson, op. cit., p. 7.

20Data from survey "Black Enrollment by States" conducted by Charles D. Moody, Sr., Director of the Center for School Desegregation, University of Michigan, Ann Arbor.

21Lindsey Gruson, "Private Schools for Blacks ," *The New York Times,* October 21, 1986, pp. C1 ff.

The Future of School Desegregation, *Charles V. Willie*

REFERENCES

Alpert, Geoffrey, H. Ron White, and Paul Geisel. 1981. "Dallas, Texas: The Intervention of Business Leaders," in C.V. Willie and S.L. Greenblatt (eds.), *Community Politics and Change.* New York: Longman, 155-73.

Alves, Michael J. and Charles V. Willie. 1986. "Controlled Choice Assignments: A New and More Effective Approach to School Desegregation," unpublished manuscript, Harvard Graduate School of Education.

Arnez, Nancy. 1978. "Implementation of Desegregation as a Discriminatory Process," *Journal of Negro Education.* 47 (Winter), 28-45.

Atlanta Journal. 1986. "Americans Today Healthier, Wealthier Than Ancestors," November 7.

Elam, Stanley M. 1978. *A Decade of Gallup Polls of Attitudes Toward Education, 1969-1978.* Bloomington: Phi Delta Kappa.

Finger, John A., Jr. 1976. "Why Busing Plans Work," in Florence Hamlish Levinsohn and Benjamin Drake Wright (eds.), *School Desegregation.* Chicago: University of Chicago Press, 58-66.

Foster, Gordon. 1973. "Desegregating Urban Schools: A Review of Techniques," *Harvard Educational Review.*

Gallup, Alex M. 1986. "The 18th Annual Gallup Poll of the Public's Attitudes Toward the Public School," *Phil Delta Kappan* 68 (September 1986), 43-59.

Hawley, Willis D. 1981. "Increasing the Effectiveness of School Desegregation: Lessons from the Research," in A. Yarmolinsky, L. Liebman, and C.S. Schelling (eds.), *Race and Schooling in the City.* Cambridge: Harvard University Press, 145-62.

Hawley, Willis D. 1981. *Strategies for Effective Desegregation: A Synthesis of Findings.* Nashville: Center for Education and Human Development Policy, Vanderbilt University.

Kyle, Regina M.J. (ed.). 1985. *Reaching for Excellence, An Effective Schools Sourcebook,* National Institute of Education. Washington, D.C.: Government Printing Office.

McGill, Ralph. 1964. *The South and the Southerner.* Boston: Little, Brown and Company.

National Center for Education Statistics. 1983. *Digest of Education Statistics, 1983-84.* Washington, D.C.: Government Printing Office.

National Commission on Excellence in Education. 1983. *A Nation at Risk.* Washington, D.C.: Government Printing Office.

Siqueland, Ann LaGrelius. 1981. *Without a Court Order.* Seattle: Madrona Publishers.

Sizemore, Barbara. 1978. "Educational Research and Desegregation: Significance for the Black Community," *Journal of Negro Education* 47 (Winter), 58-68.

Sloan, Lee and Robert M. French. 1977. "Black Rule in the Urban South?" in C.V. Willie (ed.), *Black/Brown/White Relations.* New Brunswick, N.J.: Transaction Books.

Smith, Ralph R. 1978. "Two Centuries and Twenty-Four Months: Chronicle of the Struggle to Desegregate the Boston Public Schools," in Howard I. Kalodner and James J. Fishman (eds.), *Limits of Justice.* Cambridge: Ballinger, 25-113.

Schuman, Howard, Charlotte Steeh, and Lawrence Bobo. 1985. *Racial Attitudes in America.* Cambridge: Harvard University Press.

U.S. Census Bureau, 1982-83, and 1983-84. *Statistical Abstract of the United States.* Washington, D.C.: Government Printing Office.

von Euler, Mary. 1981. "Foreword," in C.V. Willie and Susan Greenblatt (eds.), *Community Politics and Educational Change.* New York: Longman.

Willie, Charles V. 1964. "Deprivation and Alienation: A Compounded Situation," in C.W. Hunnicutt (ed.), *Urban Education and Cultural Deprivation.* Syracuse: Syracuse University School of Education, 83-92.

_____. 1978. *The Sociology of Urban Education.* Lexington: Lexington Books.

_____. 1981. *A New Look at Black Families.* Bayside, N.Y.: General Hall (second edition), 27-45.

_____. 1982. "Desegregation in Big-City School Systems," *The Educational Forum* XLVII (Fall), 83-95.

_____. 1983. *Race, Ethnicity, and Socioeconomic Status.* Bayside, N.Y.: General Hall.

_____. 1984. *School Desegregation Plans That Work.* Westport, Conn.: Greenwood Press.

_____. 1985. "A Ten-Year Perspective on the Role of Blacks in Achieving Desegregation and Quality Education in Boston," in Philip L. Clay (ed.), *The Emerging Black Community in Boston.* Boston: Institute for Study of Black Culture, Univ. of Massachusetts at Boston, 145-80.

Economic Status of Blacks 1986, *David Swinton*

BIBLIOGRAPHY

Swinton, David H. "The Economic Status of the Black Population," in *State of Black America 1986.* Washington, D.C.: National Urban League, 1986.

Symposium on Minority Youth Employment and Urban Disadvantaged Youth, sponsored by Institute for Economic Development and Shaw College at Detroit, 1980.

U.S. Department of Commerce, Bureau of the Census. *Characteristics of the Population Below the Poverty Level,* Current Population Reports (Series P-60). Washington, D.C.: Government Printing Office, various issues.

_____. *Detailed Population Characteristics, United States Summary, Section A: United States.* Washington, D.C.: Government Printing Office, 1984.

_____. *Detailed Population Characteristics, United States Summary, Section A: United States.* Washington, D.C.: Government Printing Office, 1984.

_____. *Money Income and Poverty Status of Families and Persons in the United States,* Current Population Reports, Advance Data, Current Population Survey, (Series P-60). Washington, D.C.: Government Printing Office, various issues.

_____. *Statistical Abstract of the United States.* Washington, D.C.: Government Printing Office, 1984 and 1985.

U.S. Department of Labor, Bureau of Labor Statistics. *Employment Earnings.* January, May, and October 1985 and 1986.

_____. *Handbook of Labor Statistics* (Bulletin 2217). Washington, D.C.: Government Printing Office, 1985.

_____. *Geographic Profiles of Employment and Unemployment,* Washington, D.C.: Government Printing Office, various issues.

_____. *Statistics Derived From the Current Population Survey: A Databook,* Vol. I (Bulletin 2096). Washington, D.C.: Government Printing Office, 1982.

_____. *Statistics Derived From the Current Population Survey: A Databook,* Vol. II (Bulletin 2096-1). Washington, D.C.: Government Printing Office, 1984.

Blacks, Budgets, and Taxes: Assessing the Impact of Budget Deficit Reduction and Tax Reform on Blacks, *Lenneal J. Henderson*

FOOTNOTES

[1]Charles V. Hamilton, "The Welfare of Black Americans," *Political Science Quarterly,* Vol. 101, n. 2, 1986, p. 253.

[2]Aaron Wildavsky, *The Politics of the Budgetary Process* (Boston: Little, Brown, and Company, 1979, Third Edition), pp. 132-133.

[3]Balanced Budget and Emergency Deficit Control Act of 1985, P.L. 99-177, December 12, 1985.

[4]*Representative Mike Synar et al. v. United States et al.,* Civil Action No. 85-3945, February 7, 1986.

[5]See, for example, Joseph J. Minarik, *Making Tax Choices* (Washington, D.C.: The Urban Institute Press, 1985).

[6]Lawrence C. Howard, Lenneal J. Henderson, and Deryl Hunts, eds., *Public Administration and Public Policy: A Minority Perspective* (Pittsburgh, Penn.: Public Policy Press of Pittsburgh, 1977).

[7]Warren F. Ilchman and Norman T. Uphoff, *The Political Economy of Change* (Berkeley and Los Angeles: The University of California Press, 1969).

[8]See Paul Peterson, "The Politics of Deficits," in John E. Chubb and Paul Peterson, eds., *The New Directions in American Politics* (Washington, D.C.: The Brookings Institution, 1985).

[9]Kenneth A. Shepsle and Barry Weingast, "Legislative Politics and Budget Outcomes," in Gregory B. Mills and John L. Palmer, eds., *Federal Budget Policy in the 1980s* (Washington, D.C.: The Urban Institute, 1984).

[10]Linda Willams, "The Politics of Deficit Reduction" (unpublished, Howard University, 1986).

[11]See the description of the impact of GRH on the District of Columbia budget in *Operating Budget of the District of Columbia, Fiscal Year 1987* (Washington, D.C., 1986), pp. III-1 to III-3.

[12]Lynn Burbridge, "Gramm-Rudman-Hollings and the Low-Income Population," speech delivered at Howard University, March, 1986.

[13]*A Children's Defense Budget: An Analysis of the Fiscal Year Federal Budget and Children* (Washington, D.C.: The Children's Defense Fund, 1986), pp. 60-68.

[14]Williams, op. cit., p. 4.

[15]It is important to note that some of these programs would have been targeted for elimination or reduction even if GRH had not been enacted.

[16]See essay by Georgia Persons on black state and local government officials in this volume. See also *National Roster of Black Elected Officials* (Washington, D.C.: Joint Center for Political Studies, 1986).

[17]*Representative Mike Synar et al., v. United States of America et al.,* Civil Action No. 85-3945, February 7, 1986.

[18]*Bowsher v. Synar,* July 7, 1986.

[19]Congressional Black Caucus, *The Fiscal Year '87 Alternative: The Quality of Life Budget* (Washington, D.C., 1986).

[20]Lynn Burbridge, "The New Tax Law: How Will It Benefit Black Americans," *The Urban League Review* (forthcoming).

[21]U.S., President, *The President's Tax Proposals to the Congress for Fairness, Growth and Simplicity* (Washington, D.C.: Government Printing Office, May, 1985).

[22]U.S., Congress, Joint Committee on Taxation, *Summary of Tax Reform Options for the Consideration of the Ways and Means Committee* (Washington, D.C.: Government Printing Office, September 26, 1985).

[23]Lawrence B. Lindsey, "The Effect of the President's Tax Reform Proposal on Charitable Giving," *National Tax Journal,* Vol. 39, N.1, March, 1986, p. 1.

[24]Burbridge, op. cit., p. 12.

[25]See William G. Shepherd, *Public Policies Toward Business* (Homewood, Ill.: Richard D. Irwin, Inc., 1985, 7th Edition).

[26]Albert K. Karnig and Susan Welch, *Black Representation and Urban Policy* (Chicago: University of Chicago Press, 1980).

[27]See Joshua M. Epstein, *The 1987 Defense Budget* (Washington, D.C.: The Brookings Institution, 1986).

[28]Henry Aaron and M.J. Boskin, eds., *The Economics of Taxation* (Washington, D.C.: The Brookings Institution, 1980).

[29]Thomas J. Reese, *The Politics of Taxation* (New York: Greenwood Press, 1980).

[30]Robert W. Burchell and David Listokin, *Practitioner's Guide to Fiscal Impact Analysis* (New Brunswick, N.J.: Rutgers University, 1980).

[31]William W. Ellis and Darlene Calbert, *Blacks and Tax Reform: 1985-86* (Washington, D.C.: The Congressional Research Service, 1986).

[32]John L. Mikesell, *Fiscal Administration: Analysis and Applications for the Public Sector* (Homewood, Ill.: The Dorsey Press, 1982).

[33]For a good historical examination of black participation in grants-in-aid programs, see John Hope II, *Minority Access to Federal Grants-in-Aid: The Gap Between Policy and Performance* (New York: Praeger Publishers, Inc., 1976).

[34]National Association of Home Builders, "The Impacts on Housing of the Tax Reform Act of 1986: An Overview," Washington, D.C., September 1986.

[35]Ellis and Calbert, op. cit., p. 33.

[36]Lenneal J. Henderson, "Black Business Enterprise," in Mitchell Rice and Woodrow Jones, eds., *Contemporary Public Policy and Black Americans* (New York: Greenwood Publishing Co., 1984).

[37]Henderson, op. cit., p. 132.

[38]Henderson, "Black Administrators and the Politics of Administrative Advocacy," in Lennox Yearwood, ed., *Black Organizations* (Washington, D.C.: University Press of America, 1980).

[39]John Shannon, "1984 — Not a Good Fiscal Year for Big Brother," *Intergovernment Perspective,* Vol. 11, N. 1, Winter 1985, p. 4.

[40]T.R. Reid, "State Windfalls on Tax Reform," *Washington Post,* December 16, 1986, p. C3.

[41]Gregory B. Mills and John L. Palmer, *The Deficit Dilemma: Budget Policy in the Reagan Era* (Washington, D.C.: The Urban Institute Press, 1983).

[42]Established as an amendment to the Small Business Act of 1953, Section 8(a) was enacted in 1976 to set aside federal contracting opportunities for owners of minority firms exclusively. SBA arranges with federal agencies in need of such contracting opportunities for minority-owned firms to compete only with each other on procurements "set aside" for such firms.

Black Families in a Changing Society, *Andrew Billingsley*

FOOTNOTES

[1]*Ebony,* Special Issue: "The Crisis of the Black Family," Vol. XLI, No. 10 (August, 1986).

[2]The National Urban League and the National Association for the Advancement of Colored People, *Proceedings of the Black Family Summit* (Washington, D.C.: National Urban League, 1985).

[3]U.S., Dept. of Commerce, Bureau of the Census, *Characteristics of the Population Below the Poverty Level,* Current Population Reports, Series P-60 (Washington, D.C.: Government Printing Office 1985).

[4]U.S., Dept. of Labor, Bureau of Labor Statistics, data from *Current Population Survey* (Washington, D.C.: Government Printing Office, 1985).

[5]U.S., Dept. of Commerce, Bureau of the Census, *Money Income and Poverty Status of Families and Persons in the United States,* Current Population Reports, Series P-60 (Washington, D.C.: Government Printing Office, 1985).

[6]U.S., Dept. of Health and Human Services, National Center for Health Statistics, *Vital Health Statistics,* Series 21, No. 41 (Washington, D.C.: Government Printing Office, 1984).
See also Kristen Moore, Margaret C. Simms, and Charles L. Betsey, *Choice and Circumstance: Racial Differences in Adolescent Sexuality and Fertility* (New Brunswick, N.J.: Transaction Books, 1986).

[7]Wilhelmena A. Leigh, *Shelter Affordability for Blacks: Crisis or Clamor?* (New Brunswick, N.J.: Transaction Books, 1982), p. 1.

[8]Leigh, p. 62.

[9]See article about the Catholic Bishops of Maryland in both the *Washington Post* and *The New York Times,* December 7, 1986.

[10]Sumner Rosen, David Fanshel, and Mary E. Lutz, eds., *Face of the Nation 1987: Statistical Supplement to the 18th Edition of the Encyclopedia of Social Work* (Silver Spring, Md.: National Association of Social Workers, 1987).

[11]U.S., Dept. of Commerce, Bureau of the Census, *Statistical Abstracts of the United States* (Washington, D.C.: Government Printing Office, 1984).

[12]U.S., Department of Commerce, Bureau of the Census, *Economic Characteristics of Households,* Current Population Reports, Series P-70, No. 6 (Washington, D.C.: Government Printing Office, 1984).

[13]Daniel Patrick Moynihan, *The Negro Family: The Case For National Action,* Office of Policy Planning and Research, U.S. Department of Labor, March 1965, p. 30.

[14]Ibid.

[15]Ibid.

[16]Ibid.

[17]U.S. Dept. of Commerce, Bureau of the Census, op. cit.

[18]Moynihan, *Family and Nation* (New York: Harcourt, Brace, Jovanovich, 1986), p. 146.

[19]Nicholas Lemann, "The Origins of the Underclass," *The Atlantic Monthly* (June 1986 and July 1986), p. 31 and p. 56, respectively.

[20]"Employment Policies: Looking To The Year 2000," The National Alliance of Business (Washington, D.C., 1986), p. 4.

[21]Rep. Patricia Schroeder (D-Colo.), "A Government Agenda for Today's Family," *Washington Post,* "Health" section, December 16, 1986.

[22]Lawrence Gary et al., *Stable Black Families: Final Report,* Institute for Urban Affairs and Research (Washington, D.C.: Howard University Press, 1983).

[23]Ibid.

[24]Ibid.

[25]Harriette Pipes McAdoo, *The Impact of Extended Family Variables Upon the Upward Mobility of Black Families,* Final Report, submitted to the Dept. of Health, Education and Welfare, Office of Child Development, contract no. 90-C-631(1), December, 1977.

[26]McAdoo, p. 67.

[27]James P. Smith, "Poverty and the Family," an Institute for Research on Poverty Conference Paper, presented at the Conference on "Poverty and Social Policy: The Minority Experience," Airlie House, Virginia, November 5-7, 1986, p. 56.

[28]William J. Wilson, *The Declining Significance of Race* (Chicago: University of Chicago Press, 1974) and William J. Wilson and Kathryn M. Neckerman, "Without Jobs, Black Men Cannot Support Families," *Point of View,* Vol. II, No. 3 (Washington, D.C.: The Congressional Black Caucus Foundation, 1985), p. 2.

[29]Ibid.

[30]Ibid.

[31]Ibid.

[32]Ibid.

[33]Massachusetts Department of Public Welfare, "Employment and Training Program FY 1986 Budget Narrative," 1985.

[34]U.S., *Congressional Record,* 99th Cong., 2d Sess. (1986), CXXXII, No. 83.

[35]See Joanne M. Martin and Elmer P. Martin, *The Helping Tradition in the Black Family and Community* (Silver Spring, Md.: National Association of Social Workers, 1986).

[36]Andrew Billingsley, *Black Families in White America, Revised* (forthcoming).

Social Welfare Reform, *Barbara Bryant Solomon*

REFERENCES

Brozen, Yale and Milton Friedman. *The Minimum Wage Rate: Who Really Pays?* Washington, D.C.: the Free Society Association, 1966.

Children's Defense Fund Reports, "A Beginning Look at Welfare Reform," May, 1986.

Cogan, John F. *Negative Income Taxation and Labor Supply: New Evidence from New Jersey-Pennsylvania Experiment.* Santa Monica: Rand Corporation, 1978.

Collins, Randall. *The Credential Society: An Historical Sociology of Education and Stratification.* New York: Academic Press, 1979.

Cottingham, Clement (ed.). *Race, Poverty, and the Urban Underclass.* Lexington, Mass.: D.C. Heath and Company, 1982.

Darity, William A. *Race, Poverty, and the Urban Underclass,* ed. Clement Cottingham. Lexington, Mass.: D.C. Heath and Company, 1982.

Gilder, George. *Wealth and Poverty.* New York: Basic Books, 1981.

Glasgow, Douglas. U.S. Congress. House. Committee on Agriculture, Subcommittee on Domestic Marketing, Consumer Relations, and Nutrition. *Statement for the Record.* Hearing on Employment and Training/Welfare Reform, 99th Congress, 2nd Session, September 26, 1986.

Guide to Welfare Reform. Washington, D.C.: Food Research and Action Center, 1979.

Marris, Peter and Martin Rein. *Dilemmas of Social Reform: Poverty and Community Action in the United States,* 2nd. ed. Chicago: University of Chicago Press, 1982.

Murray, Charles. *Losing Ground.* New York: Basic Books, 1984.

Ozawa, Martha N. "Nonwhites and the Demographic Imperative in Social Welfare spending," *Social Work,* Vol. 31, No. 6 (November-December 1986), 440-447.

Piven, Frances Fox and Richard A. Cloward. *The Politics of Turmoil.* New York: Pantheon Books, 1981.

Ryan, William. *Equality.* New York: Pantheon Books, 1981.

Schuman, Howard, Charlotte Steeh, and Lawrence Bobo. *Racial Attitudes in America: Trends and Interpretations.* Boston: Harvard University Press, 1985.

Sowell, Thomas. *Civil Rights: Rhetoric or Reality.* New York: William Morrow and Co., 1984.

U.S. Department of Labor. *Assessing Large-Scale Public Job Creation.* Research and Demonstration Monograph 67. Washington, D.C.: Government Printing Office, 1979.

The Black Underclass in Perspective, *Douglas Glasgow*

FOOTNOTES

[1]U.S., Dept. of Commerce, Bureau of the Census, *Statistical Abstract of the United States 1986* (Washington, D.C.: Government Printing Office, 1986), p. 457.

[2]Harrington, Michael, *The Other America: Poverty in the United States* (Baltimore: Penguin Books, 1966).

[3]U.S., Dept. of Commerce, Bureau of the Census, *Money Income and Poverty Status of Families and Persons in the United States: 1985,* Advance data from the March 1986 Current Population Survey, Series P-60, No. 154 (Washington, D.C.: Government Printing Office, 1986).

[4]Glasgow, Douglas G., *The Black Underclass: Poverty, Unemployment and Entrapment of Ghetto Youth* (San Francisco: Jossey-Bass, Inc., 1980).

[5]Nightingale, Demetra S., *Federal Employment and Training Policy Changes During the Reagan Administration* (Washington, D.C.: The Urban Institute, 1985), pp. 5-25.

[6]Simms, Margaret C., *The Economic Well-Being of Minorities During the Reagan Administration* (Washington, D.C.: the Urban Institute, 1984). Also, Tidwell, Billy J., "1985 Federal Budget: An Examination of Impacts on the Poor and Minorities" (Washington, D.C.: National Urban League, 1984).

[7]Merton, Robert K., *Social Theory and Social Structure,* (New York: Free Press, 1968).

[8]Warner, W. Lloyd, Meeker Marchia, and Kenneth Eells, *Social Class in America* (New York: Harper, 1960).

[9]Glasgow, p. 7.

[10]Drawn from "America's Underclass: Doomed to Fail in the Land of Opportunity," *The Economist,* March 15, 1986, p. 29.

[11]Lemann, Nicholas, "The Origins of the Underclass," *The Atlantic Monthly,* June 1986, pp. 31-55; Lemann, "The Origins of the Underclass," *The Atlantic Monthly,* July 1986, pp. 54-68. Kaus, Mickey, "The Work Ethic State," *The New Republic,* July 1986, pp. 22-23. Murray, Charles, *Losing Ground: American Social Policy, 1950-1980* (New York: Basic Books, Inc., 1984).

[12]Lemann, op. cit.

[13]Wilson, William J. "The 'Culture' Club" in "Welfare and Work: A Symposium," *The New Republic,* October 6, 1986, p. 20.

[14]Lemann, op. cit., June 1986, p. 33.

[15]Ibid., p. 35, italics added.

[16]Ibid., p. 53, italics added.

[17]Glazer, Nathan and Daniel P. Moynihan, *Beyond The Melting Pot* (Cambridge, Mass.: The MIT Press, 1963).

[18]Hill, Robert R., "The Black Middle Class: Past, Present and Future," in James D. Williams (ed.) *State of Black America 1986* (New York: National Urban League, Inc. 1986), pp. 43-64.

[19]Billingsley, Andrew *Black Families in White America,* (Englewood Cliffs, N.J.: Prentice-Hall, Inc. 1968), pp. 122-146.

[20]Billingsley, op. cit. Hill, Robert B., *Strengths of Black Families* (Washington, D.C.: National Urban League Research Department, 1974). McAdoo, Harriette P. (ed.), *Black Families* (Beverly Hills, Cal.: Sage Publications, 1981).

[21]McAdoo, op. cit.

[22]Wharton, Clifton R., Jr., "The Future of the Black Community: Human Capital, Family Aspirations, and Individual Motivation," *Review of Black Political Economy,* Vol. 14 (Spring 1986), pp. 9-16. Karenga, Maulana, "Social Ethics and the Black Family: An Alternative Analysis, *The Black Scholar.* September/October 1986, pp. 41-54.

[23]Valentine, Charles A., *Culture of Poverty: Critique and Counterproposals* (Chicago: University of Chicago Press, 1968).

[24]Kaus, op. cit., p. 23, italics added.

[25]Ellwood, David T., "Outside the Ghetto," in "Welfare and Work: A Symposium," *The New Republic,* October 6, 1986, p. 20.

[26]U.S., Dept. of Commerce, Bureau of the Census, *Statistical Abstract of the United States 1986* (Washington, D.C.: Government Printing Office, 1986), p. 418.

[27]Wallace, Phyllis A., *Black Women in the Labor Force* (Cambridge, Mass.: MIT Press, 1980).

[28]Tidwell, Billy J., *The Black Unemployed: A Disaggregation Analysis* (Washington, D.C.: National Urban League Research Department, 1986). McGhee, James D., *Running the Gauntlet: Black Men in America* (Washington, D.C.: National Urban League Research Department, 1984).

[29]Watson, Betty J. Collier, "Income, Employment, and Family Formation: A Pilot Study," (in progress).

[30]U.S., Dept. of Commerce, Bureau of the Census, p. 460.

[31]U.S., Dept. of Commerce, Bureau of the Census, *Money Income and Poverty Status of Families and Persons in the United States 1985,* Advance Report (Washington, D.C.: Government Printing Office, 1985), p. 60.

[32]Ibid.

[33]U.S., Dept. of Commerce, Bureau of the Census, *Changing Family Composition and Income Differentials,* Special Demographic Analyses, CDS — 80-7, 1982.

[34]Bane, Mary Jo, "Household Composition and Poverty," in Sheldon H. Danziger and Daniel H. Weinbery (eds.), *Fighting Poverty* (Cambridge, Mass.: Harvard University Press, 1986), pp. 209-231.

[35]Murray, op. cit.

[36]Plotnick, Robert D. and Felicity Skidmore, *Progress Against Poverty* (New York: Academic Press, 1975), Chap. 1; Burtless, Gray, "Public Spending for the Poor: Trends, Prospects, and Economic Limits," in Danziger and Weinberg (eds.), op. cit., pp. 18-48.

[37]Plotnick and Skidmore, op. cit., pp. 11-26.

[38]Danziger, Sheldon H., Robert H. Haveman, and Robert D. Plotnick, "Antipoverty Policy: Effects on the Poor and the Nonpoor," in Danziger and Plotnick, pp. 50-77.

[39]Ibid.

[40]Mallar, Charles, Stuart Kerachsky, and Craig Thornton, *Evaluation of the Economic Impact of the Job Corps Program* (Princeton, N.J.: Mathematics Policy Research, 1982).

[41]Betsey, Charles L., Robinson G. Hollister, Jr., and Mary R. Papageorgiou (eds.), *Youth Employment and Training Programs: The YEDPA Years* (Washington, D.C.: National Academy Press, 1985).

[42]Murray, op. cit., p. 9.

[43]Ellwood, David T. and Lawrence H. Summers, "Poverty in America: Is Welfare the Answer or the Problem?" in Danziger, op. cit., pp. 93-94.

[44]Ibid.

[45]Ibid, p. 96.

[46]Bant, Mary Jo and David T. Ellwood, *The Dynamics of Dependence: The Routes to Self-Sufficiency* (Cambridge, Mass.: John F. Kennedy School of Government, Harvard University, 1983).

[47]Greenstein, Robert, "Impact of Government Anti-Poverty Programs Declines: Benefit Cuts Increase Poverty Among Families with Children" (Washington, D.C.: Center on Budget and Policy Priorities, November 1986).

[48]Beverly, Creigs C. and Howard J. Stanback, "The Black Underclass: Theory and Reality," *The Black Scholar,* Sept./Oct. 1986, pp. 24-31.

[49]The Massachusetts Employment and Training Choices program is authorized by the WIN Demonstration Program. ET offers a wide range of work-related activities that begin with a skills appraisal and development of an employment plan, followed by participant choice of various options that can include career planning, education and training, job skills training, JTPA, on-the-job-training, and placement. Emphasis is placed on support services such as child care and transportation.

[50]Maine's Welfare, Employment, Education, and Training Program (WEET) began in 1982 as a WIN Demonstration Program. WEET was developed in response to the economic conditions of the state (nearly 40% of the population lives on the borderline of poverty), and recognition of the need for women on welfare to receive intensive training, education, and work experience. Key features of the WEET program include: support for a wide range of education and training activities, and coordination with Maine's economic development agencies to target new jobs for AFDC recipients.

[51]*Congressional Record,* "Proceedings and Debates of the 99th Congress Second Session," Vol. 132, No. 83. Washington, D.C., June 18, 1986.

[52]Bieber, Owen, Ben Hooks, John Jacob, Irene Natividad et al., *The Polarization of America: The Loss of Good Jobs, Falling Incomes and Rising Inequality,* (Washington, D.C.: Industrial Union Department (AFL-CIO), 1986.

Drug Use: Special Implications for Black America, *Beny J. Primm*

FOOTNOTES

[1]R.K. Merton, L. Broom, and L.S. Cottrell, eds., *Sociology Today: Problems and Prospects* (New York: Harper Torchbooks, 1965).

[2]Maurice Seevers, "Drug Dependence Vis-a-Vis Drug Abuse," *Drug Abuse: Proceedings of the International Conference,* ed. Chris J.D. Zarafonetis (Philadelphia: Lea & Febiger, 1972), pp. 9-16.

[3]Beny Primm, Daniel Cook, and Joseph Drew, "The Problem of Addiction in the Black Community," *Substance Abuse, Clinical Problems and Perspectives,* eds. Joyce H. Lowinson and Pedro Ruiz (Baltimore: Waverly Press, 1981).

[4]World Health Organization definition.

[5]Fred T. Davis, Jr., "Alcoholism Among American Blacks" (presented at the Meeting of Alcohol Drug Problems of North America, 1973).

[6]T.D. Crothers, *Morphinism and Narcomania from Other Drugs* (Philadelphia, 1902).

[7]Brothers, op. cit.

[8]Helmer, John, and Vietorisz, *Drug Use, The Labor Market, and Class Conflict* (Washington, D.C.: Drug Abuse Council, Monograph Services, 1974).

[9]E.M. Green, "Psychoses Among Negroes, A Comparative Study," *Journal of Nervous and Mental Disease,* 41:697-708, 1914.

[10]J.D. Roberts, "Opium Habit in the Negro," *North Carolina Medical Journal,* 16:206-207, 1885.

[11]Lucious P. Brown, *Enforcement of the Tennessee Anti-Narcotics Law in Narcotic Addiction,* eds. O'Donnell and Ball (New York: Harper and Row, 1915).

[12]Brown, op. cit.

[13]Helmer and Vietorisz, op. cit.

[14]U.S., Department of Health and Human Services Task Force on Black and Minority Health, "Drug Abuse Among Minorities," 1986.

[15]Ibid.

[16]J.D. Miller, I.H. Cisin, H. Gardner-Keaton et al., *National Survey on Drug Abuse, Main Findings 1982, U.S.* (Rockville, Md.: National Institute on Drug Abuse, 1983).

[17]U.S., Department of Health and Human Services, op. cit.

[18]Based on personal communication between Lloyd Johnston, author of the National High School Senior Survey, and the writer, November 26, 1986.

[19]"Dropout by Minorities Are Termed Epidemic," *The New York Times,* November 18, 1986, p. B3.

[20]Based on personal communication between Edgar Adams, Chief, Epidemiology Branch, National Institute on Drug Abuse, and the writer, November 20, 1986.

[21]Louisa Messolonghites, *Multicultural Perspectives on Drug Abuse and Its Prevention* (Washington, D.C.: National Institute on Drug Abuse, 1979), p. 12.

[22]Kozel and Adams, "Epidemiology of Drug Abuse: An Overview," *Science,* 234:970, November 1986.

[23]M. Harvey Brenner and Robert T. Swank, *Homicide and Economic Change: Recent Analyses of the Joint Economic Committee Report of 1984.*

[24]R.H. Rahe, J.D. McKean, and B.J. Arthur, "A Longitudinal Study of Life Change and Illness Patterns," *Journal of Psychosom. Res.,* 10:355, 1967.

[25]G. Vaillant, "Natural History of Male Psychologic Health: Effects of Mental Health on Physical Disease," *New England Journal of Medicine,* 301:1249, 1979.

[26]E.J. Khantizian, J.E. Mack, and A.F. Schatzberg, "Heroin Use as an Attempt to Cope: Clinical Observations," *American Journal of Psychiatry,* 131:160, 1974.

[27]E.E. Inwang, B.J. Primm, and F.L. Jones, "Metabolic Disposition of 2-Phenyl-Ethylamine and the Role of depression in Methadone Dependent and Detoxified Patients," *Drug Alcohol Dependence,* 1:295, 1975-76.

[28]R.S. Zimmerman, L. Pixley, and Coghlan, "Psychological Substrata of Addiction: Implications for Therapy," *Proceedings of the 30th International Congress of Alcoholism and Drug Dependence,* Vol. 1 (Lausanne, Switzerland: International Congress of Alcoholism and Drug Dependence, 1972).

[29]Eric Gnepp, "A Causal Theory of Addiction," *Psychology,* 13:13, 1976.

[30]E. Lurssen, "Psychoanalytic Theories of Addiction Structures," *Suchtgefahren,* 20:141, 1974.

[31]G.M. Carstairs, "Personality and Social Factors in Drug Addiction," *J. Med. Liban,* 25:409, 1972.

[32]Primm, op. cit., p. 710.

[33]Vital Statistics of New York City, 1985, p. 11, unpublished as of November 30, 1986.

[34]Avram Goldstein, "Endorphins: Their Physiological and Pathological Potentials: Current Concepts in Postoperative Pain," *A Special Report Prepared for Pfizer Laboratories by Hospital Practice*, January, 1978.

_____, "Therapy: Principles and Use of Drugs" (paper read as a lecture at the Stanford University School of Medicine, 1979, San Francisco, Cal.).

[35]Estimate, National Institute on Drug Abuse, *Science,* 234:972, November 21, 1986.

[36]Based on personal communication between Dr. James Curtis, Director of Psychiatry, Harlem Hospital Center, and the writer.

[37]Based on personal communication with Howard Johnson, owner, "Cellar Restaurant," New York City; and Dickie Habersham, bar owner, Brooklyn, New York, and the writer.

[38]Television interview (Channel 4) with Barbara Martin, social worker, Harlem Hospital Center, New York, New York.

[39]Based on personal communication between Dr. Harold Freeman, Chief of Surgery, Harlem Hospital Center, and Chairman of the National Advisory Committee of Cancer and the Economically Disadvantaged of the American Cancer Society, and the writer.

[40]Adam Walinsky, "Crack as a Scapegoat," *The New York Times,* September 16, 1986.

AIDS: A Special Report, *Beny J. Primm*

FOOTNOTES

[1]U.S., Centers for Disease Control, Atlanta, *Acquired Immunodeficiency Syndrome (AIDS) Among Blacks and Hispanics,* Morbidity and Mortality Weekly Report No. 42 (1986), 35:655-666.

[2]Rudolph E. Jackson et al., "AIDS Risk-Group Profiles in Whites and Members of Minority Groups," *New England Journal of Medicine,* 315:191-192, July 17, 1986.

[3]"Women and AIDS: Discussion of Precautions," *The New York Times,* November 3, 1986.

[4]U.S., Centers for Disease Control, op. cit., p. 655.

[5]"Women and AIDS," op. cit.

[6]"The AIDS Epidemic — Africa in the Plague Years," *Newsweek,* November 24, 1986, pp. 44-47.

[7]P. Piot, H. Tollman et al., "Acquired Immunodeficiency Syndrome in the Heterosexual Population in Zaire," *Lancet 2* (1984), pp. 65-69.

[8]P.J. Kanki, J. Alroy, and M. Essex, "Isolation of T-Lymphotropic Retrovirus Related to HTLV-III/LAV from Wild-Caught African Green Monkeys," *Science.*

[9]News and Comment, "Politics and Science Clash on African AIDS," *Science,* Vol. 230, December 6, 1985.

[10]Ibid.

[11]"U.S. To Restore Haitians to List of High-Risk AIDS Group," *The New York Times,* July 28, 1986.

[12]*National Institute of Justice/Research in Brief,* February 1986.
Robert Pear, "Prisons Are on the Alert Against AIDS," *The New York Times,* January 12, 1986.

[13]The National Academy of Sciences Report, "Confronting AIDS," National Academy Press, 1986.

[14]U.S., Centers for Disease Control, Atlanta, *Human T-Lymphotropic Virus Type III/ Lymphadenopathy-Associated Virus Antibody Prevalence in U.S. Military Recruit Applicants,* Morbidity and Mortality Weekly Report No. 26 (1986), 35:44.

ENDNOTES

[1]The absence of deliberate recordkeeping of black representation prior to 1970 leaves some uncertainty as to the exact number of black elected officials prior to passage of the Voting Rights Act of 1965. Some accounts report a low of 103 elected blacks in 1964. See David V. Edwards, *The American Political Experience* (Englewood Cliffs, N.J.: Prentice-Hall, 1982), p. 439.

[2]In January of 1986, there were 6,424 elected blacks, and an estimated increase of at least 100 newly elected blacks as of the end of November 1986. Data reported by the Joint Center for Political Studies, Washington, D.C.

[3]See Lawrence Howard, Lenneal Henderson, and Deryl Hunt (eds.), *Public Administration and Public Policy: A Minority Perspective* (Pittsburgh, Penn.: Public Policy Press, 1977).

[4]U.S. Commission on Civil Rights, *The Voting Rights Act: Ten Years After* (Washington, D.C.: The Commission, 1975).

[5]Eddie N. Williams, "Black Political Progress in the 1970s: The Electoral Arena," in Michael B. Preston et al. (eds.), *The New Black Politics: The Search for Political Power* (New York: Longman, 1982), p. 75.

[6]Ibid.

[7]There are, of course, instances of racial cross-over voting by whites, some resulting in the election of blacks from predominantly white districts. For a discussion of the phenomenon of racial cross-over voting by whites, see Charles S. Bullock III, "Racial Crossover Voting and the Election of Black Officials," *Journal of Politics,* Vol. 46 (Feb. 1984), pp. 239-51.

[8]*Black Elected Officials: A National Roster, 1986* (Washington, D.C.: Joint Center for Political Studies), p. 1.

[9]Ibid., pp. 4, 9.

[10]The late Patricia Roberts Harris was the first black female to seek the mayoralty of a large city, challenging incumbent black mayor Marion Barry (Wash., D.C.) in 1982.

[11]For a discussion of the dimensions of representation, see Hanna Pitkin, *The Concept of representation* (Berkeley: University of California Press, 1972).

[12]Several studies have reported this finding: see Leonard Cole, *Blacks in Power: A Comparative Study of Black and White Elected Officials* (Princeton, N.J.: Princeton University Press, 1976); Lenneal Henderson, "Administrative Advocacy and Black Urban Administrators," *The Annals,* 439 (September 1978), 68-79; and Edmund Keller, "The Impact of Black Mayors on Urban Policy," *The Annals,* 439, (September 1978), 40-52.

[13]For a discussion of the theory, processes, and impact of the incorporation of blacks (and Hispanics) into politically dominant coalitions, see Rufus P. Browning et al., *Protest is Not Enough: The Struggle of Blacks and Hispanics for Equality in Urban Politics* (Berkeley: University of California Press, 1986).

[14]For one discussion of the impact of black representation on changes in policy-making and distributive benefits, see Albert Karnig and Susan Welch, *Black Representation and Urban Policy,* (Chicago: University of Chicago Press, 1980).

[15]Peter K. Eisinger, "Black Employment in Municipal Jobs: The Impact of Black Political Power," *American Political Science Review,* 76, No. 2 (June 1982): 380-92: and Browning, et al. *Protest Is Not Enough.*

[16]*National Advisory Commission on Civil Disorders Report* (Washington, D.C.: Government Printing Office, 1967).

[17]Georgia A. Persons, "Reflections on Mayoral Leadership: The Impact of Changing Issues and Changing Times," *Phylon,* Vol. 41, No. 3 (Sept. 1985), 205-18.

[18]William E. Nelson, Jr., and Philip J. Meranto, *Electing Black Mayors: Political Action in the Black Community* (Columbus, Ohio: Ohio State University Press, 1977).

[19]Charles H. Levine, *Racial Conflict and the American Mayor* (Lexington, Mass.: Lexington Books, 1974), Chapter 6.

[20]Persons, op. cit.

[21]Studies have shown that, in some instances, white businessmen soon realized that they had nothing to fear economically from the presence of a black mayor. For an interesting discussion of the transition to black mayoral leadership in Atlanta and Detroit, see Peter K. Eisinger, *The Politics of Displacement: Ethnic and Racial Transition in Three American Cities* (New York: Academic Press, 1980).

[22]See Persons, op. cit.

[23]Ibid.

[24]See Peter K. Eisinger, *The Politics of Displacement.*

[25]For a discussion of periodic shifts in black political strategy, see Ronald W. Walters, "The Challenge of Black Leadership: An Analysis of the Problem of Strategy Shift," *The Urban League Review,* Vol. 5, No. 1 (Summer 1980), 77-88.

[26]William E. Nelson, "Cleveland: The Rise and Fall of the New Black Politics," in Michael E. Preston et al. (ed.), *The New Black Politics,* pp. 188, 198.

[27]Karnig and Welch, *Black Representation and Urban Policy.*

[28]Peter K. Eisinger, "Black Employment in Municipal Jobs: The Impact of Black Political Power."

[29]Ibid.

[30]For discussions of greater access by minorities to public sector jobs, see Joseph P. Viteritti, *Bureaucracy and Social Justice: Allocation of Jobs and Services to Minority Groups* (Port Washington, N.Y.: Kennikat Press, 1979), and Robert Freeman, *Black Elite* (New York: McGraw Hill, 1976).

[31]Interview with Keith Hinch, Staff Economist, National Conference of Black Mayors, Atlanta, Georgia.

[32]Interviews with Keith Hinch; Alvin Majors, Executive Director, Alabama Conference of Black Mayors, Tuskegee, Alabama.

[33]Interview, Alvin Majors.

[34]U.S., Dept. of Commerce, Bureau of the Census, *Expenditures of General Revenue Sharing Funds 1982-83* (Washington, D.C.: Government Printing Office).

[35]Ibid.

[36]See Joe T. Darden, "Black Political Underrepresentation in Majority Black Places," *Journal of Black Studies,* Vol. 15, No. 1 (Sept. 1984), 110-16.

[37]Richard W. Roper, as reported in Paul West, "Breaking Rules: the New Black Politics," *The New Republic* (Nov. 24, 1986), 14-15.

[38]An analysis of five case studies of black defeats in majority-black districts is provided by Robert C. Smith, *When Majority Black Districts Elect White Representatives: Case Studies in Race and Representation* (forthcoming), Joint Center for Political Studies, Washington, D.C.

[39]An analysis of the impact of the Jackson candidacy on state and local black politics is provided by Alvin Thornton and Frederick C. Hutchinson, "Traditional Democratic Party Politics and the 1984 Maryland Jackson Presidential Campaign: A Case Study" (forthcoming), in Lucius Barker and Ronald Walters (eds.), *Jesse Jackson's Campaign: Challenge and Change in American Politics* (Urbana-Champaign, Ill., University of Illinois Press, 1987).

Appendix: A Profile of the Black Unemployed, Billy J. Tidwell

FOOTNOTES

[1]C.L. Gilroy, "Job Losers, Leavers, and Entrants: Traits and Trends," *Monthly Labor Review,* Vol. 96, No. 8 (August 1974).

[2]U.S., Department of Labor, Bureau of Labor Statistics, *Employment and Earnings,* Vol. 32, No. 1 (January 1985), Table 12, p. 167.

[3]R.W. Bednarzik, "Layoffs and Permanent Job Losses: Workers Traits and Cyclical Patterns," *Monthly Labor Review,* Vol. 106, No. 9 (September 1983), pp. 3–12.

[4]Bureau of Labor Statistics, op. cit., Table 5, p. 169.

[5]For example, see R.B. Hill, "Discrimination and Minority Youth Employment," The Vice President's Task Force on Youth Employment and the Center for Public Service, Brandeis University, 1980; R.B. Hill and R. Nixon, *Youth Employment in American Industry* (New Brunswick, N.J.: Transaction Books, 1984); B. Anderson, "The Youth Unemployment Crisis, *Urban League Review,* Vol. 3, No. 1 (Winter 1977), pp. 16–21; Janet Norwood, "Some Social Aspects of Unemployment," Bureau of Labor Statistics, Report No. 469, 1976.

[6]Norwood, op. cit., p. 3.

[7]*Report of the National Advisory Commission on Civil Disorders* (Washington, D.C.: Government Printing Office, 1968).

[8]F.M. Andrews and S.B. Withey, *Social Indicators of Well-Being* (New York: Plenum Press, 1976); also, National Alliance of Black School Educators, Inc., *Saving the African American Child* (Washington, D.C.: NABSE, 1984).

[9]W.A. Darity, "The Human Capital Approach to Black-White Earnings Inequality: Some Unsettled Questions." *The Journal of Human Resources,* Vol. 17, No. 1, pp. 74–93.

[10]For a good general explanation of human capital theory, see H.M. Wachtel, *Labor and the Economy* (New York: Academic Press, 1984), Chapter 10.

[11]D. Bellante and M. Jackson, *Labor Economics* (New York: McGraw-Hill, 1979), p. 273.

[12]For example, see National Center for Education Statistics, *Digest of Education Statistics, 1983–84* (Washington, D.C.: Government Printing Office, 1983).

[13]National Center for Education Statistics, *Indicators of Education Status and Trends* (Washington, D.C.: Government Printing Office, January 1985).

[14]Darity, op. cit., p. 89.

[15]In appreciation of this fact, the Urban League is launching a broad-scale educational improvement initiative. We will allude to it again in a later section.

[16]Hill, "Discrimination and Minority Youth Employment," p. 13.

[17]D.G. Glasgow, "Full Employment: A Discussion Paper" (Washington, D.C.: National Urban League, Washington Operations, 1984); AFL-CIO, *Deindustrialization and the Two Tier Society* (Washington, D.C.: Industrial Union Department, AFL-CIO, 1984); W.J. Wilson, "Industrial Policy and the Concerns of Minorities," *Focus,* Vol. 12, No. 3 (March 1984), pp. 5–8; B. Bluestone and H. Bennett, *The Deindustrialization of America* (New York: Basic Books, 1982).

[18]AFL-CIO, op. cit., p. 26.

[19]Wilson, op. cit., p. 5.

[20]Hill, op. cit., p. 22.

[21]J.E. Jacob, "An Overview of Black America in 1984," *State of Black America 1985* (New York: National Urban League, Inc., 1985), p. v.

Acknowledgements

The National Urban League acknowledges with sincere appreciation the contributions of the authors of the various papers appearing in this publication; Tarah Hargo and Michele R. Long of Dewart, Inc.; and the special contributions of NUL staff, including Shari L. Jones and Delores Griffin of External Affairs; Cynthia Gresham, Vernice Williams, Faith Williams, Ollie Wadler, and Farida Syed of the Communications Department; Washington Operations; the Research Department; and the Program Departments.

Order Blank

National Urban League Publications
500 East 62nd Street
New York, N.Y. 10021

	Per Copy	Number of Copies	Total
State of Black America 1987	$18.00	_____	_____
Other Volumes in series:			
The State of Black America 1986	$18.00	_____	_____
The State of Black America 1985	$17.00	_____	_____
The State of Black America 1984	$15.00	_____	_____
The State of Black America 1983	$14.00	_____	_____
Volumes 1976–1982 (Available only in a set)	$150.00	_____	_____
Postage & handling: Individual volumes — $1.50 each Set of volumes — $10.00 per set		_____	_____
	Amount enclosed	_____	

Reprint of Jacob Lawrence painting, "The Builders"

Unframed poster. Size 23^1/$_8$″ by 35^3/$_4$″. Full color. $30.00 each, includes postage & handling. Number of copies _____; Amount enclosed _____

Gallery 62
National Urban League, Inc.
500 East 62nd Street
New York, N.Y. 10021

Please make checks or money orders payable to:

NATIONAL URBAN LEAGUE, INC.

Order Blank

National Urban League Publications
500 East 62nd Street
New York, N.Y. 10021

	Per Copy	Number of Copies	Total
State of Black America 1987	$18.00	_____	_____
Other Volumes in series:			
The State of Black America 1986	$18.00	_____	_____
The State of Black America 1985	$17.00	_____	_____
The State of Black America 1984	$15.00	_____	_____
The State of Black America 1983	$14.00	_____	_____
Volumes 1976–1982 (Available only in a set)	$150.00	_____	_____
Postage & handling: Individual volumes — $1.50 each		_____	_____
Set of volumes — $10.00 per set		_____	_____
	Amount enclosed		_____

Reprint of Jacob Lawrence painting, "The Builders"

Unframed poster. Size 23$\frac{1}{8}$″ by 35$\frac{3}{4}$″. Full color. $30.00 each, includes postage & handling. Number of copies _____; Amount enclosed _____

Gallery 62
National Urban League, Inc.
500 East 62nd Street
New York, N.Y. 10021

Please make checks or money orders payable to:

NATIONAL URBAN LEAGUE, INC.